Comedia Series ● No 16

Televising 'Terrorism': political violence in popular culture

Philip Schlesinger
Graham Murdock
Philip Elliott

Comedia Publishing Group
9 Poland Street, London W1 3DG. Tel. 01-439 2059
In assocation with Marion Boyars, London & New York

Comedia Publishing Group was set up to investigate and monitor the media in Britain and abroad. The aim of the project is to provide basic information, investigate problem areas, and to share the experiences of those working in the field, while encouraging debate about the future development of the media. The opinions expressed in the books in the series are those of the authors, and do not necessarily reflect the views of Comedia. For a list of other Comedia titles see page 182.

First published in 1983 by Comedia Publishing Group,
9 Poland Street, London W1 3DG.

ISBN 0 906 890 39X (paperback)
ISBN 0 906 890 381 (hardback)

Design by Will Hill and Hilary Arnott

Typeset by Red Lion Setters,
22 Brownlow Mews, London WC1

Printed by Unwin Brothers Ltd.,
The Gresham Press, Old Woking,
Surrey.

Trade Distribution by Marion Boyars,
18 Brewer Street, London W1.

US Distribution: Marion Boyars Inc.,
c/o The Scribner Book Companies.

Contents

For Martha, my mother, always an inspiration – PS

For Olwen – GM

For Wen, who kept me going – PE

Sadly, we must add to these dedications. After a long and courageous struggle Philip Elliott died yesterday, just a few weeks after the completion of this book. His is an irreplaceable loss. More will be said about his work at the right time and in the proper place. We mourn the passing of a fine friend, creative collaborator, and of a comrade who, against all the odds, believed in the possibility of a better tomorrow.

PS, GM
19 August 1983

Preface

This book is written against two orthodoxies. First, we take issue with those who are in favour of censoring television's coverage of political violence. We think that the arguments they use are both intellectually untenable and politically unsound. Our underlying assumption is that political violence needs rational analysis and wide political debate. Although, taken in isolation, political argument does not provide any solutions, we believe it to be a necessary precondition for democratic decision-making. An uninformed public is incapable of properly influencing the development of policies for dealing with political violence. As television undoubtedly has a crucial role in affecting the terms of the debate, we think that it should have more space for serious investigative coverage rather than be subjected to even further restrictions.

Secondly, we wish to challenge those who take a simple-minded view of television and its relationship to the state, and ask them to think again. True enough, broadcasting incessantly searches for the safe ground of a consensus, although this is an exercise which is proving steadily more difficult with the passing years and the growing fragmentation of British society. But broadcasting's establishment orientation does not mean that it is to be regarded as an instrument of the state. For as long as a public service broadcasting system lasts there will still be an effort to stake out some relatively autonomous ground. The system does not live up to its ideals, but that does not mean that we should fail to recognise what it can achieve. Our analysis of the coverage of political violence suggests that television's potential for dealing with some contentious issues may have been underrated.

We have written this book to stimulate some debate on this question. At the very least, we hope that it makes a small contribution to stiffening the resistance to state pressure of broadcasting's liberals – who are in the firing line – and that it offers support to, and ammunition for, broadcasting's radicals, in their battle to keep open the doors for criticism.

We have tried to write an accessible book. Chapter 1 presents the various ways in which 'terrorism' is currently interpreted and debated and the next two chapters examine how a wide range of television programmes represent these various points of view. Chapter 2 considers how 'terrorism' is covered by actuality television (news,

news magazines, current affairs programmes, documentaries), whereas Chapter 3 looks at fiction programmes (serials, series, single plays). Analysing 'fact' and 'fiction' alongside one another in this way is a novel approach, and we think it a fruitful one. Chapter 4 looks behind television's different forms, and analyses the way the system of censorship works to constrain what television can do, particularly in relation to Northern Ireland. Chapter 5 challenges the arguments of the counter-insurgency thinkers who have offered intellectual support to those seeking to impose more censorship. This examination is long overdue, and nowhere, so far, have their arguments been properly scrutinised. Whereas Chapters 1 to 5 have been written for the widest possible audience, Chapter 6 is pitched at a more academic level and intended for those interested in current debates in cultural studies and media sociology. Those who are not are advised to skip it and go straight on to Chapter 7, which draws the threads together and presents a brief restatement of our views.

We first began working on this book in 1981, when we were asked to do some research for an international seminar on the 'Representation of Terrorism on Television' organised by the Festival dei Popoli of Florence and the Verifica dei Programmi Trasmessi of Radiotelevisione italiana. As each of us had been working on relevant questions from somewhat different angles for some years, we welcomed the chance to pool our research efforts and to develop a new approach. The work we did for the Festival dei Popoli was not funded, and had to fit in with our other commitments. Our thanks to Dr. Mario Simondi of the Festival and Drs. Nicola De Blasi and Giancarlo Mencucci of RAI for getting us started. Our original monograph was published in Italy last year, together with the work of other contributors to the Florence conference.[1] Since then, our ideas have developed, and the material we have drawn together has expanded considerably.

This book has benefited greatly from the help of a number of people. Richard Paterson, John Stewart and Mairéde Thomas all kindly made available their expertise in the field of television. Colleagues at the Centre for Mass Communication Research and at Thames Polytechnic gave technical and other assistance. Both Liz Curtis and Alex Schmid generously allowed us to read and quote from the typescripts of their unpublished books. The Broadcasting Research Department at the BBC went to considerable trouble to provide us with audience data. None of these is in any way responsible for what appears below. We would also like to pay tribute to our publishers, Charles Landry and Dave Morley, for their unfailing support, genuine involvement and benevolent interest in the development of this book.

Although the research for this book was not otherwise funded, Philip Schlesinger was fortunate enough to be awarded a Nuffield Social Science Research Fellowship for 1982-83, which permitted him to take on the task of principal authorship. He would like to thank the Nuffield Foundation for its support, and is grateful to Sharon, Hannah and Tamara for bearing with him so patiently.

21 July 1983

Chapter 1

Talking about 'terrorism'

'Terrorism' has been one of the major preoccupations of recent years. Newspapers, television and radio have made reporting political violence a staple theme, and, apart from news reports, documentaries and book-length investigations, the activities of 'terrorists', and those who fight them, have been the subject of films, television fictions and novels. Terror and counter-terror have, to some, come to represent the epic struggle between Good and Evil, Light and Darkness, Democracy and Totalitarianism, Civilisation and Anarchy. Most public knowledge of terrorism is founded upon the images, definitions and explanations provided by the media.

'Terrorism' and 'terrorist' are terms which look straightforward, but actually they are shot through with contradictions. When is an action 'terroristic'; and when are its perpetrators 'terrorists'? Once we pose these questions it becomes obvious that the response depends upon our values. The term 'terrorist', as opposed to 'guerrilla', 'freedom fighter' or 'member of the resistance', implies that a given action is illegitimate and merits a condemnation as criminal behaviour. Conversely, using a term such as 'guerrilla' invites us to accept that a particular killing or bombing incident should be seen as a legitimate part of a 'liberation struggle'.

The conflict over such rival conceptions is important. Those who control the apparatus of the state have an interest in delegitimising their enemies, just as their opponents have a stake in promoting the acceptability of their armed struggle. Contests over definitions are not just word games. Real political outcomes are at stake. If the public, or sufficient sections of it, can be persuaded that the state's perspective on a given 'war against terrorism' is questionable, this might imply a weakening of support. On the other hand, if the public can be persuaded that the state is right, this helps mobilise support for transferring resources from welfare to security. Language matters, and how the media use language matters.

The definition of 'terrorism' – indeed the entire way in which the concept is represented through images, explanations, evidence – is central to the exercise of ideological power and influence in our society. In this book, we shall examine how 'terrorism' is handled in a range of television programmes, both factual and fictional.

Throughout this study we treat 'terrorism' as a term without a settled definition.

First, however, we need to look at the various contending perspectives in Britain and similar societies on the question of 'terrorism'. In our view, there are four main ways of talking about terrorism which can be given the following labels: 'official', 'alternative', 'populist' and 'oppositional'. They do not, by any means, have equal prominence in public debate.

The official perspective

The official perspective is the set of views, arguments, explanations and policy suggestions advanced by those who speak for the state. The key users of these official definitions of terrorism are government ministers, conservative politicians and top security personnel. Given their high status as news sources their opinions are assured a prominent place in media coverage. The official perspective is elaborated by certain kinds of intellectual – notably counter-insurgency theorists, academics and journalists – who are consciously engaged in waging the propaganda 'war against terrorism'. They provide what may be perceived as independent support in the struggle to win public opinion.

Although the official perspective commands the centre of contemporary debate it is by no means a monolithic, nor even a particularly coherent, set of ideas. There are considerable discrepancies in the accounts offered to the general public and the confidential briefings prepared for selected government and state personnel. There are also important differences of emphasis between the views tailored for popular consumption and those circulating among experts and elite groups. Moreover, even images and interpretations with the widest currency conflict with one another.

For example, the official perspective removes terrorism from the political arena by stressing its essential criminality. Meanwhile it places it firmly on the political agenda by presenting it as part of the Soviet Union's continuing attempt to destabilise Western democracies. There are conflicts too over the way the state should combat terrorism. On the one hand the official perspective stresses the need to maintain the rule of law in responding to terrorism. On the other it is argued that an exceptional threat to the state requires an exceptional response which may entail suspending due process and the right to trial.

The rising tide of terrorism

The notion of 'international terrorism' came into common currency at the end of the 1960s and at the beginning of the 1970s.[1] From this time a number of groups making use of violence for political reasons began to engage the attention of the media. The actions of the Red Army Fraction (Baader-Meinhof gang) in West Germany, the Red Army in Japan, the Red Brigades in Italy, the Angry Brigade and the IRA in Britain, Euzkadi Ta Akatasuna (ETA) in Spain, the Palestine Liberation Organisation (PLO) in various places, the Tupamaros in Uruguay and the Montoneros in Argentina all fed the view that a new era of terror had dawned.

Grouping these disparate movements under the unifying lable of 'international terrorism' ignores the important differences between them. They appear to be the same because they are shown as engaging in similar actions (bombings and kidnaps) with similar results (the death of innocent people). In the process, the complexity and specificity of the circumstances which have produced these various movements slides from view. They are detached from their particular histories and redefined as part of a general phenomenon of our times. This removal of political and social explanation is often reinforced by comparing terrorism to natural forces or disasters such as plagues or tidal waves. Sometimes these formulations can be quite apocalyptic, as in this passage by Christopher Dobson and Ronald Payne, two British journalists who have made 'terrorism' their speciality.

'Terrorism ebbs and flows like the tide, one moment crashing frighteningly on the foreshores of our lives, then retreating to lie quiescent, gathering strength for its next assault. It is inevitable that that assault will take place in one form or another, with greater or lesser impaet, every few years. But at no time has the assault been fiercer, more ruthless, sustained, or caused more permanent social, legal and political changes than during this decade.'[2]

A further way in which the official perspective de-politicises terrorism is by fitting it into the 'violent society syndrome'. Since the late 1960s different kinds of activity with quite different causes have come to be classified as the same, i.e., 'violent'. Thus 'mugging', the Angry Brigade bombings, IRA campaigns, criminal shootings of the police, football hooliganism, violence during picketing, rioting and political demonstrations, are all represented as symptoms of an underlying social malaise – an eruption of unprecedented criminality and lawlessness which poses a fundamental threat to peace and order.[3]

The terrorist as criminal

It is common for those who speak for the state to insist upon the simple criminality of all those who take up arms against the democratic order. Typically, referring to the killing of some British soldiers in Northern Ireland in May 1981, which she defined precisely as 'murder', Mrs Margaret Thatcher, the British Prime Minister, said:

'I hope that when their murderers have been tried and convicted no one will claim that they are entitled to special privileges – which is what political status means – when they serve their prison sentences.'[4]

The insistence on criminalising violence which might otherwise be seen as having political motivations is not just a matter of denying a more credible and acceptable label. It is not, as Mrs Thatcher once put it, that such actions are *essentially* criminal – 'a crime is a crime is a crime' was her phrase – but rather a question of adopting a conscious strategy. Assistant Chief Constable Brian Hayes of Surrey Constabulary has stated this very clearly when he argues that terrorism should not be 'over-glamourised' and that EEC police forces agree that 'existing criminal law covering such offences as fire-arms, explosives, kidnapping and extortion is quite adequate to meet our needs. In this way, terrorists are denied special status and their activities are placed firmly in the category of common – albeit serious – crime.'[5]

Along with the notion that terrorism is criminal rather than political go several other ideas. One is that it is necessarily indiscriminate. A particularly clear statement of this, coupled with the denial of political status has been advanced by Jacques Soustelle, former Governor-General of French Algeria, and a supporter of the armed resistance to decolonisation; he also, incidentally, turned a blind eye to torture on the part of the French security forces during his tenure of office:[6]

'From the beginning of the Algerian conflict in 1955 to the terroristic activities in several African countries today, from the PLO's attacks against Israeli schoolboys or athletes to the random bombing of pubs and hotels in Northern Ireland, the victims of the terrorists have been mainly children, civilians and tourists.

It should be emphasised, however, that the targets of the terrorists are not to be compared with those of the resistance fighters in France, for instance, under Nazi occupation. They are not military targets. The aim of the terroristic attacks is not to physically weaken an army, it is to create a state of psychological weakness. Terrorism is a variety of psychological warfare'.[7]

Labelling violent actions 'crimes' is no less an essential part of the strategy of psychological warfare in which both the essential irrationality and psychopathic tendencies of terrorism are also stressed. Thus, Dr Conor Cruise O'Brien, *Observer* columnist, and former Irish Minister for Posts and Telegraphs, has argued that all terrorists are possessed by their faith in the possibility of a better world and incapable of seeing the benefits of democracy. Hence, political debate with a terrorist should be refused for 'though he can argue fluently from his own peculiar premises, he is not accessible to rational argument on premises other than his own'.[8] The far-right Institute for the Study of Conflicts does not even concede as much as O'Brien:

'Those who have had experience of conversation with them can discover that one particular word, a trigger word, perhaps the name of a President or the object of the terrorists' hatred, can turn a seemingly normal man into an irrational and abnormal one in front of your eyes'.[9]

This is the province of the malign chemistry that turned Dr Jekyll into Mr Hyde. If millennarian faith, psychopathology and alchemy can explain the motivations of the terrorist it is hardly surprising that some should deny 'the notion that terrorism can be understood or explained or dealt with in terms of social causes':

'I shall say once again that the cause of terrorism is terrorists. The ability of terrorists to operate effectively depends on financial support and sanctuary by states. Terrorists may indeed have particular grievances, but they only become an effective force if they get the kind of support that terrorists such as the PLO have gotten in our day from the Soviet Union, its agents and Arab allies — financial support, training and sanctuary.'[10]

These are the words of Norman Podhoretz, editor of the right-wing US journal, *Commentary*. Like Soustelle, he was speaking at a specialised conference on Terrorism and the News Media, held in Jerusalem in 1979.[11] Such conferences are generally dominated by those holding the official view, and seek to solve the practical problem of how to win the propaganda war. They are therefore particularly good sources of the underlying assumptions of a perspective which is otherwise not generally so fully articulated.

A closer look at Podhoretz's statement, however, shows that it is deeply contradictory. On the one hand, he wishes to deny the relevance of considering the social and political causes of terrorism. At the same time he insists on the importance of the Soviet Union's material and political support in sustaining terrorist groups. He is not alone in this. On the contrary, the argument that supporting terrorism is part of the Soviet strategy for undermining the stability of liberal democracy in the West is a key theme of the official perspective.

Terrorism and Soviet subversion

A common way of looking at terrorism is to see diverse actions throughout the world as all ultimately connected, all instigated by the Soviet Union. This has two key consequences. First, it denies distinctions between different groups and different kinds of action, and second, it links the phenomenon to the Left. The concept of the 'Terrorist International' has been incorporated into the Cold War perception of international affairs. An especially clear illustration of this was given by the Reagan administration at the beginning of 1981. Mr Alexander Haig, then US Secretary of State, said: 'International terrorism will take the place of human rights in our concern because it is the ultimate abuse of human rights'.[12] Behind this statement lay a decade-long effort to establish a connection between 'international terrorism' and communism by US Congressional committees in the 1970s. By the early 1980s the existence of such a connection had become the orthodox view of the State Department and the White House.[13]

In this major shift in foreign policy, the largely ineffective disapproval of the outgoing Carter administration for repressive regimes in the 'Free World' – in particular, those in Latin America and South-East Asia – was replaced by full material and political endorsement. The practice of violent repression in Latin American client states, including torture and 'disappearances', was re-evaluated as less bad than the effects of those pursuing armed struggles to get rid of their oppressors.

According to the dictum of Mrs Jeane Kirkpatrick, US ambassador at the United Nations, unsavoury regimes who are friends, and therefore part of the 'Free World', are merely 'authoritarian', no matter what they do. They are on the right side in the fight against international communism, for whose member regimes the epithet 'totalitarian' is to be reserved. So, for example, the US interventions in Nicaragua and El Salvador were defined as part of the struggle against the Soviet design for world domination. Terrorism, in the words of the Argentinian diplomat Dr Gerardo Jorge Schamís is a 'new form of war . . . characterized by an integral strategy by means of which the Soviet Union intends to enlarge its sphere of influence . . .'[14] Moreover, for General Videla, the Argentine military government's head from 1976-1981, a terrorist was 'not just someone with a gun or a bomb but also someone who spreads ideas that are contrary to Western and Christian civilisation'.[15] This redefinition enabled him to extend the junta's self-proclaimed 'war against terrorism' and to justify the wholesale repression of Left political activists.

If the Soviet threat posed by 'international terrorism' is held to justify US intervention and extreme state repression in the Third World, the hand of Moscow must be shown to lie behind the most diverse manifestations of terrorist violence at a global level. Thus, according to Claire Sterling in *The Terror Network*,[16] the KGB evidently orchestrates the activities of the Palestine Liberation Organisation, the Red Brigades in Italy, ETA in Spain, 'The Anarchy' in Turkey, the Provisional IRA in Ireland. This thesis is part of the conventional wisdom of a good deal of journalism and fiction alike.

Sterling's book, in fact, has been actively promoted by the Reagan administration, with Secretary of State Haig distributing excerpts to a congressional committee, and the US International Communications Agency promoting it in its cultural centres abroad.[17]

But 'irrefutable proof' of the various links in the chain of terror is hard to come by, as Ms Sterling and others who argue for this view admit. So it becomes necessary to deny the existence of *direct* orchestration on the basis of the available evidence while at the same time asserting the obvious 'objective' advantages of terrorism to the Soviet Union:

'It was never part of the Soviet design to create and watch over native terrorist movements, still less to direct their day to day activities. The phantom mastermind coordinating worldwide terror from some subterranean map room is a comic-book concept. The whole point of the plan was to let the other fellow do it, contributing to Continental terror by proxy . . . The terrorists' primary value to the Kremlin lay in their resolute efforts to weaken and demoralise, confuse, humiliate, frighten, paralyze, and if possible dismantle the West's democratic societies.'[18]

Similar arguments are also made about other forms of direct political action, most notably about the anti-nuclear movement. Like 'international terrorism', the European peace movements are widely depicted as tied to Soviet foreign policy interests. Sometimes the connection is seen as a simple matter of 'Moscow Gold' and Kremlin directives, as in a letter from Robin Bruce Lockhart in the *Financial Times*. This claimed that 'the whole CND movement is manipulated by the Russians – and financed by them. Western intelligence sources believe that as much as $100m has been poured out by the Soviets over the past 18 months to fund the so-called "peace" and allied movements in Nato countries.'[19]

But more often, as with the argument on 'international terrorism', the links are seen as less direct. Hence, when women formed a human chain around the air-base at Greenham Common on 12 December 1982, to protest against the siting of Cruise missiles there, the *Daily Express* and *Daily Mail* cast them as unwitting extras in Moscow's propaganda war, with front page stories emphasising that the demonstration had been filmed by Soviet television. Underneath its main headline 'THE PEACE WAR', the *Express* added 'Russian TV cameras roll as 30,000 women ring missile base in anti-nuclear protest'. The *Mail* appended 'Russian TV crew films the big anti-missile demo' to its headline THE WOMEN OF PROTEST'. This argument – that the peace movement if not actually masterminded by Moscow is very definitely in its 'objective' interests – has recently been advanced more officially in a series of speeches by Mrs Thatcher. In her address to the Young Conservatives' national conference on 12 February 1983 for example, she explicitly compared the unilateralists to the Appeasers of the 1930's, on the grounds that both in effect supported totalitarian expansionism and thus undermined the defence of democracy.

'Those who . . . counsel the West to give up its deterrent . . . would leave the Soviet Union with a virtual monopoly of nuclear arms: that tyrannical regime, which cares not one jot for human rights, uniquely able to blackmail mankind. It is exactly fifty years since Hitler became Chancellor of the German Reich . . . If in the 1930s nuclear weapons had been invented and the allies had been faced by Nazi SS20s and Backfire Bombers, would it then have been morally right to have handed to Hitler total control of the most terrible weapons which man has ever made? . . . Would not unilateralism have given Hitler the world domination he sought?'

Through these kinds of rhetorical device a covert, but powerful, connection is established between 'international terrorism' and legitimate forms of direct action and radical critique. These links are further cemented within the official perspective by stretching the term 'terrorism' itself.

In West Germany, for example, commentators have taken to describing as terroristic the activities and demonstrations of the peace, anti-nuclear and environmental lobbies there.[20] Similarly, some British observers also claim to have detected the growth of 'terrorist' tendencies within these movements. According to Dobson and Payne, for example:

'manifestations are emerging in the field of "soft terrorisms". As some ecological and conservationist groups whose aims are in themselves peaceful and humane become more militant their activities cross the borderline into such activity. International groups of antinuclear activists have mounted violent demonstrations at nuclear power sites in France, Germany and in the United States.'[21]

The implication of this argument is clear: every radical protest movement, however well-intentioned and intially peaceful, is in constant danger of crossing the border-line from legitimate action to 'terrorism', either by design or default.

Although the designation of terrorism as a phenomenon of the Left occupies the centre of the official perspective, it has not gone entirely unchallenged. Recently some establishment commentators have drawn attention to the importance of right-wing terrorism, and its distinctiveness, as opposed to merely assimilating all terrorism indiscriminately to the KGB-manipulation model.

Professor Paul Wilkinson of Aberdeen University, one of Britain's foremost academics articulating the official perspective, has been prominent in suggesting such a revision:

'It is no surprise to find today's fascists adopting the characteristic tactics of modern terrorism. But there is a rather different pattern in the fascists' choice of targets. They have mainly concentrated on immigrants and their property, or on left-wing offices and personnel, or on Jewish targets, depending on the ideological character of the group. One particularly worrying feature of fascists' recent bomb attacks is that the perpetrators appear to have no inhibitions about causing mass slaughter in public places. Unlike the neo-marxist revolutionaries of the extreme left, they do not appear worried about turning the working classes against them.'[22]

However, at present it is quite clear that this view has not achieved a currency comparable to the one outlined earlier. Moreover, in general it does not circulate in a fully articulated form through the popular mass media, but tends to be available through more specialised publications. So, for instance, a report on 'Right-wing terrorism in Europe' compiled by the Rand Corporation in California was republished in Britain by the Centre for Contemporary Studies, a small private research body without a prestigious academic base, which aims its publications at an influential rather than a mass readership.[23]

The view from within

The elements of the official perspective discussed so far are all intended for general consumption. But those who speak for the state also produce views and assessments which circulate exclusively within the higher echelons of the governmental apparatus. One such secret document concerning the Provisional IRA was leaked in 1979. Written by Brigadier J.M. Glover of Defence Intelligence in December 1978, it was entitled 'Northern Ireland: Future Terrorist Trends'.[24] It is instructive to measure Glover's assessments against the official judgements normally on offer. Where it has frequently been asserted that the 'war against terrorism' is about to be won, Glover observes:

'The Provisionals' campaign of violence is likely to continue while the British remain in Northern Ireland . . . we see little prospect of political development of a kind which would seriously undermine the Provisionals' position'.[25]

Contradicting the notion that the IRA is just a criminal organisation, Glover cites the judgement of an earlier intelligence assessment:

'The Provisional IRA (PIRA) has the dedication and the sinews of war to raise violence intermittently to at least the level of early 1976, certainly for the forseeable future. Even if 'peace' is restored, *the motivation for politically inspired violence will remain.* Arms will be readily available and there will be many who are able and willing to use them. Any peace will be superficial and brittle. A new campaign may well erupt in the years ahead.'[26]

The report also discounts the commonly held ideas that the terrorist is *necessarily* devoid of popular support and that indigenous terrorism is *necessarily* manipulated by foreign governments:

'PIRA will probably continue to recruit the men it needs. They will still be able to attract enough people with leadership talent, good education and manual skills to enhance their all round professionalism. The movement will retain popular support sufficient to maintain secure bases in the traditional Republican areas.

'We believe that the Republic will continue to act as a haven for terrorists and they will continue to receive arms through Eire, particularly from the USA and through contacts with overseas terrorist groups. We believe that there is little risk of any foreign government giving active support to PIRA.'[27]

These assessments, which stress the popular basis for, and the

PHOTO: DUNCAN SMITH

'...the movement will retain popular support sufficient to maintain secure bases in the traditional Republican areas...'

political motivation of, violence against the state, together with its indigenous character, are central to both the alternative and oppositional perspectives. But if these views were to be more generally publicised, they might, so advocates for the official perspective argue, help to legitimate terrorism. Explanations might be mistaken for excuses, and this might weaken popular support for the state's counter-terrorist strategies. Not surprisingly, then, concern about the mass media's coverage of terrorist actions, alternative ways of comprehending them, and the likely impact of these presentations on the public at large, occupies a central place in official thinking.

The guilty media

From an official point of view, one of the greatest threats represented by terrorism is the way it undermines the credibility of the government and its perceived ability to maintain the secure functioning of the social order. Mrs Thatcher gave voice to this anxiety in May 1981, when she said:

'The world is daily assaulted by thos who seek to impose their views upon us through violence and fear. Terrorism is an attack upon the whole community ... If [the terrorist] can destroy our trust in a well-ordered society, if he can spread consternation and provoke retaliation – then he is on the way to achieving his ends.'[28]

Official spokesmen judge that maximum publicity is essential to the success of this strategy. In the words of Mr William Whitelaw, British Home Secretary,

'Terrorists and terrorist organisations seek and depend upon publicity. A principal object of their acts of violence is to draw attention to themselves and gain notoriety . . . they bomb and murder their way into the headlines.'[29]

To achieve their aims, terrorists are seen as deliberately organising their actions to fit the key news values of drama, violence, and unexpectedness. As Brian Jenkins, the Rand Corporation's expert on international terrorism puts it: 'Terrorists choreograph their violence. Terrorism is theatre.'[30] The news media, for their part, are seen as unable to resist the chance of a 'good story', so they obligingly provide extensive coverage of terrorist bombings, hijacks, kidnaps and assassinations. After a time, however, the standard terrorist performances become over-familiar and lose their news-worthiness, and, like the showmen they are seen to be, terrorists have to find new acts to keep the media interested. The result is a vicious spiral of escalating violence. This view is encapsulated by Professor Walter Laqueur of the Center for Strategic and International Studies in Washington:

'Terrorists have learned that the media are of paramount importance in their campaigns, that *the terrorist act by itself is next to nothing, whereas publicity is all.* But the media, constantly in need of diversity and new angles, make fickle friends. Terrorists will always have to be innovative. They are, in some respects, the superentertainers of our time.'[31]

The media's coverage of terrorism is therefore seen as playing into the hands of the enemies of the state, and of encouraging them to go even further. This provokes a call for tight controls over the media if they cannot control themselves. If 'terrorist propaganda' is criminal, then so are the media which uncritically relay it. In this vein, Professor José Desantes Guanter, a Spanish expert on information law, has observed:

'Terrorism today is an "information crime"; it cannot operate without the modern social communications media . . . Terrorist violence is merely the springboard for real terrorism which is communicated terrorism . . . '[32]

Implicit in this is the assumption that if political violence went unreported it would go away. It is not surprising therefore that official spokesmen view the media as especially culpable for interviewing those who have taken up arms against the state. This is seen as legitimising our enemies. Also central to the question of legitim-

the official view, the value of language as an instrument of persuasion is of paramount importance. The obvious corollary is that it should be controlled in ways that favour the definitions issuing from the state. Those who misuse language are either conscious sympathisers with the terrorist cause or dupes. Lord Chalfont, writer on defence questions, has expressed this view with some clarity:

'There are, of course, a number of journalists who actively sympathise with the criminal activities of terrorist movements, especially those dedicated to the destruction of capitalist societies. Others assist less consciously in the promotion of terrorism by accepting terrorist organizations at their own value and adopting the kind of newspeak which George Orwell made so familiar in his *1984*. Terrorists are referred to as "commandos", "urban guerrillas", or even "freedom fighters"; an organization dedicated to the violent overthrow of an elected government becomes the "Patriotic Front"; IRA murders in Northern Ireland are reported as "executions" and the brutal torture of soldiers and civilians as "trials" and "interrogations".'[33]

Dilemmas of the strong state

Criticism of 'mistaken' language is part of the pursuit of greater control of the image of the state's fight against its enemies. And this is itself subordinate to the general argument that the exceptional threat of terrorism requires exceptional measures to combat it. But acquiring special powers poses a problem for liberal-democratic states such as Britain. The state's legitimacy, after all, is founded on its adherence to due process and the rule of law. If it goes too far in its pursuit of counter-measures, and disregards publicly-acceptable limits, it risks undermining its own credibility.

This is obviously a point of great sensitivity. Some commentators argue that despite the advantages offered by efficient repression, it is nonetheless crucial not to violate the rule of law or to compromise civil liberties beyond a certain point:

'What is a reasonable response by a liberal state to terroristic violence? A response, even a legal response, which forbids almost every type of peaceful political assembly and agitation would not be an appropriate response. The wholesale arrest and incarceration of leftist and political dissidents would again not be an appropriate response. The liberal state may, for limited periods, declare martial law (a risky act at best), and it may call for reasonable guidelines in reporting news events; it cannot however, act outside "rule by law". The reasonable response by the liberal state calls for military-police maintenance of a liberal state and the democratic rights embodied in its constitution.'[34]

In Britain, the central preoccupation in recent years has been with the actions of the IRA, and to a lesser extent the INLA, although no opportunity has been lost to affirm a stand against 'terrorism in general'. A good instance was the successful breaking of the Iranian embassy siege in London in May 1980 by the counter-terrorist Special Air Service. The government spelt out the lesson of firm action: that Britain would not tolerate terrorism on the streets of its capital.

The development of the 'terrorist threat' in Britain and elsewhere has contributed to a number of changes in the state's apparatuses for countering 'subversion'. It is not 'terrorism' alone which has brought this about. The continuing economic crisis with its concomitant industrial relations struggles has also played a role.[35] The most significant changes in Britain have included:

- the refurbishing of a 'parallel' emergency state apparatus for use against external attack and internal disorder;
- major shifts in the practice of policing including the emergence of a para-military 'third force' and the strengthening of the political police;
- the increasing use of high technology surveillance against loosely-defined 'subversives' involving, for instance, uncontrolled data-banks and bugging devices;
- the use of official secrecy legislation against journalists;
- jury-vetting in political trials;
- restrictions upon, and aggressive policing of, demonstrations and picketing;
- the trial use of repressive technology and special forces in Northern Ireland, and the gradual application of the lessons learned in Britain itself;
- the development of exceptional, anti-terrorist legislation.[36]

The cornerstone of Britain's anti-terrorist legislation is the Prevention of Terrorism Act. This was originally brought in as an emergency measure in the wake of the IRA's Birmingham pub bombings in 1974 which killed 21 people and injured over 160. Its provisions suspend normal civil liberties in cases where a person is suspected of belonging to, supporting, or witholding information on, the IRA and the Irish National Liberation Army. Under the Act, amended in 1976, and periodically renewed, a police constable can arrest without warrant anyone whom he or she 'reasonably suspects' of committing these offences and hold them in custody for up to 48 hours without access to a solicitor, and for a further five days on the authority of the Home Secretary. The Home Secretary can also exclude from the UK anyone whom he believes is, has been, or is planning to be involved in terrorist activities. These provisions have been widely criticised on the grounds that most of those detained are never in fact charged or excluded and that the police use the Act for low-level intelligence gathering, to question suspects about their general political beliefs and activities.[37]

The tensions within the official perspective, around the need to have effective counter-terrorist measures on the one hand and the need to defend civil liberties on the other, emerged very clearly when the renewal of the Act was debated in March 1983. Some supporters for the official perspective, like the back-bench Conservative MP, Sir John Biggs-Davison, were firmly behind the argument that exceptional threats to the state require exceptional measures. As he told a television interviewer:

'I don't know a country in the world which is threatened by terrorism which doesn't resort to extraordinary measures, which doesn't find it necessary to act outside the normal process of law as we know it. It is unfortunate but it is necessary.'[38]

But others, including Home Secretary William Whitelaw, partly conceded the force of the civil liberties argument. And his speech advocating the renewal of the Act (and announcing plans for new legislation to deal with the incursion of 'international terrorists' into Britain) expressed perfectly the tensions in the official perspective. As he told the House of Commons:

'The means of the terrorists are abhorrent. To the degree that they become more savage, cruel and pitiless, so must we become more determined and steadfast in frustrating them. We must surely all of us resolve to beat the bombers. The clearest proof of their failure to terrorise, and of our own resolution, is demonstrated by a measured, sensible and constructive response to the threat. I believe the current prevention of terrorism legislation reflected this approach in 1974 and 1976, and that it would be unwise to jettison it now. But I also believe that its powers are unwelcome and make sad inroads into our cherished tradition of civil liberties.'[39]

At an international level, particularly in Western Europe, there have been uneven and inconclusive efforts to develop a 'counter-terrorist' strategy, in terms of a common system of extradition, a common legal zone and improved police cooperation.[40] The response conventionally advocated within the official perspective combines the streamlining of the legal process so far as trials, tradition and admissability of confessions are concerned, together with the enhancement of various specialised forms of policing, notably intelligence work. Typically, therefore, Professor Paul Wilkinson has argued that a

'useful step would be to press for speedy ratification and implementation of the Council of Europe Convention on the Suppression of Terrorism, and the parallel European Community Agreement.

A central coordinating antiterrorist cell of say half-a-dozen top security and intelligence experts . . . could add immeasurably to the precision and quality of the international response. The new unit should provide expert analyses of intelligence data, assessment of capabilities and threats, a continuing research and development backup, including work on the pooling of counterterrorist weaponry and technology, training, joint exercises in hostage rescue, and advice to ministers and security services.'[41]

However, if the state is going to use tough, even questionable means to fight its opponents, it then becomes necessary to draw firm lines between state violence and terrorist violence so that they should not be evaluated as moral equivalents. Dr. Conor Cruise O'Brien, who has been a long-standing and committed intellectual opponent of the IRA, has neatly summed up the official view: 'The force used by a democratic state is legitimate while the violence of the terrorist is not legitimate.'[42] However, it is precisely the refusal to take this division as absolute and incontestable that provides one of the major departure points for the alternative perspective.

The alternative perspective

The alternative perspective is the set of views, arguments, explanations and policy suggestions advocated by those who while dissenting from the official view of terrorism, accept that violence is not legitimate within liberal-democracies, though they recognise that it may be so in other political systems. The alternative perspective is advanced by civil libertarians, critical academics and journalists, and some politicians. Like official spokesmen and intellectuals, advocates of the alternative are concerned with the battle for public opinion, not least with trying to ensure that their own views receive a credible airing in the media.

The alternative perspective has developed in the context of the upsurge of political violence (a term often preferred to terrorism) and the growth of the repressive side of the state. While alternative views do not offer a fundamental challenge to the official claims made for a legitimate use of the means of violence, they do question the implications of excessive repression for the rule of law and democratic rights. Furthermore, the alternative perspective also questions the official strategy of repressing and exorcising terrorism, advocating instead strategies of political change and social engineering designed to defuse the violence and tackle its causes.

The alternative perspective is argued from a position which is both defensive and subordinate. It is defensive because those who argue officially accuse those who do not of being 'soft on terrorism'. It is subordinate because the orthodoxy is well entrenched, as has been indicated by Dr Alex P. Schmid of Leiden University. Author of a comprehensive survey of work on 'political terrorism', Schmid has remarked:

'In terms of research focus, left-wing terrorism has been given almost exclusive attention and the focus has often been on questions which are more interesting to secret services and counter-terrorist agencies than to the social sciences.'[43]

Such constrained perceptions are not limited to research alone, but extend across the field of public debate.

Contesting the terms of debate

As the label suggests, the alternative perspective runs counter to the official picture of 'terrorism'. First of all, it treats the very term 'terrorism' as partial, harnessed to propaganda purposes rather than offering any sort of analysis.

The most developed critique along these lines has come from Professors Noam Chomsky and Edward S. Herman. Like the proponents of the official view, they recognise the importance of language. But rather than endorse the liberal-democratic state as absolutely different from the communist enemy, Chomsky and Herman point to US support for repression in the Third World and the ideological function of 'human rights' rhetoric. At any given time, they contend, US policy towards Third World states provides an ideological framework within which 'the spectrum of acceptable and unacceptable bloodshed' may be defined. Central to this framework are 'the words "terror" and "terrorism"' which 'have become semantic tools of the powerful in the Western world.'[44] These terms 'have generally been confined to the use of violence by individuals and marginal groups. Official violence which is far more extensive in both scale and destructiveness is placed in a different category altogether.'[45]

In the course of their analysis Chomsky and Herman develop a provocative distinction. 'Official violence', that produced by states, results in what they call 'wholesale terror'. On the other hand, 'unofficial violence', that of individuals and small groups, is characterised as producing only 'retail terror'. Chomsky and Herman's redefinition implies a complete re-evaluation of the place of state terror in the contemporary world. The abstract conceptual point is illustrated tellingly, a typical example being the following:

'At the first Latin American Congress of Relatives of the Disappeared, held in San José, Costa Rica, January 20-24, 1981, the estimate given for disappeared men, women and children in Latin America over the past two decades was 90,000. By contrast, the CIA's most recent (newly inflated) estimate of the total number of deaths resulting from "international terrorist" violence for the period 1968-1980, numbers 3,668, or about 4 per cent of the number of "disappearances" for Latin America alone.'[46]

But perceptions such as this, argue Chomsky and Herman, hardly ever appear in the mass media – at any rate in the United States – where the officially-endorsed terminology 'has been institutionalised as a device to facilitate the exclusive preoccupation with the lesser terror of the alienated and the dispossessed, serving virtually as a disguised form of apologetics for state terror and client fascism'.[47]

In this version of the alternative perspective, then, 'international terrorism' of the official accounts is recodified as the explicable frustration of 'the wretched of the earth', to use Frantz Fanon's phrase. Such a revised interpretation also entails explaining the origins of the epidemic of *state* terrorism. Edward Herman has set out to do this very directly, by taking head on Claire Sterling's Soviet-backed terror network thesis. In *The Real Terror Network*, published as a direct riposte to Sterling and her colleagues, Herman declares the official account to be no more than a fabrication. The 'real' network of US-backed state terrorism in Latin America and other states such as South Africa, Israel and Indonesia is contrasted with the one denounced by Sterling. This, Herman argues, is simply a pseudoscientific product of the current Cold War campaign of disinformation.

Herman considers the thesis of Soviet manipulation of terror implausible, since terrorism in the West is incompatible with Soviet goals in pursuing detente. Furthermore, he points out, Sterling's account lacks adequate detail on how the Soviet Union is supposed to control the diverse actions of its alleged 'proxies' throughout the world.

Most important, though, is the alternative account he offers of what lies behind the 'real' terror network:

'there is a *system* of terroristic states . . . that has spread throughout Latin America and elsewhere over the past several decades . . . which is deeply rooted in the corporate interest and sustaining political-military-financial-propaganda mechanisms of the United States and its allies in the Free World. The mechanisms protecting this network are extremely potent, combining military force, economic power and coercion, and a vast apparatus serving to engineer consent. The United States has *needed* Polish martial law, Gulag and other Soviet sphere crimes and abuses to distract attention from the escalating reign of terror under its own sponsorship.'[48]

Instead of Soviet efforts to destabilise the West, we are asked to focus on US efforts to secure domination at the price of human rights. This strategy is grounded in an economic and political logic which involves the mobilisation of consent at home, not least by raising the distracting spectre of continual advances by the enemy.[49]

Terrorism as political action

The alternative perspective invites us to look at the system of international relations in other ways too: for example, that political violence pursued on nationalist grounds results from the failure of the international community to recognise legitimate aspirations. Thus, for instance, the Congolese Ambassador to the UN argued, in 1972:

'We cannot separate (the Palestinians') actions from the circumstances that have engendered them. They were born in conditions that we have made favourable by ignoring their rights, by dissociating ourselves from their fate, and by throwing them into a ghetto like the dregs of humanity. If the Europeans of 1972 no longer blow up trains and bridges (like the Resistance), it is because their countries are free. Palestinians in a Palestine regained will go to the Olympic games, not to take hostages but to compete with other nations in the stadium, just as Palestinians in a Palestine regained will no longer have any reason to hijack aircraft.'[50]

A further variant of this argument looks at the failings of the nation state. The Italian political scientist, Professor Luigi Bonanate has argued that if a society produces terrorism

'this means that something is going wrong . . . A society that knows terrorism is a *blocked society*, incapable of answering the citizens' requests for change but nevertheless capable of preserving and reproducing itself'.[51]

This kind of analysis, especially prevalent amongst those arguing for alternative approaches in Italy and in West Germany, centres on the failings of the political system and its inflexibilities. Such arguments, which pin responsibility for political violence on those who rule rather than those who revolt, are the target of official spokesmen and women who inveigh against 'terrorist sympathisers'. Acknowledging this response, the Italian political analyst Alessandro Silj has observed:

'Unless the Italian political forces find the will, the imagination and the ability to lead their society towards social justice and shared objectives of economic and social growth, urban guerrilla activity can only continue and expand. Unfortunately, Italy's politicians today do not appear to have the moral authority that alone can rally the country and start a process of renewal. Moreover, most of them would shrug off this analysis as too "sociological" and "soft".'[52]

Since the alternative standpoint is argued from a position which has been delegitimised, it is hardly surprising that many alternative writers have felt impelled to insist upon their proper democratic credentials. Sebastian Cobler, West German lawyer and social scientist, has pointed out that the attack on alleged sympathisers is designed to

'silence or incriminate anyone who unreservedly embarks on a discussion of the sociopolitical origins of the phenomenon referred to under the heading of terrorism, along with anyone who makes the demand – which can by no means be taken for granted in the Federal Republic – that the state preserve the most elementary civil and human rights even of those who would trample those very rights underfoot.'[53]

It is illuminating to see what happens when arguments that recognize the political dimension are proposed. One instance was provided by *The Guardian* in a New Year editorial in 1983, titled 'The year of the terrorist'. The writer argued that treating terrorism as a law-and-order problem alone was too simple, and, that in the case of the IRA its political motivations needed to be recognised. A New Year's resolution was offered in conclusion: 'to recognise the motives of all forms of terrorism for what they are, and by understanding help to end them. In other words, know thine enemy'.[54]

This brought a damning response from Dr Conor Cruise O'Brien writing in *The Observer*:

'When we are summoned to make an effort to understand them, I don't think this is really a call to cognitive effort. Rather it is a way of deflecting indignation and preparing surrender – "know thine enemy" may be a first stage in giving in to him . . . It is an invitation in fact to acquiesce in legitimising terror . . . The IRA must interpret public endeavours to understand them and recognise their motives as a sign of cracking will. What can that do except to encourage them to greater efforts?'[55]

This is an excellent example of how the official view tries to recoup lost ground. The exchange, given the two papers concerned, was addressed to liberal and progressive readerships.[56] The constant reaffirmation of the official perspective goes hand in hand with the effort to marginalise both the impact and the legitimacy of the alternative to it. Not surprisingly, alternative spokesmen and women have seen this as threatening the more general freedom to debate controversial questions in liberal democracies, and as related to the emergence of a 'strong state' in such regimes.

From preventing terrorism to state repression

According to the official view, the 'war against terrorism' justifies exceptional measures and emergency legislation such as Britain's Prevention of Terrorism Act. Such legislation enables the government to proscribe organisations, to 'exclude' individuals from the British mainland (in effect to exile them), confers enhanced powers of police search, detention and arrest. Similar steps have been taken elsewhere. In West Germany, anti-terrorism legislation of an even more draconian nature was part of an offensive against the employment of radicals and 'subversives'. The Law for the Protection of Communal Peace has the far-reaching intention of punishing the 'giving of support and approval to violence' by means of words, publications and films 'likely in the circumstances to disturb the public peace'.[57] This law has been used to ban writings judged socially harmful. The most celebrated such banning, perhaps, concerned the confessional autobiography of ex-terrorist 'Bommi' Baumann.[58] In Italy emergency laws empower long periods of preventive detention. Those accused of terrorist offences can be detained for up to five years and four months before their first trial and up to 10 years eight months before the second.[59]

Such legislation is justified as regrettable but necessary by official spokesmen. It is never represented as the use of *state repression*, rather, in a significant linguistic twist it is presented as the 'prevention' of terrorism or its 'suppression'. The alternative view directs attention to ways in which such responses are socially harmful. Thus for instance, the National Council for Civil Liberties gave a classic alternative response to British terrorism legislation when arguing for its repeal. However, it was careful to distance itself from the use of violence and avoid the charge of 'sympathising':

'Our opposition to terrorism is in no sense compromised by our opposition to laws such as the Prevention of Terrorism Act which were supposedly introduced to curb terrorist activity. Our position has often been misrepresented by those who believe that criticism of emergency legislation must imply support for the terrorists. Nothing could be further from the truth. We oppose emergency legislation because it diminishes the rights of *all* citizens by providing the Government, the police and the army with powers unchallengeable in the courts, and by corrupting the standards which are central to the administration of justice.'[60]

Similar concern that the pursuit of order might – and does – tip over into manipulation of law was well to the fore in the Labour Party's opposition to renewal of the Prevention of Terrorism Act in March 1983. Some argued that the Act's suspension of civil liberties was counter-productive and served only to strengthen the terrorist case. As one MP told the House of Commons:

'The best way of fighting terrorism and anything associated with it is by open justice and not by secret activity on the part of the state. Having reached this stage with the Prevention of Terrorism (Temporary Provisions) Act 1976, there has been a victory for political terrorism and not for democracy. The Act is the very form of legislation that political terrorists in Britain or in any other country or society wish to see a democratic state give way to introducing. It is their way of subverting a state that is otherwise democratic. It is their way of justifying much of the terrorist style of politics.'.[61]

Others, like Shadow Home Secretary, Roy Hattersley, claimed that such legislation was in fact a step towards totalitarianism:

'in a free society you can't arrest people without being able to charge them in court and imprison them even though they've been convicted of nothing. It's quite terrifying to say "well we can't actually take these men into court but we happen to know they're guilty and therefore we are going to keep them inside". That's totalitarianism.'[62]

Efforts to achieve international agreements which threaten civil liberties have also come in for criticism. Professor Willem Nagel, the Dutch criminologist, has argued against ratification of the European Convention on the Suppression of Terrorism of 1977. One point he makes is that 'Without explaining what must be understood by acts of terrorism, the European Convention goes straight on to recommend extradition for terrorists'. He also objects to the lack of clarity in the definition of a 'political offence'. According to him it is possible

'to include as terrorism a variety of acts of different degrees of "seriousness", ranging from severe acts of violence such as homicide to participation in a peaceful demonstration, for example against the construction of a nuclear power plant; it might also be interpreted to include press reports intended to defend the organisers of the demonstration and criticism of the police if the latter were to resort to violence to break up the demonstration.'[63]

In Nagel's view, countries with more liberal legal provisions would be compelled to adopt the standards of the most repressive.

The alternative view also expresses concern about the use of violence by the state. As noted earlier, 'National Security States' such as Chile and Argentina, while formally in the 'Free World', are expected to violate human rights because of their very nature. However, quite different expectations apply to the metropolitan liberal-democracies when special powers legitimise the use of torture and assassination. Pierre Vidal-Naquet, the French political analyst and man of letters has expressed this concern in his criticism of French state-sanctioned torture during the Algerian independence struggles:

'When the Algerian war broke out, the French authorities could choose between two policies: to accept that the Algerian problem needed an overall political approach, or to think that it would be resolved by military and policing techniques. The adoption of emergency legislation indicated that the government – and the National Assembly – had chosen the second option, and that, in fact, they were capitulating before the torturers. Far from strengthening itself, the state destroyed itself: policemen, and then soldiers became its sole representatives. Between the head of state and the users of the water pipe or electric shock equipment a complicity in the act itself was established.'[64]

Such remarks could apply equally to Northern Ireland, where, for instance, there have been documented cases of systematic torture and ill-treatment in British interrogation centres.[65] It has been demonstrated that such actions violate internationally binding conventions on human rights, and therefore democratic norms. Alternative spokesmen and women have raised questions about the use of the armed forces in Northern Ireland, not least about their undercover activities. It was the celebrated siege at the Iranian embassy, and its violent resolution by the use of a special force, the SAS, in May 1980, which first brought 'home' to the British mainland some pressing questions about the nature of such groups. The spy novelist, John le Carré expressed these typically 'alternative' sentiments when he wrote:

'We have learned a lot in the last few days of how SAS recruits are tortured, immersed in ditches filled with sheep's entrails, hooded, strapped to boards, trained to endure, to kill, to foreshorten their humanitarian impulses. In the past fifteen months, we are told, four of them have died in the course of this training. Theirs is scarcely the courage of the untrained passer-by who "has a go" at a thug. It is the courage of the tough guy put to social use. At Princes' Gate counter-terror vanquished terror. We should indeed be thankful that the extreme recourse succeeded. But we should be scared stiff by the sight of shock-troops storming into London's streets, and a little ashamed of having them billed as our national – racial? – champions.'[66]

Incidents such as the Iranian embassy siege bring the conflict between terror and counter-terror to the centre of the media's attention. Those arguing from the alternative perspective may often criticise the media for their shortcomings. But they are also concerned to maintain the existing possibilities for analytical coverage, to try and extend these further, and to impede further encroachments by the state. We shall return to these questions in some detail in Chapters 4 and 5.

The populist perspective

The claim is frequently made officially that a 'war against terrorism' is being fought nationally and internationally. But at the same time official views also stress the defence of the rule of law and assert the political and moral advantages of democratic rule. The war against terrorism, therefore, cannot be total. No democratic state can openly advocate torture, assassination or arbitrary imprisonment on poor evidence; nor can such practices even be admitted to exist as other than aberrations from a law-abiding norm by 'bad apples' amongst the security forces.

But this means that the official perspective is open to a charge of inconsistency. If there is warlike walk, what about warlike action? Why not kill the terrorists, whether by military operations, or by imposing the death penalty after they have been captured and convicted? Proponents of this view take the metaphor of war seriously. We have labelled the framework in which it is developed the 'populist' perspective.

It has much in common with the present government's hard-line 'law and order' rhetoric which provides one of the lynch pins for the 'authoritarian' populism which defines their general style and stance.[67] Both Thatcherism and the 'reactionary' populism we are concerned with here, trade upon popular stereotypes of civil libertarians and Left politicians as ineffectual and 'soft' on violence. Both work with essentialist categories of good and evil and both insist that combating terrorism and restoring order requires a tough and uncompromising response. But whereas those who pursue these themes from within the official perspective continue to claim (however rhetorically) that the rule of law must be upheld, 'reactionary' populists are prepared to drop this caveat and call for a full-blooded 'war against terrorism' aimed at restoring order by whatever means may be necessary. Moreover, it is argued, if the state refuses to take such action, people are entitled to fight back themselves, by force if necessary. At this point the populist perspective on terrorism shades into the more general advocacy of popular vigilantism as a way of combating violent street crime. As we shall see, this view is not as central as the other two perspectives to television's representation of 'terrorism', though it does occupy a secure niche in popular fiction.

There are abundant illustrations of the populist perspective in Northern Ireland. A rich source has been the paramilitary loyalist organizations which draw upon a long tradition of militant armed opposition to a British 'sell-out' to Irish nationalism, from Edward Carson's day, when the first private army of resistance to Home Rule was organised, to the present.

A clear expression of populist sentiments came when the loyalist leader, the Reverend Robert Bradford, was assassinated in 1981. There were calls for the creation of a 'third force' on the model of Carson's Volunteers which would take on the IRA. Dissatisfaction was expressed with the inability of the security forces to root out the terrorists. John McMichael, a leading figure in the paramilitary Ulster Defence Association expressed reactionary populist outrage very clearly when he said: 'The Israelis have the right attitude. You seek out your enemy and you destroy him. The British government seems to think there is some sort of crime wave here. In fact there is a war.'[68]

Loyalist politicians have repeatedly advocated a 'get tough' security policy to solve the present round of troubles. The Ulster Unionist MP, Harold McCusker, gave voice to these sentiments in November 1982:

'I think a government's responsibility is to protect its innocent population and to preserve law and order in the community. And if the normal rule of law cannot deal with people like [Gerry] Adams and others who are I think the godfathers of violence, then they should be taken out of society by other means. And I'm not talking necessarily about shooting them. I'm talking about internment . . . '[69]

Throughout the conflict, loyalists have repeatedly expressed their dissatisfaction with the prosecution of the war effort. In 1972, Mr William Craig, a former Home Affairs Minister under the Stormont regime, advocated a strategy for dealing with the failures of British repression:

'We must build up dossiers on those men and women in this country who are a menace to this country because one of these days, if and when the politicians fail us, it may be our job to liquidate the enemy.'[70]

Such statements cannot be made by the spokesmen for a democratic order; not in public anyway. As private armies and vigilantism represent something of a threat to the state's claim to the monopoly of the legitimate use of force, they must be formally disowned. A typical denunciation of the 'third force' approach came from Mr James Prior, Secretary of State for Northern Ireland, in November 1981:

'It has long been the only objective of the IRA to make not only this province of the United Kingdom but ultimately the whole of Ireland ungovernable within the democratic tradition. The IRA has not succeeded and will not succeed. Extremists on the other side of the sectarian divide now utter precisely the same threat to the rule of law and to the democratic parliamentary system. The Government's response is exactly the same. The rule of law must prevail. Unless it prevails there can be no future for us or our children. Terrorism can and must be defeated. but that is not all. We must not, in the end, lose the war for the preservation of our democratic way of life.'[72]

This is precisely what one would expect from the spokesman of a state which proclaimed itself above the fray. Even so, it earmarks only the 'terrorist' enemy by name, the IRA, whereas the other enemies of democracy go under the unspecific label of 'sectarian extremists'. This points to a problematic ambiguity: the good must sometimes fight the bad with the assistance of the ugly.

But official spokesmen speak with more than one voice. As we saw earlier, for example, Brigadier Glover's defence intelligence report offered a picture close to the alternative view of terrorism as politically-motivated violence. But this is an unpublicised perception, unless it somehow leaks out. In much the same way, the use of 'dirty tricks' by special forces remains unspoken, and, in practice, because it puts the demands of order before those of the law, it is very close to the public populist advocacy of rooting out the enemy. Very occasionally, members of the security forces are prepared to give anonymous voice to such sentiments, as did a 'world weary major' quoted in one newspaper report, who said: 'Some people believe in selective internment. I believe in selective assassination.'[72]

Such tactics are officially denied, but critics continue to discount the denials and to accuse the authorities of slipping into virtual terrorist tactics themselves. One such allegation concerning recent security policy, for instance, came from the leader of the Social Democratic and Labour Party, John Hume MP:

'It is quite clear that a section of the RUC and the British Army have now been authorised to shoot to kill anyone about whom they are suspicious. No-one objects to any person being arrested for any crime for which they are suspected, charged and brought before the courts – that is the due process of law. But to authorise their instant execution or attempted execution, as has now happened on five separate occasions in recent times, is in effect to abandon the rule of law completely and give official sanction to what is in fact legalised murder.'[73]

This is precisely what the populist perspective advocates when it puts the demand for order above the need for strict legality. Such openness is not available to official spokesmen – whatever the agents of the state may in fact do – for they would sacrifice the claim that the violence of the state is always legitimate.

The oppositional perspective

The oppositional perspective justifies the use of violence in the pursuit of political ends. It is put forward by those who perform acts of politically-motivated violence, or by those who either directly speak for them or share their objectives. Those arguing the official perspective are concerned to ensure that oppositional views, inasmuch as they provide a rationale for violent acts, receive as little publicity or credibility as possible. In that way the actions – which generally result in death and injury and damage to property – may be allowed to 'speak for themselves'. The less they are placed in context by oppositional spokesmen and women, or by communiqués, the more they are subject to explanation in official terms, as criminal, barbarous and irrational.

Two main kinds of justification surface in the communications of those employing anti-state political violence. The first is that politically and economically the state is a repressive instrument which so constrains those within it that any other form of political action is either impossible or ineffective. The aim, therefore, must be the complete overthrow of the state and the political and economic system which it maintains.

The second justification offered is that political violence is necessary in struggles for national or sectional liberation in circumstances where the state may be said to have adopted a colonial role towards another people or towards a section of its own population. The subjugation of other peoples may take the form of economic imperialism rather than direct colonial administration and so be carried out through client states and dependent governments. In this second case, warfare becomes a realistic metaphor for the insurgents to adopt, although it is constantly rejected by the authorities. It is a metaphor which confers legitimacy upon the insurgents by making their struggle one for territorial self-determination. The 'terrorist' therefore claims the role of an enemy with defined but limited war objectives.

A current example of anti-system political violence is provided by the Red Brigades in Italy, a group with the avowed aim of 'striking at the heart of the state'. Their greatest *coup* was the kidnapping, and, after some two months of holding him captive, the assassination of Christian Democrat leader, Aldo Moro. What makes this case particularly relevant for our purposes was the fact that in many respects it was an event in which the media played an important role. The kidnapping was part of the Red Brigades' effort to establish their presence on the political scene as a legitimate party to discussion with those controlling the state. At the time, in 1978, there was much debate about whether or not the press and other media should report the Red Brigades' communiqués. This crystallised around the suggestion of media guru Marshall McLuhan that 'the plugs should be pulled out' on terrorists who thrived on publicity.[74] One can readily understand why such anger and anxiety were generated in official circles by the publication of the Red Brigades' messages, as their captive was described as a 'prisoner' undergoing 'trial' and his eventual killing was characterised as a 'death sentence'.

'The interrogation ... proceeds with the absolute collaboration of the prisoner. His answers clarify ... the counter-revolutionary line being pursued by the imperialist centrals ... The information we have been able to obtain ... will be made known to the revolutionary movement which will make good use of it in the continuation of the TRIAL [OF] THE REGIME ...'[75]

Putting the regime 'on trial' through one of its leading personalities presumes a counter-legitimacy to that of the state. While the communiqués set out the Red Brigades' political rationales, they did so, as some commentators noted, and as the above quotation illustrates, in language so alien to most that they could hardly be persuasive.[76]

In Britain there have been a few cases of this anti-system type, the most notable being the Angry Brigade at the beginning of the 1970s. Most armed action, however, has been of the second 'liberationist' type, either carried out by the agents of foreign groups operating against their own targets on British territory, as for instance in the case of the Iranian embassy siege, or by the agents of one of the separate nationalities included in the British nation-state, the Scots, the Welsh, and pre-eminently, the Irish. The distinction between different types of insurrectionary activity is important, and while it is emphasised by alternative analysts, the official view rejects it as irrelevant and focuses instead upon the general consequences of 'terrorism', in particular the loss of life or the material and psychic damage produced by acts of violence.

A particularly illuminating confrontation between official and oppositional views occurred when Lord Mountbatten, the Queen's uncle, was assassinated by the IRA at Mullaghmore in the Irish Republic in the summer of 1979. The press coverage in Britain was highly reverential because of his kinship to the Queen. Mountbatten was presented as the epitome of the finest British qualities: soldier, hero, noble, statesman, family man *par excellence*. His passing was widely referred to as 'the end of a legend'. The newspapers and television and radio programmes ran stockpiled obituaries, interviews with friends and acquaintances and tributes from across the globe. The act of killing was widely interpreted as irrational, as that of 'evil men' (*Daily Mail*), 'wicked assassins' (*The Sun*), 'psychopathic thugs' (*Daily Express*), 'murdering bastards' (*Daily Star*), as 'cowardly and senseless' (*Financial Times*) and as the product of 'diseased minds rather than political calculation' (*Daily Telegraph*). There was, therefore, a counterpoint between, on the one hand, the irrational and evil forces threatening the state and, on the other, the virtues of an exemplary citizen whose death was inexplicable.

Much less prominence was given to the simultaneous disaster which befell the British Army, namely the killing of eighteen crack soldiers in an IRA ambush. A close reading of some papers disclosed that sources in the security forces did not see the two linked incidents as senseless and irrational. Rather, they took them to indicate a more sophisticated strategy of armed struggle. Only one newspaper printed in full the IRA communiqué which specified the reasons for Mountbatten's killing. This talked of his assassination as 'one of the discriminating ways we can bring to the attention of the British people the continuing occupation of our country'.[77]

Against this kind of picture it is instructive to set out the opposi-tional one. The justifications for killing Mountbatten were offered at some length in an interview published in France by a member of the Provisional IRA's Army Council:

'First of all, he was a member of the Royal Family, of a monarchy which has done nothing other than bring misery to our people. He had considerable stature within the British military machine which for the past eight centuries, and especially during these past twelve years, has enslaved Ireland. But apart from his membership of the British Royal Family, he was also an absentee landlord – that is to say a landed proprietor in the old English tradition in Ireland, who, while living in London, benefits from the exploitation of the lands of his great house in Ireland, living there just once a year, during August.

So killing this man had the aim of making the world understand – and first and foremost the British – that there's a state of war in this country. Given his personal importance there was inevitably going to be enormous publicity attached to this operation . . . we had no hatred for him as a person. It is the society, the military and political machine he symbolised that we were aiming at.'[78]

Clearly these are political calculations being offered, agree with them or not. The definition of the offensive act as part of a wartime campaign is central to the claim of legitimacy (a point, as we have seen, well recognised by those arguing the populist case, and covertly accepted officially). The implications for publicity are important.

ENGLISH GUTTER PRESS
IN AN EVIL AND
MURDEROUS MOOD,
THE MORNING AFTER

Republican News, September 1st, 1979

In fact, the press reaction to the killing was a cause of some satisfaction to the IRA, as it focussed attention on them. The interviewee went on:

'The outburst of hysteria in the British press . . . exposed all the falsifications in the . . . reporting of the war in Ireland . . . The explosion of hysteria wasn't a surprise to us, especially on the part of the conservative newspapers . . . British phlegm took quite a blow . . . Through such operations we have raised the Irish liberation struggle to a new international level, one which it has not reached for several years, giving the IRA the chance to explain itself, to make sense of the war we have been fighting for the past ten or more years.'[79]

Even negative coverage, then, is worth having on this account. Moreover, the references to criminality, brutality and psychopathology in the press reactions are countered with assertions of the legitimacy of the struggle as one of popular resistance:

'For the German armies, French or Polish resisters were "terrorists". Today, they are heroes . . . It would be unthinkable for anyone today that they should not have dynamited the Wehrmacht's trains because those are "terrorist" activities . . . Even if Britain does not recognise that we are an armed force because it's not in her interest, that is nevertheless the case . . . our prisoners are condemned to heavy periods of detention for acts of conscious resistance to an oppressive system. They are not victims of a conflict between personal interests and a given system, but fighters who are completely committed to an armed struggle, which you can criticise if you want, but certainly not define as motivated by the lure of reward or by personal interests . . . Demanding recognition for political status is all of a piece with the war we are fighting, and you can measure its importance by the fact that London refuses to give it to us with such tenacity.'[80]

With these quotations we have come full circle. The oppositional view articulates a systematically contrary account of the rationale and legitimacy of political violence to that of the official view. As such it threatens the state, for if it were widely believed it would undermine the state's authority.

From perspectives to programmes

These then are the four main perspectives on terrorism currently 'in play' in political debate. How are they presented on British television? First we need to look at two pairs of terms which play an important role in the discussion which follows. Each pair distinguishes between different types of programmes but in ways which cut across the conventional division between actuality and fictional programmes, and across the normal subdivisions which are made within these categories; between news bulletins, current affairs, and documentaries for example, or between serials, series, and single plays. We label these cross-cutting dimensions *open* and *closed*, and *tight* and *loose*.

These distinctions were prompted by our discovery, as we researched this study, that presentations of terrorism on British television were a good deal more diverse and complex than simpler assumptions about television's relation to the state and to dominant ideology predict. Some types of programming, for example news bulletins and action-adventure series like *The Professionals*, are relatively *closed*. They operate *mainly or wholly within the terms of reference set by the official perspective*. But other forms, such as single-plays and 'authored' documentaries, are relatively *open* in the sense that *they provide spaces in which the core assumptions of the official perspective can be interrogated and contested and in which other perspectives can be presented and examined*.

Open and *closed* then, are static concepts based on whether the programme deals with one or more viewpoints.

To this we need to add the dynamic distinction between *tight* and *loose* formats. This distinction focusses on the internal organisation of programmes and the way the various elements within them are arranged and presented. A *tight* format *is one in which the images, arguments and evidence offered by the programme are organised to converge upon a single preferred interpretation and where other possible conclusions are marginalised or closed-off*. A *loose* format in contrast, *is one where the ambiguities, contradictions and loose ends generated within the programme are never fully resolved*, leaving the viewer with a choice of interpretations. Not surprisingly there is a fair degree of overlap between these two pairs of distinctions. Most *closed* programmes are also *tight* while many *open* programmes are also *loose* but there are some interesting exceptions. As we shall see, some *open* programmes, which contest the official view, are organised in a very *tight* manner in order to mobilise the audience behind the alternative perspective.

The next two chapters look in detail at the way these processes operate in the major types of programmes. We have not attempted a full-scale analysis of how often the topic of terrorism appears on British television. Nor is this a full survey of how prominently the various perspectives, and their component themes, are featured. The present study was conceived as an exploratory exercise aimed at raising questions for debate and suggesting productive lines for future research. More particularly, we set out to do two things.

Firstly, we have tried to widen the terms of the current debate about television's relation to the state and to political life. So instead of concentrating exclusively on news and current affairs coverage, as most previous studies of television and politics have done, we decided to look at television fiction as well. This has several advantages. It provides a rather more comprehensive picture of the ways that television represents the issues around 'terrorism'. It enables us to explore the continuities and breaks between the rhetorics, imagery and explanations offered by fictional and actuality programming. And it helps to pin-down what is unique and specific to a particular programme form and the forces shaping it as well as what it shares in common with other kinds of programmes. So, although our selection of examples is not exhaustive it is systematic. In technical terms it is based on a quota sample. We took the conventional divisions between the major programme types as our sampling frame and looked for representative examples of each category. Our analysis therefore includes action-adventure series, drama serials, and single plays, as well as news bulletins, current affairs programmes and documentaries.

Secondly, by focussing on the representation of terrorism and the state's responses to it, we hoped to move the discussion beyond the entrenched concern with party and parliamentary affairs and the electoral process.

Chapter 2

Reporting 'terrorism'

How is 'terrorism' handled on actuality television? That is, in the different forms of news, current affairs and documentary programming. Once we begin to examine individual programmes we can see how the four perspectives outlined in the previous chapter come into play. But the ways in which those perspectives appear in different types of programme seems to vary. In this chapter we attempt to show how and why they do so.

We have drawn in varying detail on some 15 different programmes for our illustrations, all of which, with two exceptions, come from 1981–82, the period in which we gathered most of our material. We are not in any way claiming that this is an exhaustive survey which carries statistical implications. But we do think that most regular watchers of British television would accept that our systematic sample does fairly represent the range of actuality programming presently on offer.

There is another limitation on the way in which we have handled the selected material which readers should take into account. A full qualitative analysis of a television programme takes up a great deal of space. One instance of such detailed work may be found in Hall, Connell and Curti's study of an edition of *Panorama* during the 1974 General Election.[1] Another is Davis and Walton's study of the news bulletins of six different networks in three countries on the day Aldo Moro's body was discovered.[2] Each of these offers a detailed account of the overall programme structure, spoken vocabulary and visuals. We have decided against offering such a technically detailed account as it would restrict the range of material that we could examine in the space available.

Given the constraints we have adopted, we have focussed most upon the spoken vocabularies of the programmes selected, and we have paid particular attention to the structuring of interviews, an area which has been somewhat neglected.

Forms of actuality television

Actuality television divides up into a number of programme forms which have developed over the years from the initial distinction between 'news' and 'current affairs' output (see Table 1). Reading across we can see that the main types of output can be classified as the news bulletin, the news magazine, the current affairs programme and the documentary. These are the working distinctions within television itself. These different programme forms offer a range of programme spaces. For instance, the documentary form can be relatively more open to alternative and oppositional views than the news bulletin. But there is nothing hard and fast about this since it depends, in turn, on the kind of documentary. The table summarises, in a very schematic way, the argument of this chapter. In essence, this is that as you move across the forms of television, with their different production constraints, and their different public identities, there are systematic variations in the way in which the question of political violence is dealt with.

Television news

Television news is probably the main source of images of terrorism for most people. It commands very large audiences and is widely seen as having considerable potential influence on public opinion. In Britain, both BBC and commercial television are formally obliged to present their news with due accuracy and impartiality, and to preserve impartiality in all programmes dealing with matters of public controversy. Such 'impartiality' is defined in practice in terms of positions taken in relation to the British political system and its underlying social and economic order. Since terrorism, particularly that which makes its presence felt on the domestic scene, is seen as threatening the social order, this is one field of coverage where broadcast journalism cannot remain impartial.

Though there has been relatively little work on the news coverage of terrorism or political violence in Britain, news itself – both on television and in the press – has been the object of a great deal of research during the past fifteen years. Numerous areas of coverage have been analysed, ranging from parliamentary politics through industrial news to crime and civil disorder.[3] On the basis of this, a number of quite general points may be made about the nature of television news.

The news output of organisations such as the BBC and ITN attracts keen attention and scrutiny from politicians and is therefore one of the points at which the authority and credibility of the broadcasting organisations is most exposed. Consequently, adherence to the practices and techniques which define 'impartiality' is as much a matter of institutional survival as one of external pressure. The more the broadcasters sustain an image of political responsibility the more they strengthen their claims to autonomy and so forestall attempts to impose more stringent controls on their operations.

Table 1: The major forms of actuality television

	Programme form			
	news bulletin	news magazine	current affairs	documentary
Examples	*News at Ten* (ITV) *BBC News*	*Nationwide* (BBC1) *Newsnight* (BBC2)	*Panorama* (BBC1) *TV Eye* (ITV)	*Heroes* (John Pilger)
Frequency	daily	daily	weekly	irregular
Item length	short (news story)	short (programme item)	long (programme theme)	long (programme subject)
Production techniques	visual clips brief interviews	short film report/studio interview	film report studio discussion	film report
Presenter's rôle	reader	reporter/ interviewer	reporter/ chairperson/ interviewer	storyteller
Programme identified with	the broadcasting organization	the production team	the production team	an individual presenter/ producer
	relatively closed			relatively open
	Programme space			

But these constraints result in a form of news which presents itself as a merely factual report of events in the world. News bulletins tend to be rendered in a style that conceals the processes of selection and decision which lie behind the reporting, and which allows little room for comment or argumentation. The opinions which are presented are almost always confined to the holders of power in major institutions: government ministers and politicians from the major parties; senior members of the police force and the judiciary; trade union leaders and the heads of employers' organisations; and those who speak for 'accredited' pressure and interest groups such as churches and professional organisations. As a result, news is one of the more 'closed' forms of presentation, and operates predominantly within the terms of the official perspective.

News about terrorism

The socio-political impasse in Northern Ireland has contributed to a wider crisis of legitimacy within the British state. Together with government's continuing inability to restore profitability to capital and its repeated confrontations with organised labour, this has led towards a more authoritarian structure of rule, aspects of which were outlined in Chapter 1. We have some sympathy for the argument, developed by Stuart Hall and his associates, that the media have played an important role in winning consent for the shift from the social-democratic consensus to the law-and-order state.[4] The development of the authoritarian populism articulated so ably by Mrs Thatcher has in part been based upon the development of something of a siege mentality, in which the social order is seen as gravely threatened by various forms of 'violence' and dissent. A good deal of media coverage has contributed to the present climate, one in which the smack of firm government is evidently a welcome reassurance to many.

Incidents such as hijacks, assassinations, sieges and bombings — especially where they are directed against important people such as Lord Mountbatten or Mr Airey Neave — can provoke a sense that the entire society is under threat, and they evoke ritualised responses from the media. The analysis in the last chapter of the reaction to the killing of Lord Mountbatten is an instance of this. The society as a whole is invited by its leadership to stand united against a terrorism which is evaluated as inhuman and irrational, as the very embodiment of chaos.[5]

The coverage of Northern Irish affairs in the British media has tended to simplify violent incidents, to avoid historical background, to concentrate on human-interest stories and to rely heavily on official sources. Even during periods of the most intense constitutional activity, such as election campaigns, the story has been pre-eminently one of violence, and of irrational, inexplicable violence at that.[6]

Similar points are made by David Paletz, John Ayanian and Peter Fozzard who have studied the ways in which the IRA, the Red Brigades and the Puerto Rican Fuerzas Armadas de Liberacion Nacional (FALN) were covered on the three US networks from 1977 to 1979. Their analysis demonstrates that, during that period, just over one of every two stories 'from or about Northern Ireland, Italy and Puerto Rico concerned the actions of terrorists'.[7] Most news coverage focussed on spectacular events: the Moro affair, the assassination of Airey Neave, FALN bombings in New York city. Paletz and his associates argue that the way in which television packages stories about terrorism into 'round-ups' tends to create 'the general impression that terrorism is widespread around the world'.[8] This magnifies the importance of left-wing anti-state terrorism whereas right-wing terrorism and repressive state actions in countries friendly to the US are almost never mentioned. Their overall conclusion tends to support the view that the official perspective on political violence is largely reproduced by US television news:

'Terrorists enjoy attention, but they are not endowed with legitimacy by television news. With the occasional exception of the IRA, the justness of the terrorists' causes are denied. Most of the stories about the insurgents' actions are provided by the authorities and concern governmental responses to the violence, or the actual terroristic acts themselves. The underlying objectives of the violence are rarely explained, almost never justified. When tactics are emphasised without discussion of motives, objectives, goals or precipitating social conditions, then context is discarded, and political justifications are denied. The terrorists are identified with criminal violence and seen simply as bent on terror.'[9]

This picture seems broadly convincing and supports other research findings. Paletz and his team studied *news* broadcasts, however, and were not making claims about other forms of television journalism.

In one other recent study, with a far smaller empirical base, much more far-reaching claims are made. Howard Davis and Paul Walton have analysed the way in which the main news bulletins on one day in Britain, the United States and West Germany reported the discovery of Aldo Moro's body in Rome on 9 May 1978. Drawing on their earlier work in the Glasgow Media Group, they pursue the argument that broadcasting systems are the central location in which a social consensus is elaborated and in which what they call a 'moral closure' is effected against what are defined as disruptive forces in the state and society. We agree with their argument that since terrorism is outside the consensus, broadcasters do not feel obliged to treat it in a balanced or impartial manner. That is hardly very contentious and is documented elsewhere.[10] Davis and Walton demonstrate that the main news bulletins of the six networks they examine used similar narrative structures, visuals and verbal language for telling the story of Moro's discovery. This similarity, they argue, is dictated by a 'need for closure', that is, a way of demonstrating the apartness of terrorist groups from normal political life. The reports they examined consistently removed legitimacy from the Red Brigades by implying their political marginality, by labelling them as 'terrorists' (sometimes as 'criminals' and 'killers') and by representing them as psychopaths. All of these techniques are typical, we would agree, and we have documented them in our earlier studies and do so later in this book.[11]

Davis and Walton further argue that it is the spoken word rather than the visual element of news which is of predominant importance in establishing the kind of 'preferred' interpretation which the viewer comes to accept. But as we shall see not all forms of programming offer an unambiguous 'preferred' reading.

Our disagreement with their account arises when they draw from these very particular data a quite unwarrantable conclusion. They say:

'...the evidence from the reporting of the Moro story in the press and the television networks *points to a universally assumed consensus* (in Western media) within which, with some cross-cultural variation, the complex causes and impact of armed opposition and revolutionary violence are reduced by the inferential frameworks of "law and (dis)order", the "violent society", the threat to democracy, and international terror, to *a simple picture* of a temporary and unprovoked outbreak of irrational violence in an otherwise ordered and peaceful society.'[12]

This is a very sweeping statement. First of all, there is no serious analysis of press coverage, so we must discount that from the claim. Secondly, it is surely going too far to talk of a 'universally assumed consensus' because that presumes that *all* forms of dissent and armed opposition, wherever they may occur, are going to be treated equally in all Western countries. Recent divergencies over the interpretation of guerrilla actions in El Salvador and Nicaragua between European governments and that of the US have been reflected in divergent analyses in the press and broadcasting. Moreover, to take an example nearer home, the IRA has been represented as a *political* force with a rational cause and a social base on Italian and Swedish television.[13] How could one account for this if a *'universally* assumed consensus' existed? Obviously, it does not. Davis and Walton have failed to note the importance of the way in which *distance* from a particular conflict and therefore from state pressure, permits more dispassionate reporting. Their statement reflects, in our terms, what the official perspective tells us. But it is absurd to claim that the official perspective is the *only* one in play.

What Davis and Walton's analysis shows, in fact, is that news is a relatively 'closed' form and that it benefits official explanations. These are bound to be enhanced when a set-piece event is taken which mobilises ritual forms of reporting, such as the assassination of Moro or of Mountbatten. However, other kinds of reporting do not manifest this presumed 'universal consensus'; nor indeed is 'moral closure' as easily effected as this style of analysis supposes.

News magazines, current affairs programmes and documentaries

The study of news in isolation from other forms of television journalism is apt to lead us up such blind alleys. While we would not dispute that broadcasting journalism is constrained in the way in which it can deal with a hot subject such as terrorism, it is not all constrained in the same ways or to the same degree. As we indicate in Table 1 above, different programme forms may dispose of more space in which to deal with such contentious subjects.

News magazines and current affairs programmes have developed as a complement to the news bulletins and are designed to provide space for longer, more reflective treatment of the day-to-day issues of social management. Nevertheless, they remain closely tied to news priorities and are subject to many of the same constraints. They generally take their topics from some recent or forthcoming news event, and they tend to draw on the same cast of spokesmen and women. Although the rubric of balance and the easing of time constraints ensures that a wider spread of opinions is presented, the range generally remains confined to the positions taken up within the main political parties and 'accredited' interest groups and comparatively little attention is paid to views falling outside it. Occasionally, these bounds are broken as in the instance (discussed below) when a spokesman for the Irish National Liberation Army was interviewed on the BBC daily news magazine *Tonight*. But these cases are the exception rather than the rule and they invariably provoke heated debate on the legitimacy of giving air-time to enemies of the state.

Within the 'normal' confines of the standard news magazine and current affairs formats, however, there are still important variations of emphasis. These can be seen in the different ways in which presenters perform their roles of chairing and interviewing. They may, for example, present themselves as populist spokesmen and women, articulating what they take to be the prevailing fears and preoccupations of 'ordinary viewers', basing their questions on some supposed commonsense consensus on the issue (which places the discussion firmly within the parameters of the official perspective). Or, they may choose the role of devil's advocate, quizzing their Establishment witnesses from a perspective which incorporates alternative or even oppositional elements. Though, here again, there are significant variations in the way this role is performed. Presenters may be deferential and apologetic, prefacing their remarks with phrases like 'Some people would argue . . .'. Or they may be more direct and obtrusive as in 'But surely you do not mean to tell me that . . .'. The aggressive style is most apparent when the witness is putting an alternative or oppositional view, as in the interview with the Sinn Fein spokesman on *Newsnight* discussed below.

In choosing between these various roles presenters are constrained in important ways by the programme's place in the schedule and by the kind of audience it is aimed at. The BBC's early evening news magazine, *Nationwide*, for example, goes out on the Corporation's main channel (BBC1) directly after the early evening national news bulletin and regional news round-ups, and plays a key role in building and holding a mass audience for the rest of the prime-time output. This strategic position in the ratings battle pushes the programme towards populist forms of presentation and discourse which work with the most widely held images and assumptions in the interests of mobilising the largest possible audience.[14] *Newsnight* in contrast, is transmitted on the minority channel (BBC2) in a slot (10.55-11.40 pm) which is out of prime-time. This location gives it an audience concentrated among those with post-school education and professional and managerial jobs. And since the presenters can assume that they are addressing people much as they would like to see themselves – well informed, open-minded, and sceptical – they feel freer to present issues in a more complex way which allows greater scope for the consideration of alternative views and positions.

Nevertheless, this flexibility remains subject to the constraints which stem from the BBC's 'special relationship' to the state and subject to notions of nationhood. In Britain there is an important sense in which the BBC, in spite of its formal independence from the state is the *national* broadcasting organisation in a way in which the programme companies making up the ITV network are not. This means that the BBC's general current affairs and documentary output is more closely identified with the organisation, the organisation is more exposed to political and other criticism and its regular current affairs output is more closely tied to the political agenda of the day. The weekly *Panorama*, for example, is regarded as the BBC's 'flagship' in current affairs. Its topics and techniques are particularly exposed to political scrutiny and censure. It is expected to act as a national forum and deal with the important issues of the day. The regular current affairs output on ITV on the other hand has more freedom to select its own agenda.

Although documentaries are often grouped in a series or occupy a regular time-slot, they are less constrained than the regular current affairs output to follow the political issues of the day. They draw their agenda more widely across the range of social, political and economic questions and often take the form of enquiries into the workings of particular organisations and social institutions. They rely less on studio presentation of those speaking for various legitimate views and opinions, more on sequential reports of the material that the producer has managed to put together on a subject. The balance requires the producer to take note of the major currents of opinion within the field he or she is investigating. This requirement has relaxed, however, as the notion of 'balanced output' has taken precedence over that of 'balanced programme', implying that balance need not be achieved within the single programme but in the output taken as a whole. The space opened up by this relaxation is at its maximum in the 'authored' documentary.

Whereas the news and most of the regular current affairs output are so closely identified with the broadcasting organisations as to be seen as 'their' products, for which they bear collective responsibility, 'authored' documentaries are ascribed to an individual reporter or producer and presented as their particular view of the subject. Accordingly, the commissioning organisation is usually at pains to distance itself from the programme, by, for example, announcing at the beginning and end that it represents the personal opinions of the makers. This disavowal in turn licences the presenters to ignore the normal constraints of balance, and to offer their individual views backed by whatever material they can command. In the process, they move out of the normal roles of observer and reporter and into the role of 'author', a role they share with the creators of television fiction, and more particularly with the writers of single plays.

Reporting terrorism: some examples

Television news, because it deals with immediate events, presents the 'Who, what, where and when' of the latest incident in its reporting of terrorism. Because it cannot be present at every violent event, it often makes use of pictures of the aftermath, and this directs the audience's attention to the connection between terrorism and its horrible consequences. In particular, television like the press tends to focus on those victims who are most vulnerable and innocent: women, children and animals. Where the victims are members of the security forces or the police, attention is drawn to their lovable human qualities. PC Lock, the captured policeman in the Iranian embassy siege, is the quintessential example of this.[15]

The London bombings

The BBC's 5.40pm News on 20 July 1982 began with the following headline:

'IRA bombers return to London. Their target – British soldiers, but civilians die too. At the bandstand in Regent's Park six people are killed at an army concert and three more die in Knightsbridge as the household cavalry ride past to change the guard. Injuries are terrible. Nearly 50 people are taken to hospital.'

Returning to the story after the other headlines, the newsreader announced:

'In all 9 people died in the two bomb explosions in central London this morning. 50 more were injured. Both explosions were aimed at targets where tourists would be watching the army. The IRA said they were responsible for both bombs.'

The reporter at Knightsbridge said:

' . . . the blast in mid-morning started a day of carnage and confusion in London. As well as the three guards killed, 13 were injured. Many were shielded by the horses, seven of which were killed or later destroyed. In all 21 people were taken to hospital, several of them civilians who had simply been passing by.'

The report from Regent's Park also focussed on the death and injury, referring to the presence in the Park of holiday makers and London office workers: ' . . . six people died instantly. 25 were injured, some seriously.' The bulletin referred three times to the fact that 'people' had been killed, but only once identified those people as soldiers.[16]

The news bulletin established the two locations with aerial shots and a map of Central London. The newsreader warned the audience that there were going to be 'horrible pictures'. There were scenes of devastation at the bandstand and in Park Lane, of covered-up bodies and of dead horses, of the emergency services at work. The bulletin, therefore, established the dreadful effects of the bombing, the loss of both human and animal life, the disruption of everyday life and the destruction of property. There was also some effort to account for the IRA's action in a background commentary by TV reporter Michael Sullivan:

'When it comes to shaking the British public, the IRA work on the principle that one bomb in London or another major English city is worth several in Belfast or Londonderry. Publicity is their aim rather than outright military success with any one bomb and for that reason even soldiers engaged on ceremonial duties are satisfactory targets, though civilian by-standers are also likely to die. Bombings in London have come in a series of campaigns . . . '

The IRA's purpose was presented, therefore, as a pure quest for publicity in which a rather indiscriminate approach to 'soft' targets prevailed. Aside from offering this off-the-shelf explanation so prevalent in the official view, the broadcast also carried condemnatory reactions from the House of Commons, where Mrs Thatcher gave a clear statement of the official view: 'These callous and cowardly crimes have been committed by evil and brutal men who know nothing of democracy.' Commander William Hucklesby, head of the anti-terrorist branch of the Metropolitan police, described the London bombings as 'such horrible things' when giving his reaction to the news.

If we now turn to *Nationwide*'s reporting of the same incident (BBC1, 20 July 1982), a number of the general points outlined in our table become apparent. The news magazine began with a review of the death toll and previous campaigns. It was introduced by Frank Bough, the studio presenter, thus: 'Eight dead; many more injured. We're asking is this the start of a new terror campaign and what can be done to keep the bombers out of Britain?' This was followed by a report which noted security force successes against the IRA, in particular the jailing of Gerard Tuite 'their master bomber'. Giving more background than the news, the reporter referred to the Provisionals sinking into 'relative obscurity' as a result of the Falklands crisis and the forthcoming assembly elections in Northern Ireland which Northern Ireland Secretary Jim Prior 'had hoped would woo militant republicans to the ballot box and away from the bullet and the bomb'. Following this report, Frank Bough interviewed David McKittrick, London bureau chief of the *Irish Times*. The use of a journalist expert is a familiar device in television and radio current affairs programmes, but almost never a part of news bulletins. Bough first asked whether the bombings were 'simply publicity'. McKittrick suggested that it might be revenge for the jailing of Tuite or possibly a more militant new man 'at or near the top of the IRA' which explained the action. There then followed an exchange which neatly illustrated the official premise of irrationality and inhumanity lying behind Bough's question together with McKittrick's attempt to offer an alternative insight into the IRA's motivation:

Bough: Now why do they do it in this sense, because if you can explain if they have any feelings at all, why do they do it? Because all they've done today is arouse a great deal of hatred, and a great determination not to be overcome by it. Now, that, as was said in the House of Commons this afternoon, is totally counter-productive. So why do they do it?

McKittrick: Well you have to remember that the Provisionals look at things in a very different way from the way you and I would. One big factor for them is that when they set off a bomb like this in London whatever the damage it might do, as we would see it, to their cause, the fact is that it is tremendous for the morale of their volunteers, the low down guys back home. They see it as a blow struck at the soft underbelly of the enemy. The other general factor is that I gather at the moment that there was some criticism in the ranks of the fact that the IRA didn't do very much during the Falklands campaign when it might have been thought that they had an opportunity to strike at the heart of Britain.

The action, therefore, is explained in terms of hitting at the wave of patriotism aroused by the Falklands episode and as maintaining support back in Ireland. The language of rationality and calculation counters the language of sentiment. Later in the interview Bough asked whether the bombings had been on a 'sudden impulse', further pursuing the assumption of irrationality. McKittrick's reply was that he thought that 'this is something that has been looked at and studied carefully for quite some time'.

The contribution of the 'expert', then, placed the bombings in the context of a rational tactic, if not strategy. An alternative appraisal of the armed opposition to the state was played off against a largely official line of questioning. The programme was also a vehicle for reaffirming the political unity at Westminster against the terrorists. After citing Mrs Thatcher in the Commons saying 'We shan't rest until they are brought to justice', Bough then turned to Roy Hattersley, Shadow Home Secretary. At first, in response to Bough asking whether the Commons had been in a 'sombre' mood Hattersley offered a ritualised official denunciation:

Hattersley: Yes, the House of Commons was shocked as it always is when it hears of these episodes of awful and mindless violence. Partly because of the simple horror of eight human beings being killed and very many more being injured and partly because we don't understand the irrationality of it. I understand why you try to analyse the IRA psychology but very clearly as you said this puts their cause back and that people should behave in this unspeakably brutal way for absolutely no rational reason is in itself horrifying, I think.

This passage completely dismisses McKittrick's attempt to provide some sort of rational answer and moves the depiction of the action back into the heartland of the official perspective: irrational, brutal, horrifying – and pointless to try and understand the motivations ('IRA psychology'). The interview moved on to discuss the possible security measures that might be taken to prevent a recurrence. After Hattersley had urged greater public vigilance the questions shifted to legislative repression. Bough questioned Hattersley on whether he thought there were sufficient police powers and over divergences between government and opposition over the use of the Prevention of Terrorism Act. The interview concluded with Hattersley reaffirming his view that the Act was injurious to civil liberties – a typical alternative argument – but this was fused with the equally typical official view that the negative features of the act would be exploited in the propaganda war:

' . . . stopping Irish men and women getting off the boat at Liverpool on suspicion, holding them without any evidence against them, then perhaps releasing them after four days or requiring them to go to Belfast . . . actually helps the IRA because they go back to Belfast and they say there is no justice in England. If you speak with an Irish accent you are likely to be arrested and one of the principal objections to the PTA is the publicity advantage that it gives to people who ought not to be given that sort of privilege.'

In this programme, therefore, the presenter aligned himself throughout with variants of official thinking, but there was unquestionably space for the alternative view to be put by McKittrick. The relevance of this was dismissed by Hattersley, whose fusion of hard-line official and mild alternative views demonstrated very clearly that the various perspectives we have outlined do not necessarily appear as pure types in television's discourse.

The *Nationwide* example illustrates our thesis that as one shifts from hard news to current affairs the scope for articulating alternative views increases, and that this is, in part, a function of the form of the programme. But one should also note the strong continuities which nevertheless exist between the news angles and definitions which are pursued in the most frequent and popular forms, news bulletins and daily current affairs programmes. A particularly strong feature of news reporting, whether on television or in the press, is its concentration upon the 'human angle', notably the tragic consequences of acts of terrorism. This is also a characteristic of daily current affairs output. *Nationwide* (BBC1, 24 September 1981) provided a routine example from the Province itself in a feature on 'How one family is coping with the human tragedy of Northern Ireland'.

The feature opened with a shot of a minister of the church speaking at the funeral of the victim, John Proctor, whom he characterised as follows:

Minister: John Proctor, a father, a son, a brother, a colleague, a parishioner, a loved one.

The programme cut to an interview with Proctor's widow, June, in which she was clearly and understandably distressed:

June Proctor: It's awful, it's awful, it is. He was just getting into the car, he'd bought a new car, and he was getting into the car, so it was, and they shot him in the back. In the back. Of all places in the back.

Next, the programme cut to a reporter standing outside the hospital in which Proctor died:

Reporter: Twenty-five years old, John Proctor, married with a two-year-old son had been in the police full-time reserve for a year.

Only at the end of the introduction did the reporter reveal why John Proctor was a target, and then in such a way as to minimise his association with the police force. The rest of the introduction was devoted to establishing the victim's credentials as a human being, and so to underlining the misery and misfortune of his death. This instance illustrates recurrent themes in such aftermath reporting: the family connections of the victims, their bravery compared to the cowardly nature of the attack, and the unfinished business left by sudden death. Later in the feature, the reporter took up the latter theme as the widow's father showed us around the house into which his daughter and son-in-law had been about to move:

Reporter: Today would have been John and June's fourth wedding anniversary. They were due to move into a house of their own for the first time. June's father had helped get it ready . . . (father shows reporter round the house) . . .

Reporter: What are your feelings about what happened?

Father: Oh very strong feelings. I'd like these men to be caught. I would indeed. People like that. Bombing and killing. Awful killings. Look at the sorrow it leaves behind. Endless sorrow.

Reporter: What can be done to stop all this killing in the long term?

Father: It's hard to know. This has been going on so long, so long.

Reporter: What sort of initiative could people like yourself take?

Father: Oh, oh, I wouldn't like to be taking any initiatives. I leave it to the authorities and I think maybe this new man [James Prior appointed Secretary of State for Northern Ireland, 15 September 1981] coming, this new Secretary of State. We've had letters from both him and his wife. Very, very deep letters, we think he'll take it on.

This is an affirmation of confidence in the British government's legitimacy and ability to solve the problem. It offers us a message that constitutional remedies are available and that there is no place for the violent pursuit of political ends.

It is not only human tragedies which provide good, moving, copy. One noteworthy obsession of television and press alike has been the health and welfare of animals, particularly those loyal to the state. In the aftermath of the London bombs in July 1982 much attention was lavished upon one four-legged survivor of the attack: Sefton, an elderly cavalry horse. Apart from numerous reports in news bulletins – even a year after the event – a whole Television South West documentary, *Sefton, A Household Name*, (ITV, 7 December, 1982) was devoted to this equestrian hero. The programme introduced Sefton and his rider, Trooper Michael Pederson, who had saved his mount's life by pressing on its severed jugular vein. The scenes of that day, when eleven soldiers were killed, 50 people injured and ten horses were killed or had to be destroyed, were 'burned into the memory of the nation'. A nail from the nail bomb was displayed as 'a reminder of that morning', and to film of Sefton the commentary went on:

'Nineteen year old Sefton, his jugular vein severed in the blast, became a symbol of the nation's outrage and compassion. The cavalry vets managed to staunch his wounds and save his life, and by the end of August he was running free again in the grounds of the Royal Army Veterinary Corps hospital at Melton Mowbray. Gifts, sweets and telegrams and cards poured into the cavalry barracks

Daily Mirror, July 24th, 1982

from all over Europe and the progress of Sefton's recovery became the subject of almost nightly bulletins on the TV and radio.'

Aside from focussing on the struggle against the horrific consequences, the programme also offered a powerful reaffirmation of the British will to survive, one that extended even to anthromorphised animals. Part of the documentary consisted of an interview with Colonel Andrew Parker-Bowles, commanding officer of the Blues and Royals, Sefton's regiment. The Colonel, dressed in full regimental uniform with decorations, observed: 'the mind boggles that anyone could pack these nails round explosive in order to kill and maim horses . . . ' However, these dangers had to be looked in the eye:

Colonel: Every time any terrorist organisation commits an outrage, their aim is to disrupt ordinary everyday life. And our aim must be to continue as normal.

This statement reaffirmed the official view of terrorism as an essentially meaningless eruption threatening order. To film of the Blues and Royals passing the spot, the commentary reinforced this message:

'And the July outrage has added a new tradition to regimental life. Each time the Life Guards and the Blues and Royals pass the scene of the bombing they salute in honour of their dead and injured fellow soldiers.'

Thus, we are told, what the enemy inflicts is as nothing weighed against the ancient ability of the military to turn the scars of battle into memories worth saving.

Sefton was not unique. Aside from televised celebrations, many features were run in the press and the horse now even enjoys his own full-length biography. One might note the not dissimilar treatment accorded Rats, the dog who befriended British troops stationed in the beleaguered outpost of Crossmaglen in South Armagh. He too became a media hero, subject of a biography, decorated and happily pensioned off in England, to be trotted out now and again.[17]

Dog-soldier Rats, according to his biographer Max Halstock 'had served longer in one of the world's most troublesome and dangerous spots than any other individual British soldier, and he bore with him more than his fair share of battle scars.'[18] If Sefton has been the 'symbol of suffering' (as one newspaper headline had it), the Rats has represented the doughty determination of the squaddie in adversity.

Concern with animals has even extended to our feathered friends. After the conclusion of the siege at the Iranian embassy,

Nationwide (BBC1, 13 May 1980) ran a feature about a family of ducks which had pluckily stayed on in Prince's Gate until the SAS blew their way in through the windows. Fortunately, mother duck and her brood found a new home in St. James's Park.

Such treatments reach deeply into popular culture, and resonate with that well-known aspect of British 'national character', the love of animals. Clearly, this feature of the popular projection and understanding of nationhood needs serious investigation. The pertinent point here is that popular sentiment about animals can seemingly be mobilised in ways that support official views of terrorism, so it is only superficially amusing, sentimental and trite. Scratch beneath the surface and you find the propaganda war.

Interviewing outlaws

There have been very few interviews with Irish republican 'terrorists' on British television – certainly no more than eight since the beginning of the 1970s. On virtually every occasion that the BBC or IBA have permitted such an interview to take place – and the conditions are tightly controlled – there has been a fierce political row at Westminster.

There is an important distinction to be made between interviews with a 'terrorist spokesman' and interviews with those speaking for a legal organisation which is described as the 'political wing' of an illegal armed group. In some respects interviews with 'terrorist spokesmen', although politically highly charged, are relatively unproblematic for the broadcasters. The interview is quite clearly identified as beyond the pale of decent, democratic politics. The problems arise much more intensely with the legal political face of banned armed organisations. The difficulty is compounded where interviewees are elected representatives of a duly constituted assembly of the state. For, in that case they are quite legitimately entitled to speak through the public media, but what they stand for from an official point of view – criminal terrorist violence – is not legitimate.

An analysis of the adversarial current affairs interview demonstrates very clearly the terms under which oppositional views are directly admitted on to television, and the techniques and tactics employed to signal the standpoint which the broadcasting organisations are themselves taking.

Fury as IRA hunger striker becomes an MP

Elected: The Hon. Member for Violence

Sands: After victory he expects death

By JOHN LEY and ANDREW TAYLOR

THE Government prepared last night to counter massive IRA propaganda following election of a hunger-striker as an MP.

Robert Sands, in the hospital of Ulster's Maze Prison on the 42nd day of a fast, will never take his seat at Westminster for Fermanagh and South Tyrone.

The House of Commons could unite to vote to expel him. Sands might resign—but anyway he expects to die in the next few weeks.

FRIGHTENED

The 27-year-old IRA man, serving 14 years on firearms charges, heard the result on radio in the Maze where he was leader of the "dirty" protest.

His 30,492 votes gave him a 1,446 majority over Official Unionist candidate Mr Harry West (29,046) in a big turnout of 86·8 per cent in the by-election caused by the death of Republican Frank Maguire.

There were 3,280 spoiled papers, perhaps from Catholics frightened to be seen absent from the poll.

A neighbouring Unionist MP, Mr

Now parties may unite to get him thrown out—

Harold McCusker, referring to Tuesday's shooting of a young wife collecting census forms, said : "The result was equal to 30,000 decent Catholics standing at the graveside and giving three cheers for her murder."

A shaken Mr West said : "We now know the type of people we live among."

Sands's mother, Rosaleen was "overjoyed" but said she would not try to make him end his fast.

The IRA's propaganda line across the world will be that the vote indicates not only support for political status for Republican prisoners — the issue on which Sands's campaign was fought — but an endorsement of the 11-year terrorist campaign.

Daily Express, April 11th, 1981

The INLA interview

In 1979 a great deal of controversy was aroused by the screening of an interview on *Tonight* (BBC1, 5 July 1979) with a member of the Irish National Liberation Army (INLA), the group which killed the Conservative MP and Northern Ireland spokesman, Airey Neave. In the course of the interview the INLA spokesman denied that his organisation had 'murdered' Neave, saying instead that he had been 'assassinated' or 'executed'. The interview was conducted on a hostile, adversarial footing. Following the interview, the studio presenter, Robin Day, re-established the point that this had been murder before inviting two Northern Irish MPs to comment.

Robin Day: Following the interview by David Lomax with one of the self proclaimed murderers of Mr Airey Neave I have with me the Reverand Robert Bradford, the Official Unionist MP for Belfast South, who is in our Belfast Studio, and here in the studio Mr Gerry Fitt, leader of the SDLP and MP for Belfast West.

Mr Bradford, first of all may I ask you for your comment on that interview.

Robert Bradford, MP: Well I'd like to say first of all that my immediate reaction was to decline the invitation to join you on this programme because of the interview which we've just heard. But when, having established that I wouldn't actually have to talk to this creature, I think I should take the opportunity to say on behalf of all the people of Northern Ireland that this subhuman creature will be pursued by us, by the security forces, and we will do everything in our power to put this kind of people to death and make sure that they do not inflict the hurt and the death and the anguish on the community in Northern Ireland for a minute longer than is possible.

Robin Day: Mr Fitt what is your comment on that interview?

Gerry Fitt, MP: I don't think it was wise of the BBC to allow such an interview to take place. I know that in Northern Ireland the interview that has just gone out will have inflamed protestant and loyalist opinion . . .

In a variety of ways, this interchange introduces the terminology of the official and populist perspectives counteracting thereby the public's exposure to oppositional views. Whereas Day used the language of criminality – 'murderer' – the Reverend Robert Bradford subhumanised the interviewee. He went further and gave clear voice to reactionary populism when he announced that 'this creature . . . will be pursued by *us*', the loyalists, only then mentioning the security forces. For his part Gerry Fitt introduced a standard official argument, namely that the interview was irresponsible. None of this, then, worked to evaluate the interview's political content: it was simply denied.

Interviewing Provisional Sinn Fein

The parliamentary by-election victory of one of the IRA hunger strikers in the H-blocks, Bobby Sands, pointed up the ambiguities surrounding the status of armed Irish republicanism. His election conferred legitimacy, but his imprisonment on arms charges denied it. Following Sands' death on hunger strike, *Newsnight* (BBC2, 27 October 1981) interviewed Danny Morrison, a spokesman for Provisional Sinn Fein. We have quoted the interview at some length as it revealingly shows the programme presenter John Tusa consistently working to maintain the idea that terrorists are criminals against the offensive of oppositional definitions offered by Danny Morrison.

First of all Morrison challenges the legitimacy of the British presence in Northern Ireland and the administration of justice:

Danny Morrison: . . . there are two sets of law operating in Northern

Ireland, one set for the British Forces, who, when they kill people, as they did, they killed three teenagers last week . . . nothing. They weren't charged, and yet Bobby Sands for possessing a gun got fourteen years in jail.

John Tusa: There is no evidence that those teenagers were killed by the security forces, and I think inquiries are still going on.

Danny Morrison: (interrupts) Well, what about Bloody Sunday, well people on Bloody Sunday were killed by the British Army and none of them were charged.

The interviewer then tries to move the discussion away from this politically embarrassing point-scoring to the death of Sands. However, Morrison again refuses to accept the terms of the argument, insisting on redefining the label of criminality which has been fixed on the hunger strikers. Morrison also succeeds in introducing the idea that the imprisoned IRA-men are fighting a war for political reasons and that they should therefore be accorded political status. It is precisely these terms of reference which the official view denies.

John Tusa: The question was put to Mr Atkins just now: 'Can the British government cope with three more Bobby Sands?' Can the Republican Movement cope with three more Bobby Sands or even more?

Danny Morrison: Well, the British government hasn't got a leg to stand on. This argument that these people are criminals without support among the local community . . .

John Tusa (interrupts): Are they or are they not criminals first of all? Francis Hughes, can you really say that somebody who committed what he did deserves political status . . . for the murder of a soldier?

Danny Morrison: Well, there's a war going on in the North of Ireland.

John Tusa (interrupts): You say there's a war going on in the North of Ireland.

Danny Morrison: The British, the British, well, Reginald Maudling, who was Home Secretary in 1971, declared war on, the IRA.

John Tusa: That does not make it a war situation; that does not justify the use of violence in return, but still, I want to go on.

Danny Morrison (interrupts): In the legislation, in the legislation, which convicts these political activists in the non-jury courts, it is stated that what distinguishes them from ordinary prisoners is the fact of their political motivation. Margaret Thatcher voted for that legislation, and then she gets up and makes this stupid statement, makes an ass of herself: 'A crime is a crime is a crime' . . .

John Tusa: But is that not the case, that, after all . . .

Danny Morrison: No.

John Tusa: . . . That if soldiers are killed, are murdered, are you suggesting that somehow because you call that a political event that gives you the right to move it into a different sphere of law altogether?

Danny Morrison: Has the British Army ever murdered anybody in Ireland? Has the RUC ever murdered anyone in Ireland? You journalists are employed . . . You won't tell the British public.

The presenter once again tries to realign the direction of the interviews, gets side-tracked by the force of Morrison's interventions, and then finally succeeds in directing Morrison into stating his political objectives. Here again, however, the terms in which the answer is couched refuse absolutely any accommodation with the official view. Even the final reference to the propaganda war is turned round:

John Tusa: That is, that is, that is not the question. These are the legitimately constituted forces. They are the legitimately constituted forces of the realm.

Danny Morrison: You won't explain to the British people what's going on over here . . .

John Tusa (interrupts): That has often been explained if you read the papers. But I want to hear what you have to say. Will the other three now go through with their strike?

Danny Morrison: Yes, they will carry it through because there was another republican hunger-strike, that of Terence McSweeney, who was MP for Mid-Cork and died on hunger-strike in 1920. And he left the Republicans a saying: 'It's not those who can inflict the most, but those who can suffer the most who will win in the end'.

John Tusa: Can you say to people what you think you have gained by this; what in hard concrete political terms do you feel that you are gaining, apart from losing people whom you see as comrades?

Danny Morrison: The spotlight is on the prison-camp and the arguments which Margaret Thatcher puts for suggesting that these people are criminals, and that argument does not stand up, and all the journalists that I have spoken to from around the world are sympathetic and understand the situation. They've seen it before in

Nicaragua, they've seen it before in Latin American countries, and they are sympathetic and they realise that Bobby Sands was a political prisoner.

John Tusa: So you feel that you are getting the propaganda victory from this, you're getting propaganda mileage out of it?

Danny Morrison: Yes, there's publicity about this case, and Britain is a political leper in the eyes of the world.

John Tusa: Danny Morrison, thank you.

At the time of the *Newsnight* interview Morrison was not, as he is now, an abstentionist member of the Northern Ireland Assembly. The problems of dealing with such an elected representative, and the techniques for trying to handle it, emerged very clearly in a *Panorama* (BBC1, 22 November 1982) interview and profile of Sinn Fein Vice-President, Gerry Adams (now an MP), after his election to the Northern Ireland Assembly as representative for West Belfast.

This programme was an instance of how a 'tight' structure was used to try and sustain the official position that Sinn Fein is simply a front organisation for the Provisional IRA. It also sought to establish that Adams, despite his election, had been a Provo with a long record of involvement in terrorist acts, and that he was still a key figure in the military command structure. The problem faced by the presenter, Fred Emery, is that there is no firm evidence for the official view, so the interview is an attempt to manoeuvre Adams into admitting his guilt and involvement. Adams, however, consistently subverts the situation to put across the 'oppositional' view of the republican movement.

The programme set the scene with this depiction of Adams:

'From the Provo on the run, repeatedly picked up by the police and the army, the face has subtly changed of the man the authorities suspect of masterminding most of the past five years' terrorism. Suspect but can't prove. The authorities simply have no evidence that will stand up in court. Now Adams assumes a studious legitimacy. But however well groomed he's become, his opponents reckon they know their man.'

The opponents were brought on to state their case. Amongst others, the Reverend Ian Paisley, Democratic Unionist MP, and Merlyn Rees, former Northern Ireland Secretary, stated their view that Adams is still a key figure in the IRA. In the concluding sequence, the terms of reference were framed by an extract from an interview with Ian Paisley in which he stated that Sinn Fein 'is just a political front for the IRA' which has committed itself to murder under the slogan of 'armed struggle'. The view that armed struggle equals murder was then taken up by the interviewer:

Fred Emery: At what point does what you call the armed struggle, this campaign essentially of murder, at what point does that cease?

Gerry Adams: Sinn Fein doesn't advocate a campaign of murder. Sinn Fein supports politically and defends the right of people, as legitimate action, to resist British rule.

Fred Emery: But it also has a resolution that you read out at your party conference only last week, that all its candidates must be unambivalent in support of the armed struggle. Now that is a campaign of murder, surely?

Gerry Adams: No. No, let me just . . .

Fred Emery: And it was passed without anybody . . .

Gerry Adams: Of course it was passed and that's always been the Sinn Fein position and it's nothing new. Now the British Government are unambivalent in their support of what happens in this country. There's no-one goes along and awards IRA men medals when they kill civilians, yet the British Government, when British troops wantonly and deliberately and consciously opened fire and killed civilians in Derry, the British Government awarded the person in charge medals.

Fred Emery: It brought them to trial.

Gerry Adams: Let me finish. No it didn't bring the people in Bloody Sunday to trial. It's OK if the British Government go and murder people in the Argentine and to be applauded for their actions . . .

Fred Emery: That is another argument.

Gerry Adams: It isn't another argument. If it's legitimate for the British Government to resist what they see as oppression by the Argentine, certainly, very very certainly it's legitimate for Irish people in their own country.

As with the Morrison interview, there is a systematic attempt by Adams to invert the terms of reference. British misdeeds in Derry are disinterred and the analogy of war and legitimate resistance to oppression placed firmly on the agenda.

Proximity and distance

So far, we have concentrated exclusively on examples which deal with Irish republican political violence. The greatest problems for actuality coverage arise when the 'terrorism' with which it deals is at home, *proximate*, within the boundaries of the British state. In other contexts, where the imperatives of national security recede (and with them the threats of censorship or other state intervention) the possibilities of openness expand. We have illustrated varying degrees of openness to alternative and oppositional views in a number of programmes. We have also shown the implications of tightness and losseness: one way, for instance, of trying to further discipline a maverick interview such as Morrison's is by anticipating it and erecting a tight framework of interpretation and evidence around it.

To a certain extent there is more scope for openness, even with the same subject matter, when the events with which programmes deal are more distant in time. Historical distance, very occasionally, has permitted the portrayal of economic exploitation and military brutality and the admission of *past* mistakes and excesses on the part of the British state.

In depicting the contemporary situation, however, proximity and distance feature in two other significant ways: geographically and ideologically. Other states' problems with terrorism may attract an altogether more critical gaze, and that is by no means just a feature of British television.

Recent Italian research on current affairs programmes broadcast by RAI-TV has shown that political violence outside Italy is handled in ways which differ significantly from such activities at home. Dr Donatella Ronci has found that in the case of the IRA and the Corsican separatists there was a tendency to examine the social causes at work and to recognise the legitimacy of violent dissent, without thereby giving it a positive image.[19] In a supporting analysis Luciano Li Causi has commented that when Italian television looks abroad (with the possible exception of West Germany) terrorists cease to be the authors of crazed messages and are treated as political actors, even as individuals: 'Foreign terrorism isn't some kind of aberrant spectacle coming from nowhere or out of the heads of third-rate ideologists. It has roots, causes, objectives. Its actions can be understood by the television audience, even if not justified.[20]

Geographical distance is heavily overlaid with ideological criteria. Thus, television presentations are likely to be at their most 'open' to oppositional accounts when an insurgency takes place within non-democratic states in which legitimate channels of dissent are either restricted or non-existent and in which state repression is a prominent feature of the system of rule. In such cases, where violence against the state may be seen as justified as a tactic of last resort, the label 'terrorist' is likely to be replaced with one which accords legitimacy, such as 'guerrilla' or 'freedom fighter'. In other

words, attitudes towards insurgencies are inextricably tied to attitudes towards the regimes in which they take place. Feature films,
documentaries and popular television series (such as the BBC's
Secret Army), for instance, constantly celebrate violent acts of
resistance to the Nazi occupation of democratic Europe, which, in
other contexts, would be unambiguously condemned as terroristic.

We have seen the adversarial frameworks within which programmes such as *Panorama* have dealt with Irish republicanism. Let
us consider some other cases which indicate how the proximity
factor may operate. One edition of *Panorama* (BBC1, 29 June 1981)
examined the propaganda war between Israel and the Palestine
Liberation Organisation. The programme set out to show how both
the Israelis and the PLO organised their international propaganda
efforts and their sources of funding and support. A central theme
was how, from being 'the world's most ruthless band of murderers'
and 'synonymous with horror' a decade before, the PLO was now
treading the road of respectability.

The question of what was to count as 'terrorism' was therefore
somewhat ambiguous, because the PLO was represented both as
having a terroristic past and as now being a quasi-state engaged in
diplomacy, with illustrative visuals of Yasser Arafat meeting leading
EEC figures and prominent social-democratic politicians such as
Bruno Kreisky and Willi Brandt. In the course of a series of interviews, the contestation over definitions of terrorism came over
clearly. The Israeli prime minister, Menachem Begin, in an interview
near the beginning of the programme, said:

'We do not recognise that so-called PLO, it is not a liberation organisation, it is a blood-thirsty, terrorist, Nazi organisation which is
bent on the destruction of Israel. Its aim is genocide and they want to
destroy our country and people.'

Later on, in a sequence which examined the PLO's activities at the
United Nations, the following, strikingly different, definitions were
counterposed, first of all from Professor Yehuda Blum, Israeli
ambassador to the UN:

'Irregular privileges granted to them at the UN are in flat violation of
the UN's charter and its rules of procedure. But beyond that how can
you expect the UN to contribute anything to fighting international
terrorism when it glorifies the leading component within the terrorist
international?'

John Stapleton, the reporter, then asked Zehdi Terezi, PLO representative at the UN:

'What would you say to those people who would argue that an organisation like the PLO which is associated with terror has no right to be a member of an august body like the UN?'

To which Terezi replied:

'I cannot really draw a line between one or the other. We are working on more than one front – diplomatic, political and the military front. After all you seem to forget that we are under occupation. That the fate of four million Palestinians seems to have been forgotten and these Palestinians are fighting for their survival. So the word terrorism actually is a bad quotation let's say. I don't want to be offensive to you but I can understand when a state drops bombs at refugee camps, that defend themselves against the planes, that's not terror that's legitimate self-defence.

The way in which the question was posed to Terezi was decidedly different from the engaged style of interviewing Irish republicans indicated above. His reply contained the rarely made point, if not quite explicitly, that states may be said to practice terrorism too. The equation of state terror and insurgent terror is impermissible nearer home.

A further example comes from an edition of *Panorama* on the armed conflict in South Africa (BBC1, 15 June 1981). South Africa, with its clear-cut racism and rejection of equality before the law, is a regime which can make no claim whatever to liberal-democratic legitimacy (although it can, and does,claim to be part of 'the West' in its struggles against 'international communism'). Here the ideological space for accepting the legitimacy of anti-state violence against state repression is at its maximum and contestation over definitions hardly figures at all.

The programme examined the roots of armed resistance to the apartheid regime and its steady growth during the later 1970s. There was only one point at which the official view of 'terrorism' was raised, and that in the context of an interview in which an alternative definition – 'terrorists' as human beings pushed beyond endurance – was allowed to prevail.

Peter Taylor (reporter): Suppose [the guerrillas] came to you for food, assistance, medical supplies. Would you encourage the mission to give them what they wanted?

Solomon Sente (Lutheran Bishop of Northern Transvaal): In a situation of need like that I think I would even not want to know who they are. I would simply see them as people, see the need that they require from me and we will do everything we can to assist them.

Peter Taylor: Even if you knew who they were?

Solomon Sente: Well I think it would still not change my attitude. They are humans and I'd give them the type of assistance they required.

Peter Taylor: Even if you knew they were terrorists?

Solomon Sente: (Embarrassed laugh) I think I would do that (more embarrassed laughter). It is a bit ... er ... difficult but if you start considering, that it may be your son, it may be your uncle, it may be your nephew. You would be bound from human compassion I think to do that.

Peter Taylor: That they are your people?

Solomon Sente: Because they are my blood. They are my flesh. They are part of my emotional experience. I think this is very important. In a way, one may not say very, very, very loudly but I think they are part of my agony.

This example, and the contrasts in the treatment of domestic and foreign political violence it demonstrates, may be pursued further. An instructive comparison may be drawn from the television coverage of the funeral of Bobby Sands in Northern Ireland and that of Pallas Mallangu, a black striker in South Africa.

On the *Nine O'Clock News* (BBC1, 7 May 1981), Kate Adey reported Sands' funeral thus:

'To the tens of thousands who watched his coffin to the grave this was the burial of Bobby Sands, martyr ... An army helicopter grinding relentlessly overhead all but drowned the tones of the Irish pipes and there were shouts by the stewards as they tried to supervise the coverage by the world's press. Tens of thousands of people from all over Northern Ireland and from the South, a grim-faced demonstration of support for the political aims of the hunger strikers, overtaking the private grief of the Sands family ...

Outside a shopping centre in Andersonstown came the symbolic moment for the Republicans. Three masked men stepped forward and obeyed orders in Irish to fire a three volley salute. Illegal uniforms. Illegal shooting. All grist to the mill for the convictions of republican and loyalist.'

The Sands funeral is admitted to be a tragic symbol for his supporters but, according to the reporter it is a symbol arranged for the media which has no more than propaganda value for a cause which we, the reporter and her audience, cannot support. The Mallangu funeral on the other hand is a 'political demonstration'. In that case the reporter (*Panorama*, BBC1, 15 June 1981) develops the story to show how workers and guerrillas are united in the same movement, pursuing the same cause, the 'liberation of the black man'.

'*Peter Taylor* against background of chanting mourners at funeral procession: 'Many black workers see themselves as comrades, fighting the same war as the guerrillas. Pallas Mallangu's funeral became a political demonstration. To the crowds who followed his coffin Pallas Mallangu was not just a martyr to the workers' cause. He was a martyr to the cause of black liberation. It's the political message of scenes like this, a mixture of anger and grief, which makes the government ever more anxious about the power of the black trade unions. Many black workers see themselves as comrades, fighting the same war as the guerrillas. They share the same enemy, they share the same end. Only the means are different.'

Liberation is the oppositional justification which may be allowable in less proximate contexts, so that 'terrorists' become 'guerrillas'. In Northern Ireland however the claims of, for instance, Danny Morrison in the interview cited above, for political status for the IRA were vigorously denied by the interviewer.

The violence of the state

It is possible, and more comfortable, to raise the question of state violence given geographical, temporal or ideological distance. The hard truth, whether at home or abroad, is that state bullets inflict death and injury in just the same way as terrorist bullets. The weight of the argument against terrorism is that it causes suffering. If the state and its agents also cause suffering then there is some explaining to do. One answer is that state violence is legitimate, but this is used relatively rarely as it accepts that state violence occurs and has nasty consequences. Even in discussions of the state's preparations for war against a conventional enemy, euphemisms and technical terms are used to disguise the fact that war means death and injury, starting from the initial and ubiquitous euphemism of defence. By comparison, arguments that suffering caused by state violence was an isolated mistake, that under provocation some retaliation may be necessary, or more general attempts to deny that the incident took place or that state forces were responsible are more common. A favourite British device, which has been used in cases like Bloody Sunday, when British troops shot dead 13 demonstrators, or following allegations of torture in Northern Ireland, is to 'resort to Widgery', to set up legal inquiries which, over a period, redefine the problems into acceptable terms. These the media can then report with relatively few problems. In the case of Bloody Sunday, Lord Widgery found that there had been 'shooting by the army which bordered on the reckless'. Sir Edmund Compton redefined torture as physical ill-treatment.[21]

To take a more recent illustration, in a *Panorama* programme on Northern Ireland (BBC1, 21 October 1981), the latest problem of civilian deaths from plastic bullets, supposedly used as a method of riot control, was set out as an understandable consequence of mistakes and retaliation. During a sequence dealing with street riots and petrol bombings, the reporter, Peter Taylor, commented:

'Almost inexorably the violence from these mobs has provoked violence in return. Under a hail of petrol bombs, the security forces were bound to retaliate. In an attempt to control the riots they fired plastic bullets. These are meant only to deter but they can be lethal.

The IRA has never been slow to exploit mistakes. Plastic bullets have killed seven people since Bobby Sands died. This has only deepened the alienation the Catholic community already feels.'

The programme went on to illustrate this point by interviewing the mother of a young girl killed while innocently bringing home some shopping. State violence, therefore, we would argue, is generally defined according to its proximity, and although alternative and oppositional views are demonstrably permitted space in television's coverage of domestic political violence they are subject to tighter forms of contextualisation and control than similar violence abroad.

The personal view

Actuality programmes which most confirm the official perspective are both relatively 'closed' and tightly constructed: the news and documentaries such as *Sefton* are cases in point. But tight structuring my also be a feature of relatively 'open' programmes which argue for an alternative perspective. In 'authored' documentaries, which are clearly signalled as the personal viewpoint of their writer/presenter, dominant definitions of terrorism may be both contested and subverted, particularly if they bear on violence that has either passed, even if only recently, or which happened in areas remote from the immediate sphere of British interests.

In a *Pilger Report*, produced by ATV, on the current plight of Vietnam veterans in the United States, the journalist John Pilger drew out the implications of their conditions for current American policy in El Salvador (ITV, *Heroes*, 6 May 1981). In the course of this programme Pilger dealt with the same repertoire of meanings and definitions found in other coverage of terrorism. But he systematically inverted the official meanings and definitions and provided a clear statement of an equation which is the precise opposite of the dominant view of terrorism. In official accounts insurgent terrorism leads to unacceptable human misery. In Pilger's alternative statement it is state terror which produces unacceptable human costs:

'Missing from this film are the other witnesses to the Vietnam period, the Vietnamese. We hear very little about them these days and the American veterans speak little about them perhaps because what was done over there was so terrible that only the victims can afford to speak about it. Such has been the politics of vengeance, that the people of Vietnam are now almost completely isolated, with only the waiting arms of the Russians to turn to, whom they rightly distrust as much as they distrusted the Americans, the French, the Japanese and Chinese who came to their country selling noble causes.

So here is the news from Vietnam. In the wake of the war's devastation there is now famine. Rations are less than ever during the war years, about half the food needed for a healthy survival. There is no milk any more for children over the age of one and un-exploded bombs and mines kill children every day.

Like its refusal to help its own victims of the war the American government has denied all help to the people of Vietnam and so too has the British government.

On the other hand both governments are building the greatest military machine in preparation for a war that may well end all wars, and for that our heroes need not apply.'

Throughout the programme the official discourse on war is systematically inverted. In drawing a parallel between Vietnam and El Salvador Pilger used US Ambassador White to redefine terrorism from insurgent terrorism to state terrorism. He then, in an El Salvador sequence, underlined the point by comparing the tragedy of the El Salvadorians and the Vietnamese, both victims of the state's military machine. The camera closes in on a book he is holding:

'This book is a collection of *New York Times* front pages which trace the American involvement in Vietnam and reading it now is an eerie experience. The same headlines are appearing today. The same jargon such as escalation, and light at the end of the tunnel. The same delusions. Delete Vietnam and write in El Salvador and the stories seem almost identical. Like the politicians then – Kennedy, Johnson and Nixon – the politicians now, Haig and Reagan, see the world in the same arrogant, simplistic terms, speaking of dominoes as if nations were blocks of wood. Not societies riven with their own differences and animosities. Today as before, honest men pay with their careers. The American Ambassador in El Salvador, Robert White, has said that the war in that country is caused by social injustice and that the real terrorists are the regime backed by Mr Reagan and Mr Haig and supported of course by the British government . . .

For speaking the truth the ambassador was sacked. Here is an announcement of US advisers going to Vietnam and US troops going to protect them. The advisers have already arrived in El Salvador. As in Vietnam the people who are dying in the streets and jungles of El Salvador are nameless stick figures on a television news or between the commercials in a re-run Hollywood movie. The American veterans of Vietnam have much in common with them for they too have been declared expendable.'

This is a rare statement in actuality television that there is a problem of state terrorism. In the next chapter, as we shall see, a central concern of television fiction dealing with terrorism is the state's use of violence, although this is handled in a variety of ways.

Television looks at terrorism on television

How news and current affairs programmes cover political violence has been the subject of periodic discussion on television. It has also figured on the radio and in the press. Such attention has been episodic rather than sustained, and has usually occurred in response to a controversy about television somehow overstepping the mark.

There have been very occasional opportunities for debate on programmes such as LWT's now defunct *Look Here*, the BBC's *Did You See?*, and latterly Channel Four's *Eleventh Hour* slot. All of these have provided commentary, more or less critical, on television's output. Even less frequent has been the televised 'hypothetical', in which real-world decision-makers act out a plausible scenario which exposes the relationships between the media, the government and the security forces on the lines of Granada's *Bounds of Freedom* series in 1979. Occasionally too, the dilemmas of journalism are dramatised, as in Channel Four's *Giro City*.

In his comment on the INLA interview, Gerry Fitt charged that television itself would be responsible for causing suffering as screening such sentiments would inflame passions. This is a particularly sensitive point for broadcasters, and similar charges were levelled on an edition of *The Editors* two years later by Dr Richard Clutterbuck, a counter-insurgency expert (BBC1, 28 June 1981), who declared the INLA interview an 'irresponsible and reckless use of the medium'.

In the programme, two journalists, Anne McHardy of *The Guardian* and Jeremy Paxman of BBC television, put their case for interviewing terrorists while the presenter, John Morgan, elaborated the official perspective. In essence, he argued, if terrorists are criminals then there is no need for in-depth investigation of their motivations.

John Morgan: I'd like to ask you both, Anne McHardy, would you yourself think it proper as a citizen as well as being a journalist to interview terrorists at length and frequently.

Anne McHardy (The Guardian): Yes I think it's entirely proper. I've obviously thought about it long and hard and talked about it often. I don't think that I could possibly, as a reporter working for a British newspaper write about Northern Ireland with any kind of authenticity if I didn't talk to terrorists.

John Morgan: Would you think that applies to television as much?

Jeremy Paxman (BBC Panorama): Absolutely. It seems to me that the basic perception of the problem in Northern Ireland is that it is a problem of irreconcilable political aspirations compounded by a problem of law and order. Now, if that is the case you cannot have political dialogue without reporting political differences and therefore it seems to me absolutely essential that however much you may disagree with these people you have to talk to them. You have at the very least and at the most basic level to understand why it is that people are being killed.

John Morgan: But that is making the assumption that they are not, as some people would argue, mere murderers or thugs as well as being enemies of the state and that you would then have an obligation to go to the security forces whenever you meet such people.

Jeremy Paxman: It is my judgement as a journalist that these people are not murderers and thugs, although they may be, solely, although they may be that as well. There are political motivations at work and that we have to understand those if we are to understand what is happening in Northern Ireland. And it seems to me if you are going to say that we should not be talking to these people then what you are really saying is that there is a state of war and that we should impose military censorship. And if that was the case, and it is the case in many other wars which I've covered, then that's fair enough because we'll all know where we stand.

McHardy's statement encapsulates the argument that effective journalism needs a variety of sources, however unpalatable some may be. Paxman's points offer a much more extended elaboration of an alternative perspective, beginning with the assumption that there is a pre-eminently political character to the violence and that criminality is definitely subsidiary. It is also revealing that the crucial question of declaring war surfaces in his answer. War confers legitimacy on the enemy and that is a high price to pay for the effective conscription of the journalist.

In Granada's 'hypothetical' on terrorism, 'a television producer receives an invitation. It is from a man who has escaped police custody. He is thought to be a terrorist leader, responsible for bombing and assassinations. He asks the producer to interview him in a neighbouring country and not tell the police'.[22] As the INLA interview has indicated, such is the substance of current journalistic dilemmas. The scenario of the 'hypothetical' was also part of the story-line of Karl Francis' Channel Four movie *Giro City* (1 December 1982).

Hard-bitten television reporter O'Malley, 'the conscience of the company', is invited to interview the chief of staff of the Provisional IRA, David Flynn, a figure evidently modelled on David O'Connell. The film sets out to demonstrate the political pressures faced by senior broadcasters and the ways these are mediated through the organisation, via legal advice, to end, effectively, in censorship. These processes are considered in Chapter 4. What is of immediate interest is the way in which the 'terrorist case' is represented in the film. The interview with Flynn, conducted in a secret location in Dublin, is not very convincing. If we lay it alongside the adversarial stratagems adopted against Adams and Morrison, Flynn has it far too easy, and puts words in his interviewer's mouth when he would, in reality, be fighting for his corner:

David Flynn: Most actions are political whether the British government likes it or not. The misuse of terminology in the face of death is an abomination.

O'Malley: The British government – indeed a majority of the British people would say . . .

Flynn: . . . would say we are murderers but I assure you that we are not. It is our belief that the majority of the British people want a united Ireland and want a withdrawal of troops in the North.

The point, however, is that the film's scenario permits Flynn to set out an oppositional case in full, but much of it ends up on the cutting-room floor, and he is balanced in the studio presentation by a government minister who is given a soft reporter just to make it easy for him to dismiss the IRA's political claims. It is a plausible enough scenario. Aside from offering its audience the political logic of the oppositional case, the film also permits the disenchanted journalist, in discussion with his equally disillusioned producer, to argue the alternative perspective:

O'Malley: All I know is that when we suppress the truth we create the violence.

Producer: And what happens when we tell lies?

O'Malley: And when we tell lies, we use law and order to justify it.

Producer: I think I would put justice before law and love before order.

A film such as this, like Pilger's *Heroes*, is exceptionally open to those arguments which run against the official perspective. Similarly, it is constructed tightly, to offer an indictment of the ways in which journalism works as the servant of the state. Obviously, this picture is at fundamental variance with the premises of most of the criticisms that surface on television. The fact that it is developed in an 'authorial' product, and one transmitted on the least orthodox of the channels, is not unimportant.

A somewhat less nuanced treatment of much the same story line was offered by three consecutive episodes of Granada TV's lunchtime series, *Crown Court* (ITV, 19-21 April 1983), written by Janey Preger.

The scenario was as follows. A bomb goes off in an English country town killing a woman and seriously disabling two children. The police, on the basis on an eyewitness and forensic evidence, attribute the incident to two well-known IRA-men, issue pictures of them and initiate a man-hunt. John Dickens, current affairs reporter with a regional television company, is invited to talk to a Provisional spokesman, who, disguised in a manner similar to the INLA interviewee, denies responsibility for the bomb, which he alleges was planted to discredit his organisation. He also gives a statement of the Provisional line, expressing regret for any harm befalling civilians, but warning that a new bombing campaign is on the way unless the British withdraw.

Dickens asks the police to comment and he and his company are requested to hand over uncut film, which they refuse to do. Dickens is consequently charged under the Prevention of Terrorism Act (1976) for withholding information which might lead to the capture of terrorists. He is brought before the court, pleading 'not guilty'.

The jury (made up of real-life citizens, not actors) is asked to decide on Dickens's guilt. It sees a videotape of the interview, in which Dickens is first seen introducing the story by concentrating heavily on the injuries and death suffered by the innocent victim of the bombing. As the case unfolds Dickens is cross-examined by the prosecution, and in response argues that without such interviews essential information on IRA policy and plans would simply not be known to the public. His defence lawyer then asks the following question:

Defence lawyer: How do you answer the charge that you were giving this man a platform for IRA propaganda?

Dickens: I would say look at the way I introduced the film by spelling out the death and injuries caused by the Fulchester bomb. I would say, look at the way I handled the interview, how I interrupted him when he started going on about the British army murdering people, how I expressed total disbelief at his claim that it wasn't an IRA attack. And I would say look at the comments made after the film when I said the denial of responsibility by the IRA was not being taken seriously, and I expressed the view that it was an IRA bomb.

The jury evidently found this convincing, as Dickens was 'acquitted'. Rather like *Giro City*, the programme permitted a statement of journalistic ideology, and space for the oppositional view. The latter, however, was more tightly framed on this occasion, and the way it was represented was through the more sinister INLA-type interviewee rather than the more plausible Flynn, modelled on David O'Connell.

Conclusion

Different forms of television journalism may handle the question of political violence with varying degrees of openness to arguments which depart from official orthodoxy. This is important since there is a readiness to assume that news coverage is the paradigm case of all actuality television. The main consequence of this assumption is to limit our understanding of how the television system as a whole works. Our argument is that television is shot through with contradictions – the contradictions of liberal-democracy itself. News is a particular form of communication. It is very important and has rightly attracted a great deal of academic study. But the academic orthodoxy – one to which we have ourselves contributed in the past – is in danger of missing the wider and more complex picture. News coverage attracts the largest audiences, and therefore is likely to predominate in forming public views of political violence. Further, the occasions on which oppositional views (as opposed to alternative ones) are aired are few indeed. But they are aired, and given more room for manoeuvre than any reductionist generalisations from news alone would lead us to expect. If we want to understand television we need to take this into account.

The Iranian embassy siege-bust in May 1980 thrust the SAS—Britain's most secretive army unit—into international prominence. The masked man in black became the symbol of counter-terror at work: the anonymous state agent, identity shrouded for reasons of national security.

But the face of the Provisional IRA and other such groups is also masked and anonymous, hiding its identity from the forces of law and order. So the black mask is ambiguous: it conceals terror and counter-terror alike.

Since the SAS's televised eruption into British domestic politics, the siege-bust motif has been continually reproduced. But look hard at those images. Where does fiction begin and fact end? And what should we make of the comedy of terror?

May 1980: men in black end the Iranian embassy siege before the television cameras. (5.5.80)

September 1980: a fictional siege bust in London Weekend Television's *The Professionals*. (14.9.80)

March 1982: the SAS destroy a
shipboard lavatory in London
Weekend's *Whoops Apocalypse*.
(21.3.82)

July 1982: a televised advertisement
for a serialised feature in the *Sun*.

September 1982: the men in black
attack social security scroungers in a
Guardian cartoon.

Chapter 3

Dramatising 'terrorism'

From actuality to fiction

Despite the firm line usually drawn between them, there are strong links between television fiction and journalism. Contemporary fictions frequently draw on news events for plots while news stories are often presented like fictions.

Like popular fiction, news deals in dramatic events and heroes and villains, and uses vivid imagery and human interest angles to catch and hold the reader's attention. As Robert Park has remarked

' "News story" and "fiction story" are two forms of modern litera-ture that are now so alike one another that it is sometimes difficult to distinguish them'.[1]

For television newsmen like Reuven Frank of NBC, this convergence is a welcome weapon in the ratings battle and one worth developing. As he told his staff, 'every news story should (ideally), without any sacrifice of probity or responsibility, display the attributes of fiction, of drama'. They should be built around the triad 'conflict, problem, denouement', they should have 'a beginning, a middle and an end' and they should feature rising action which builds to a climax.[2] These "fictive" qualities of television news were well to the fore in the coverage of the SAS's successful breaking of the siege at Iran's London embassy in Princes' Gate on 5 May 1980.[3]

Both the BBC and ITV cut into their normal programmes to cover the action live, although not from the very beginning.[4] The story has since been symbolised by the dramatic moment of entry into the embassy: the footage of armed, masked men in black on the first floor balcony, a huge explosion, clouds of smoke, the dis-appearance of the troops into the building. The superbly spectacular qualities of this denouement became the organising principles for the fuller coverage of the main bulletins which followed the rescue of the hostages. The BBC, for example, opened their 9.40 pm bulletin with the headline 'Dramatic end of the six day siege', while ITN's opening commentary was 'presented entirely in the present tense: taking us through the screams, shooting, attack, dogs barking, sirens, fire, firemen and hostages.'[5]

The siege-bust made the SAS into popular heroes. Television fiction rapidly exploited the images deriving from actuality cover-

age, and not surprisingly, the SAS has most frequently been represented by the actions of men in black. This image has been used not
only in drama, but in comedy, popular history, novels, cartoons and
a film. One of the most secretive units in the British military has
therefore become the object of considerable attention and firmly
lodged in popular culture.[6] The veteran director and producer,
Raymond Menmuir has commented shrewdly on this:

'Before the Iranian Embassy siege, there was a great deal of caution
about the SAS. But from that moment attitudes began to change.
There was that national 'boost'. Before, there had been a mystery
about them. Did they travel incognito? Did they speak 38 languages?
Suddenly, they became part of the overall 'law and order' framework of our society . . . our freedom to tell stories about such areas
was very welcome.'[7]

Quite soon after Prince's Gate, television dramas began to feature
SAS type figures and siege situations. They appeared first in *The
Professionals*, a top rating crime series centred on a fictitious special
unit, C15. The episode entitled *Wild Justice*, which went out in
September 1980 (just four months after the actual event) featured a
group of masked agents on a training exercise, storming a building
almost exactly like the Iranian Embassy, while a second group role-
play Arab terrorists holding hostages inside. An SAS-type action
against terrorists also provided the climax to *Blood Money*, a BBC
series broadcast in September 1981. We shall be looking at the way
these programmes handle the issues in more detail later on, but for
the moment we want to focus on *Who Dares Wins*, which was the
most extensive attempt to exploit the fictional possibilities of the
siege scenario.

Although a feature film, *Who Dares Wins* is relevant to the
present discussion. There is a steady flow of ideas, styles and personnel between the film and television industries in Britain and *Who
Dares Wins* draws particularly heavily on television talent and know-
how. The story-line was devised by thriller writer George Markstein,
an ex-intelligence officer who has written extensively for popular
television series, including *The Avengers* and *The Prisoner*. The
director Ian Sharp was chosen for his work on *The Professionals*,
while Lewis Collins who plays the male lead was already very well
known to British audiences as one of the stars of *The Professionals*,
where he plays a similar role. The result, not surprisingly, is a film
very like an extended episode from a television action-adventure
series using many standard plot and character devices.
Consequently, it offers a useful way of introducing some of the ways
this central fictional form handles actuality materials.

From Princes' Gate to Pinewood Studios

The initial idea for *Who Dares Wins* came from Euan Lloyd, one of Britain's most successful independent film producers, and probably best known for *The Wild Geese*, based on the real-life exploits of white mercenaries in black Africa. He lived near the embassy and caught the atmosphere at first hand but it was watching the siege bust on television that decided him to make a movie based around the central image. The next day he telephoned his agent in New York asking him to register possible titles, including the one that was eventually used, *Who Dares Wins*, the SAS's regimental motto. The Home Secretary, William Whitelaw, had already praised 'the meticulous efficiency and great skill of those involved' while the Prime Minister was quick to add that the operation made one 'proud to be British'.

As Lloyd later told a journalist, it was this sense of national pride that he most wanted to capture:

'I was thrilled by the live action on the television, and proud that it was happening in Britain. I'm determined that this should be a British film, as it was a British triumph.'[8]

The film was shot at Pinewood Studios and on location in various parts of the country. It received a Royal premiere in London in August 1982, and despite having less than half a year at the box office did good enough business to make it one of the ten most successful films of the year. By a lucky piece of timing its release coincided with the high tide of patriotism that following the retaking of the Falkland Islands which put its advocacy of the 'resolute approach' to attacks on the British way of life in a new and powerful context.

The film's plot centres on SAS captain Peter Skellen, who is detailed to infiltrate The Peoples' Lobby, a terrorist group, backed by Moscow, trained by an East Germany agent and financed via Libya, who are using the Peace Movement as a cover. He does this by seducing the group's female leader, Frankie, but he is unable to stop them from taking over the US Ambassador's official residence in Regent's Park and holding hostage a number of high ranking military and political figures from both countries. The group threaten to kill the hostages unless the government drop a nuclear device on the submarine base at Holy Loch to demonstrate the horror of nuclear war. Skellen however manages to flash a message to his commander using a bathroom mirror and at dawn the SAS arrive in helicopters, crash through every available door and window, shooting the terrorists dead, and liberate the hostages unharmed.

This denouement draws heavily on the imagery of the embassy

siege bust. The same masked SAS men break into the same kind of elegant, balconied building. But unlike Princes' Gate, this is an operation against home-grown terrorists (albeit directed by Moscow and led by an American heiress), and as such it touches on the central tension in official thinking; between the demands of efficiency and order on the one hand and the requirements of legitimacy and law on the other. According to the promotional material, this tension is never resolved within the film, rather it:

'encapsulates the problem in one extreme confrontation between a radical anti-nuclear faction and the SAS. On the one side are campaigners for peace willing to resort to terror tactics. Against them are ruthless men, committed to stamp out terror with terror . . . In the words of producer Euan Lloyd: ''Arguments are presented but by no means resolved. We cannot and do not draw conclusions.'' Drawing conclusions is left to the viewer.'[9]

In fact the audience is pushed towards certain, very definite conclusions.

In the first place, the plot provides space for reactionary populist sentiments that put order above law, though these are more prominent in James Follett's best-seller based on the story line (*The Tiptoe Boys*) than in the finished film. Here for example is Skellen complaining to Frankie about the way that politics inhibit the 'war against terrorism' in Northern Ireland.

' . . . those cringing wankers at Westminster put me and my mates in there to clean up their shit. But are we allowed to fight as soldiers are trained to fight? Christ, no. We've got to ride round like fucking human targets and be shot at first. Then we're allowed to shoot back if we're still alive, but we musn't use too many rounds and there's fucking hell to pay if we do. You reckon the Provos do that? Do they hell. They're laughing at us . . . Skellen stopped. The anger and frustration in his voice was genuine. His feelings were shared by many servicemen who felt that they had been sent in to do a job with their hands tied.'[10]

Conversely, the story-line allows virtually no space for the alternative perspective's critique of the strong state. Doubts about the mass media's celebration of the siege bust and the shooting of the terrorists are voiced by a politician at the very end of the film. But directly afterwards we see him meeting the Libyan courier who passed on the money for the operation. It is clear from their conversation that the honourable member is part of Moscow's terror network, but to avoid any ambiguity the film ends with a freeze frame of them walking, overprinted with a list of terrorist attacks on the embassies of western powers, with 'The Red Flag' playing on the soundtrack. The message is crude but clear; anyone who expresses doubts about the need for a tough response to terrorism is helping 'our' enemies and is more than likely to be in their pay.

This ending puts the final touch to a narrative that has been organised from the outset to enlist support for the film's celebratory view of the SAS and the strong state. This movement towards closure and convergence begins with the very first frames. These open with shots of Boadicea's statue with Big Ben behind and of a war memorial, followed by footage of The Peoples' Lobby marching in a real CND demonstration through London (with Communist Party banners well to the fore), and ending with a terrorist shooting an SAS undercover agent dead with a crossbow. These initial images establish the key oppositions around which the rest of the action revolves. They draw a firm ideological line between the legitimate force used to defend Britain against her enemies (by Boadicea, the fallen of the two World Wars, and the SAS) and the violent tactics of the terrorists, fellow-travelling Communists and anti-nuclear activists who are bent on undermining 'our' democracy and way of life. They also suggest that since The Peoples' Lobby is prepared to murder in cold blood, it can only be countered by what the film's publicity blurb calls 'violent, ruthless men, committed to stamp out terror with terror'.[11] True, Frankie is given a long scene in the ambassador's residence to explain the political ideals behind her actions, but her arguments are deflected by the general thrust of the film. As a flawed idealist her death might have appeared tragic. As a murderous fanatic in the pay of a foreign power it simply appears necessary and as Markstein told an interviewer:

'Remember, you are going to appreciate far more the awe inspiring power and professionalism of a fighting force like the SAS when you are made aware of the dedicated life-and-death fanaticism of their opponents.'[12]

Who Dares Wins is an excellent example of the standard action-adventure format that dominates a good deal of popular television fiction. It produces a consistently closed and tight treatment of the issues. But television fiction also works with formats, genres and narrative structures which allow for rather more openness and ambiguity.

Varieties of fiction

Despite the similarities in imagery and form between news and certain kinds of popular drama, television fiction enjoys significant advantages over journalism which make it, potentially at least, more flexible in the way it can deal with the issues.

In the first place, it can show two key groups of actors who almost never appear in actuality programmes: terrorists and members of the security services. As we have seen, interviewing terrorists or their supporters poses considerable problems for current affairs producers and documentary makers whereas fictional programmes regularly feature terrorists as central characters, probing their motivations, and political philosophies. Similarly, they don't have the same problems of access to state personnel or high security operations and units, and can therefore provide an 'insider' view of the 'secret state'. This difference emerged particularly clearly in a television discussion of a BBC play *Psywarriors* (discussed below) which dealt with a secret anti-interrogation course employing the techniques of modern psychological warfare to test potential recruits to an elite anti-terrorist unit. As Roger Mills, one of the country's best known actuality producers, explained during the discussion, although he had tried to get access to make a documentary programme about such courses, his request had been denied.

Mills: I've met servicemen throughout my BBC career who've told me about courses that they've gone on, anti-interrogation courses . . . and I've tried to get permission from the Ministry of Defence to make documentaries about them and I've got nowhere.

Chairman: Did they tell you why they wouldn't let you do that?

Mills: Just that it generally wasn't in the interests of the army for us to do this sort of film.[13]

Fictional programmes not only show us more of the struggle between terror and national security, they deal with it in a greater variety of ways, since they are not bound by the requirements of objectivity and balance that govern television journalism. However, there is no simple relationship between the added scope for personal viewpoints and openness to alternative or oppositional perspectives. This is so because some producers and writers subscribe to the official perspective, and in any case the intentions of programme makers are only one of the forces shaping fiction production. They are also subject to the commercial pressures of the rating battle and by the constraints and possibilities of the genres and narrative styles they adopt.

Commercial pressures operate with particular force on the popular series and serials that are central to the rating battle between the two main networks, BBC1 and ITV. To attract a mass audience they need to work with images and ideological themes which are already accepted by the widest range of potential viewers. Consequently, they tend to draw most heavily on the official perspective (and on reactionary populism) since these are the best publicised and most pervasive perspectives. This tendency towards closure is further reinforced in productions like *The Professionals* aimed at the international as well as domestic markets. The makers have to work with material which will be intelligible across cultures, particularly in the United States, since success in the American market is the key to profitable overseas sales. In contrast to popular series and serials, single plays are not in the front line of the battle for audiences or programme exports and so they are not under the same pressure to work with the most prevalent ideological themes or to deliver predictable pleasures to the largest possible number of viewers. On the contrary, the makers of single plays are expected to fulfil the role of 'authors' and to express their particular viewpoints and commitments in their own distinctive voice and style. In the words of David Reid, ex-Head of Drama at ATV and now chief of the BBC's drama department, 'at best' [the single play] is the individual voice being heard loud and clear which implies that its content and tone cannot be expressed in any series episode'.[14]

This notion of the author's right to free expression, including the right to challenge official orthodoxies, is one of the key principles of public service broadcasting, and as such it provides an important buffer against both commercial imperatives and internal pressures.[15]

As the well-known television director, Roland Joffé has pointed out:

'... there is an enormous difference between current affairs censorship and play censorship and that's to do with the way our culture has grown. Artists have been allowed a fair amount of freedom ... the ideas of free speech and art go very importantly hand in hand ... So a play is a lot more sacrosanct: it's not as safe to interfere with the writer's right, as to say well this journalist did this but we have decided not to put it out.'[16]

As a result, single plays are one of the main spaces within contemporary television where the official perspective can be interrogated and the alternative and oppositional perspectives presented and worked through. This does not mean that all single plays or 'authored' films are equally open and critical. Nor does it mean that all popular fictions are equally closed. In fact, they handle the perspectives on offer in a variety of ways.

In general the series format, which features the same main characters in self-contained stories, is more closed than the serial form where the narrative unfolds over a number of episodes. The ratings success of a series largely depends on the extent to which the audience identifies with the central characters (and the stars who play them) since it is this attachment that keeps them watching from week to week. The invitation to identify is announced in the programmes' titles – *The Return of the Saint, The Avengers, The Professionals* – reinforced by the way the shows are publicised in the popular press and the weekly TV guides, and cemented by the way the narratives are structured. The plots always revolve around the central characters. They are the heroes. They are on screen for most of the time and the action is seen from their point of view.

The villain's function is to disturb the social and moral order and present the heroes with problems to solve. The villains do not need to be rounded characters to fulfil this role. They simply have to personify threats to the established order in a readily recognisable form. They appear abruptly at the beginning of the episode and are purged at the end. But since there are only fifty minutes or so to do this, we get to know very little about their background or motivations. The narrative is moved along by what they do not what they say. In the popular series, actions nearly always speak louder than words. Conversely, we know a good deal about the personalities and past experiences of the heroes since each new story can trade off the knowledge presented in past episodes.

Because threats to the established order are seen exclusively through the eyes of its defenders, there is little scope to explore the critiques offered by the alternative and oppositional perspectives. Whilst the need for the central characters to return unsullied next week means that the narrative tends to end with a simple unambiguous triumph for order over subversion.

In contrast, the more relaxed narrative pace of the serial where the action may be spread over three hours or more, allows more space to explore the background and motivation of terrorists and more scope to probe the tensions between law and order in the state's response. These differences in programme format are often reinforced by differences in narrative style between action-adventure plots and what we can call puzzle plots.

Whereas action-adventure plots rely on simple clear-cut oppositions between good and evil, the state and its enemies, puzzle plots present the central characters with an enigma or mystery which they must unravel. In the process they probe behind appearances. People are not always what they seem, and the defenders of order may turn out to be conspiring to overthrow the system. In a puzzle plot nothing can be taken for granted. Ambiguities and uncertainties are introduced into the presentation of the state and its agents. Because of the space they need to unfold, puzzle plots are more often used as the basis for serials, while action-adventure plots are characteristic of series. To these differences we also need to add variations in genre. The 'problem' of terrorism appears in popular fiction in two main genres – police thrillers and secret service thrillers – both of which structure its presentation in important ways.

Take, for example, the 'Appointment in Florence' episode from the last series of *Return of the Saint*, a very successful British crime show (ITV, 15 August 1981). The episode begins with the Saint enjoying a ski-ing holiday in the Alps with his old friend Christian von Essler. Essler is kidnapped by a splinter group of the Red Brigade and a ransom demanded. Payment is delayed on the advice of the police and Essler is delivered shot through the head with a note pinned to his chest reading 'Delay kills, Monopoly Capitalism kills'. This is the only political statement the terrorists make in the entire episode, but it is immediately defused by the next scene in which the head of the anti-terrorist squad briefs his men on the prime suspect, Manfred Niessen, the group's leader. We hear nothing more about Niessen's political ideas. He is described solely in terms of his crimes.

'The insignia on the death note belongs to a splinter group of the Red Brigade. Manfred Niessen their leader (indicating a slide on the viewing screen). Born 1942. Was arrested in 1973 for arson. Released while appeal was pending and fled the country. Wanted for murder, bank robberies, smuggling arms out of Switzerland, and accused of at least four kidnappings.'

This scene could have come from any standard crime film where the police chief talks his men through the 'most wanted' list.

In contrast, the secret service thriller places 'terrorism' firmly within a political context, though this is often the Cold War, which produces an equally 'closed' presentation. But these tendencies towards closure do not operate automatically. The secret service thriller has undergone important changes in recent years which have opened up a new perspective on the secret state and its response to 'terrorism'.

Gentlemen and proletarians, players and professionals

The secret service thriller emerged in its classic form during the Edwardian era when the security of Britain was widely seen as under attack from external enemies (beginning with Germany and moving on to the Soviet Union) and alien forces within the state, most notably Irish republicans and emigré anarchists.[17] Within the genre, these threats were opposed by upper class gentlemen who represented everything that was best about the English way of life. Some, like John Buchan's Richard Hannay, were amateurs, serving their country out of love and duty. Others, like William le Queux's Duckworth Drew, were full-time members of the newly formed intelligence and security services. But all were gentlemen. They had no formal training. Their skills and qualities had been acquired on the playing fields of the public schools. They fought by the Queensberry Rules and killed only as a last resort, though they were all excellent shots.

These stock ingredients of alien incursion and 'invisible export' from Ireland and Germany still feature prominently in the way terrorism is portrayed in popular television fiction. So too does the image of the secret service agent as English gentleman. It is most obvious in the various *Avengers* series, where the main male character John Steed, displays his 'Englishness' through the universal signs of the gentleman – the bowler hat and the rolled umbrella. But it is also evident in *The Saint*, whose hero, Simon Templar, comes from a long line of debonaire defenders of the realm. These continuities drag along with them an ideological baggage packed in the heyday of Empire but the way in which the genre has changed in response to movements in the political and ideological climate is equally significant.

The early 1960s saw an important shift in the public image of the 'secret state'. In the classic secret service thriller, the conspiracies that threaten democracy are always located *outside* the social order. They are the work of foreigners, agents of hostile powers, or people possessed of 'alien' political beliefs. The intelligence services appear as institutions of unquestioned integrity and patriotism, the main bulwarks against anarchy and subversion. With Kim Philby's defection to Moscow in 1963, however, this image was severely dented. The discovery that a high-ranking intelligence officer had been a long-standing Soviet agent introduced a permanent note of suspicion and doubt which found its way into the thriller in two important themes: the possibility that conspiracies could originate *inside* the security services themselves, and the increasingly negative evaluation of the gentlemanly amateurs who ran the service and served as agents.

The declining ideological fortunes of the gentleman have been accompanied by the professionalisation of the 'secret state' within the thriller. This shift entered the mainstream of popular fiction with the Bond films (starting with *Dr No* in 1961), where the classically gentlemanly figure of the 1950s novels is 'refashioned as the very model of the tough, abrasive, unsentimental professionalism which according to the rhetoric of Heath and Wilson, was destined to lead Britain into the modern, no illusions, post-imperial age'.[18] Despite this new professionalism the screen Bond retained a gentleman's taste for high living, good food and expensively tailored suits. This sense of style was carried into television by Steed of *The Avengers*, which also began transmission in 1961. But alongside this glamorous version of the new professionalism (so characteristic of the general iconography of the sixties), television was developing a seedier, grittier variant in the person of *Callan*, an expert and ruthless assassin with extensive underworld contacts. He did the secret service's dirty work for them but he was not a regular agent. As television entered the seventies though, these new style no-nonsense operatives were incorporated into the regular agencies of law and order in a string of series featuring special units. They included *The Sweeney, Target, The Sandbaggers* and *The Professionals*.

The Professionals was devised in 1977. It took the highly success-ful formula of *The Sweeney* – a strong emphasis on action centred on two male heroes willing to bend the rules to get the job done – and transposed it from the world of regular police work to the clandes-tine world of the secret state. The show was developed by Brian Clemens and Albert Fennel who had worked on the original *Avengers*. But it operated with a very different ethos. Unlike Steed, CI5's chief George Cowley is definitely not part of the old boy network and we are told that as soon as he got the job

'He had weeded out the old concepts of 'who you know' and replaced them by 'know how'. The day of the amateur was long gone. He had turfed out the languid dross and replaced them with tough, hard men to deal with the new, tough, hard situations all too frequently encountered at the latter end of the Twentieth Century.'[19]

Bodie and Doyle of CI5, along with the most of the new style operat-ives, are hardly out of the top drawer. They lack the traditional social graces and they don't fight by the old rules, but they are effect-ive. The prototype was Harry Palmer, the hero of Len Deighton's novel *The Ipcress File* (1962) a tough, insubordinate working class northerner who exposes his elegant, languid public school superior, Dalby, as a traitor. But this new social type also draws on changes in the American hard-boiled crime thriller.[20]

This genre has always had a strong reactionary populist thrust which is well represented by Mickey Spillane's best-sellers like, *I the Jury* and *Vengeance is Mine*, where freelance operatives seek retribution untrammeled by the police rule book.[21] In the seventies though this current found a forceful new popular expression in a series of successful movies, beginning with Clint Eastwood's *Dirty*

Harry in 1971, featuring cops who behaved like vigilantes. Their motto is: 'Forget what's legal. Do what's right'.[22] Their excesses may earn them a reprimand or even a suspension, but there is no doubt who the heroes are. *The Professionals* takes this official vigilantism a stage further. Bodie and Doyle are not rogue operatives. Their actions are officially sanctioned. The whole show is based on the premise that exceptional threats to order and democracy require exceptional measures. As Cowley tells them, their brief is to contain these threats 'by whatever means necessary. That's our loophole . . . Like an alley fight. That's what this is, an alley fight, so hit him first, do unto others what they're still thinking about.'[23]

At the same time, the characterisation of state agents as violent avengers embodies a suggestion of undue even uncontrolled violence. Indeed their very success in restoring order often depends on them overcoming criminals, 'terrorists' or other enemies of the state by using even greater force and dirtier tactics, and this presents a problem of sustaining the legitimacy of official violence.[24]

Sanitising the strong state

This problem is compounded by the fact that the forces of order and the agents of subversion are often depicted in the same terms, as in these two descriptions of the SAS. The first is from the flyleaf of a novel about a fictional operation against the IRA, *Whisper Who Dares*, the second is from a *Sun* feature on their exploits in the Falklands War.

'The SAS and the IRA: each in its own way a mysterious and deadly organisation. One capable of terrorising an entire nation; the other practised in feats of combat beyond our wildest imagination.'[25]

'By night they came. Paddling small boats through stormy seas, or dropping from helicopters out of wild skies. A young Argentinian soldier was found dead the next morning. No one knew what had killed him until they found a thin red line round his neck. He had been garotted with a steel wire. *The Special Air Service, silent and unseen, were spreading their terror.'*[26]

Not only do they come from the equivalent clandestine organisations and use the same methods, the SAS even look like the forces of violent disorder. In popular imagery, even in comics, they are almost always shown wearing masks, usually some kind of balaclava helmet. There is of course a firm tradition of masked avengers in popular fiction, including the Lone Ranger and Batman, though they normally wear carnival masks covering only the eyes. The more immediate comparisons are with violent criminals, especially bank robbers, and with the IRA, both of whom are often shown wearing exactly the same kind of balaclava as the SAS. But if the most celebrated agents of order look like the best known forces of disruption and use the same tactics, how are we to tell the difference between them? What makes the violence of one legitimate and the other not? Popular fiction has a number of ways of resolving the problem through narrative devices and key images.

In the first place, it is always the terrorists who initiate the plot with a violent attack on the existing order (such as the assassination at the beginning of *Who Dares Wins*). Hence, the state's violent *response* always appears as defensive, regrettable but necessary to defeat the threat and restore the status quo. However, since this still requires the use of equivalent or even greater force, it is necessary to further reaffirm the moral and personal differences between the two sides. This is normally done by humanising the state's agents. Before he goes undercover for example, Skellen in *Who Dares Wins*, is shown at home with his wife and child as a typical family man. And later, having cornered Frankie, he can't bring himself to shoot her and it is left to an anonymous masked operative to finish the job. Like Bodie and Doyle of *The Professionals*, he is not a faceless instrument of state force, but an ordinary decent man doing an extraordinary and dirty job. His work sets him apart from normality but his character and off-duty life make him one of 'us' and we are invited to identify with him and his dilemmas.

Conversely, the 'terrorist' opposition is usually defined as abnormal, inhuman and alien to the British way of life. The simplest device is to make the terrorists into physical aliens, foreigners who have arrived from elsewhere and don't share our political ideals or way of doing things. Images of 'foreignness' and the residual racism and xenophobia on which they trade are still central to a good deal of popular fiction about terrorism. Similarly, home-grown terrorists are often depicted as having embraced alien beliefs and working to undermine the nation and overthrow democracy, probably with the help of a hostile power. This stereotype of the terrorist as 'foreigner' is often played off against idealised images of 'Englishness'. Landscape is particularly important here. In a number of the programmes we looked at, terrorists were shown disrupting quintessentially English settings such as vicarages in rolling parklands, the Kent orchard country, and elegant eighteenth century buildings and squares.

Terrorists are further separated from 'us' by being presented as fanatics and psychopaths who lack the normal human qualities. Images of women often play an important role in securing these stereotypes. This was certainly the case with the coverage of the Angry Brigade, England's best publicised modern exponents of the anti-system terror practised by the Red Brigades and the Baader-Meinhof group. Although four members of the Brigade were convicted at the trial in December 1972, the popular papers concentrated on the two female defendants, Anna Mendleson and Hilary Creek, and based their stories on the contradiction between violence and femininity.[27] This contrast is also the stock-in-trade of popular fiction. In *Who Dares Wins*, for example, Skellen's wife and child are held hostage by Helga, the East German weapons expert who has been training the group. Unlike Jenny Skellen, she lacks all the conventional 'feminine' attributes of the wife and mother. As James Follett makes clear in the novelisation, 'she would never allow a weakness for attractive men to undermine her objectivity and efficiency for the simple reason, that as far as Helga was concerned, there was no such thing as an attractive man'.[28] Moreover, when the baby won't stop crying she threatens to kill it.

The East German woman terrorist from 'Who Dares Wins'

This contrast between fanaticism and femininity picks up the powerful anti-feminist current in popular iconography, with its association of independence and aggression. It finds a particularly powerful expression in the masculine world of the 'hard boiled' thriller, with its suspicion and even contempt for women and its celebration of male camaraderie and macho values.[29]

These devices are common in popular television fiction but by no means universal. The more 'open' and 'loose' programme forms allow for a more critical view of the state's recourse to violent force and a more rounded picture of terrorists as political actors. In the standard action-adventure series however, these devices are deployed to the full to close the narrative around official thinking and nowhere is this more evident than in *The Professionals*. As one of the most popular and successful action-adventure series produced for British television in recent years and the one that has most consistently featured terrorism, *The Professionals* was an obvious choice for detailed study.

'Forget the political, vicar, just concentrate on the force': the world of the professionals

Almost all of the episodes of *The Professionals* have featured in the top ten most popular programmes and the series has been sold in most of the major overseas markets. The action centres around Bodie and Doyle, the two top agents of CI5, a clandestine criminal investigation unit. According to the promotional material for the series:

'Anarchy, acts of terror, crimes of violence – it's all grist to the mill of the formidable force who make up CI5.'[30]

'CI5 breaks all the rules: no uniforms, no ranks and no conscience – just results. Formed to combat the vicious tide of violence that threatens law and order, its brief is to counter-attack. And when there's a hijack, a bomb threat, a kidnap or a sniper, men from CI5 storm into action.'[31]

'Dedicated, highly trained and ruthless – they play the criminal at his own game. They're part of the new generation of crime fighters who will stop at nothing to keep crime off the streets for good!'[32]

These descriptions underscore two key themes in the official perspective. Firstly, they place terrorism firmly within a criminal rather than a political frame and define it exclusively in terms of the violence it entails. And, secondly, they legitimate the state's use of violent countermeasures by arguing that exceptional threats to the social order require exceptional responses in which consideration of civil liberties, democratic accountability, and due process, are held in abeyance in the interests of efficiency. Within this perspective the end of re-establishing order justifies the use of dubious and even illegal means, and licences the men of CI5 to use the same dirty tricks as their adversaries. We are told that Bodie and Doyle: 'would think nothing of kidnapping a kidnapper, or chaining a bomber to his own bomb and leaving him to defuse it'.[33]

The Professionals' tight format and reactionary populist version of the official perspective allows very little space for alternative or oppositional viewpoints. As script editor Gerry O'Hara has explained:

'... because we set out to make the show 'move', the action content had to be given its head. You plant action or intrigue in the teaser; then you work towards the first commercial break and have to bring up the action line, and again at the end of the second act and very much so at the end of the third ... We keep our pauses as short as we dare, we rarely let our actors stand still.'[34]

Moreover, as in all action-adventure series, threats to the social order are seen exclusively through the eyes of the heroes. As Brian Clemens' original brief to writers for the series put it: 'Set up the story, set up the problem CI5 have to deal with and then let's see how they solve the apparently insoluble.'[35]

But, since they are agents of the state popular support for their strong-arm tactics cannot be entirely taken for granted.

Hence, while it operates firmly within the terms of the official perspective, the programme must also work *actively* to head off dissent and enlist the audience's support for powerful counter-measures by underlining the exceptional nature of the terrorist threat and the irrelevance of alternative and oppositional perspectives on state violence. This process of ideological mobilisation is well illustrated in the episode entitled *Close Quarters* (ITV, 5 June 1981).

The episode opens with the assassination of a British politician, Sir Denny Forbes, at a check-in desk at London airport, killed with a syringe of poison by the leader of the Meyer-Helmut terrorist group. This introduces four central themes: the essential criminality of terrorism; its identification with the Left; its characterisation as an alien incursion originating outside Britain; and the absolute contrast between the legitimate pursuit of interests through parliamentary representation and the illegitimacy of direct action. The assassination is a direct attack on the 'body politic' and on the 'British way of life'.

Having announced these themes in the opening sequence, the

Bodie (having burst into the vicarage and secured the doors and windows, turns to the vicar and his housekeeper): In the heat of the moment I forgot my manners. This is Julie my girlfriend and I'm Bodie. May we have a drink. I think we all need one.

Meyer (with heavy sarcasm): May we have a drink vicar. So polite vicar. Let's all have a little tea party. You English are all insane.

Bodie: Not like the Meyer-Helmut group eh? They just bomb and hijack and shoot the odd plane and hostages.

Meyer: It's a necessary part of our strategy.

Bodie: The end justifies the means eh?

narrative immediately begins to elaborate them. The audience has already been invited to see Meyer's act as essentially criminal rather than political since CI5 is a *criminal* intelligence unit. To reinforce the point the scene immediately after the credits shows Cowley briefing his men in a facsimile of the scene in *Return of the Saint* (already referred to):

Cowley (standing in front of a blackboard filled with photos of the group): Sir Denny Forbes, businessman, politician, deceased. He took a hypo in the thigh. Two grains of pure poison. Yes, murder, and a murder proudly proclaimed by the Meyer-Helmut group . . . anarchists, fanatics. They've killed or maimed at least a hundred innocent people in the last two years. Now they're in Britain and I want them.

Although Bodie attends the briefing he is excused active duty because of an injured gun hand, and he decides to take his girlfriend Julie for a picnic on the River Thames at Henley. While on the water he recognises Meyer standing on the bank. He follows him to the cottage he is using as a safe house and arrests him. But the other members of the group arrive and give chase. Bodie eludes them and makes his getaway in a stolen car. The group pursue him and he barricades himself in a country vicarage which the group, heavily armed, surround.

The key visual images in this sequence underscore the essential alienness of terrorism by counterposing the menacing figure of the German, Meyer, with idealised representations of traditional England and the British way of life – rowing on a sunlit River Thames at Henley and the elegant eighteenth-century vicarage set in rolling parkland.

After this action sequence the dialogue again takes up the two core themes; the irrationality and criminality of terrorism and its essential alienness to the British way of life.

Meyer: You don't understand. You will never understand.

Bodie: No. Not if I live a million years.

Meyer: We are the Meyer-Helmut group. We are not trash.

Vicar: Who are those people outside?

Bodie: He just told you, a bunch of killers.

Meyer: We are a political force.

Bodie: Forget the political, vicar, just concentrate on the force.

The group's utter ruthlessness is confirmed when they shoot the vicar in cold blood as he is climbing out of a window in an effort to reason with them. This incident clinches the central ideological theme of the narrative; you can't bargain with terrorists. Faced with their arbitrary violence, the state is justified in using similar tactics. Popular support for this position is mobilised through the common-sense response of the housekeeper and Bodie's girlfriend. The audience is invited to identify with the women's situation in the narrative, innocent by-standers caught up in events they do not fully understand, but who recognise the state's moral right to combat terrorism with all the weapons at its command.

Meyer (addressing the girlfriend and the housekeeper): How does this concern you. You have no conception of what this fight is about. It's not your fight.

Housekeeper: I don't understand your politics, but I understand good and evil. You kill without cause. You kill people who cannot possibly stand between you and your ideas. You don't even know who they are.

Julie (addressing Meyer): You're right. I have no idea what you're fighting about. I just know it means violence and killing and someone's got to stop you.

Despite these protestations Julie still has reservations about the legitimacy of Bodie's use of violence (after he has shot two members of the group as they attempted to enter the vicarage).

Bodie: I'm doing this to protect you, people like you.

Julie: You live by violence, just like him (indicating Meyer).

Bodie: Yes, well you fight fire with fire in this job.

But when the chips are down, Julie overcomes her qualms. As the last member of the gang storms the room where they are hiding, Bodie is disarmed by Meyer and it is Julie who picks up his gun and shoots. The ideological circle is finally closed, around the official perspective.

In contrast to the 'imported' terrorism of the Meyer-Helmut group, an episode entitled *No Stone* (ITV, 6 February 1983) deals with domestic terrorists, the model being the Angry Brigade rather than the Red Army Fraction. The group is led by an English girl, Judy Wynant, who has changed her name to Ulrike Herzl (after Ulrike Meinhof). She is the classic mental alien.

As the narrative opens Jimmy Kilpin, the son of a self-made industrialist, is in prison for his involvement with the group. In return for a reduced sentence he has provided information which has secured long sentences for several group members, and has just told CI5 where to find one of the group's main arms dumps. But the group is tipped off by Kilpin's lawyer (a sympathiser) and when CI5 take Kilpin to dig up the guns they are ambushed. Several agents are shot and Kilpin is captured. He is tried by a kangaroo court in a Kent Orchard for informing on his ex-comrades, found guilty and hanged. The group then put into action their major plan to disrupt the legal system by placing car-bombs outside several London courts. One blows up, but after pressuring Kilpin's lawyer into revealing Ulrike's whereabouts, Bodie and Doyle arrest her at the airport and trick her into admitting the location of the other bomb. It detonates just as a disposal expert goes to defuse it killing him outright.

Unlike *Close Quarters*, *No Stone* does allow the terrorists to put their political case: the present legal system is an instrument of ruling class domination which fails to deliver the promise of equal justice for all. A communiqué to the press claims:

'We've suffered the violence of the system for too long. The legal system in this country is a perversion of the word justice. The law protects corporate crime, big business, the multinationals, the rich, the powerful, the law has nothing to do with justice.'

Here again we see how popular television fiction constantly borrows images and scenarios from news reporting. The original brief for *The Professionals* urged its writers to 'steal situations from the headlines'.[36] In this case some of the phrases were borrowed as well. The first sentence of Ulrike's manifesto is almost identical to the opening words of the Angry Brigade's sixth communiqué which began; 'We have sat quietly and suffered the violence of the system far too long'. Both statements are classic examples of the anti-system variant of the oppositional perspective which argues that terrorist violence is a response to the institutionalised violence of the society aiming to reveal the repressive reality behind democratic rhetoric. As with the popular press's reporting of the Angry Brigade however, this political content is dismissed out of hand and Ulrike's group are cast simply as 'bomb happy destructionists' bent on throwing 'Britain into bloody chaos'. Like Frankie's speech in *Who Dares Wins*, Ulrike's communiqué is inserted into a narrative whose whole structure is designed to discredit it as a political argument. Its function is to confirm the group's extremism.

Their separation from 'us' is reinforced soon afterwards by their kangaroo trial of Kilpin which demonstrates that their brand of 'popular justice' is even more arbitrary and brutal than the system they oppose. Moreover, it is made clear that they are part of the international terror network 'capitalised by the KGB and trained by the PLO', as Cowley puts it, and that their attack on the legal system is part of an orchestrated attempt to destabilise the European democracies. Hence they appear not as misguided idealists but as fanatics in the pay of Moscow.

In the world of *The Professionals*, idealism is prompted by social experience and a genuine concern for justice and equality. Fanaticism is the product of external influence or personality disorders. Idealists retain their capacity to choose. They are open to doubt and reclamation. Fanatics are beyond rationality, driven by compulsion. This distinction is elaborated through the contrasted characters and careers of Ulrike and Kilpin.

We are told that Kilpin grew up watching his father buy favours from the police and the law on his way to the top, and this formative experience makes his desire for radical change entirely intelligible, even admirable. As Cowley tells his father, Jimmy's idealism may be 'half-baked' but it is 'idealism none the less'. After a youthful flirtation with terrorism however, he comes to see that his ideals are at odds with such methods. He changes sides, joins the fight against his former comrades and himself becomes the victim of their arbitrary violence. In contrast Ulrike is consistently shown as a fanatic. Her callous disregard for innocent lives is confirmed when Bodie questions her about the whereabouts of the last car-bomb.

Bodie: People are going to get killed. Kids are going to lose eyes and limbs. Do you want that?

Ulrike: Yes.

Bodie: Well it won't help you.

Ulrike: Not us. It'll help the others. Today England, tomorrow Germany, France, Holland. In a year's time there won't be a court-room in Europe working properly.

But by this point in the plot the audience already knows that her actions have less to do with political convictions than with the fact that she is a psychopath who gets pleasure from killing. As she tells Kilpin just before he hangs, 'putting a gun on a man, is the greatest sexual turn on of all. No, second greatest. Killing's the greatest.' Her abnormality is further underlined by the contrast with the wife of the CI5 agent killed in the ambush. Directly after we see Ulrike shooting to kill we see Doyle going to tell Judith Cook of her husband's death. He finds her in the kitchen, pregnant, and preparing her husband's favourite meal. Here again, we can see how popular iconography points to the 'unnaturalness' of terrorism by counterposing female terrorists who totally lack the normal attributes of wives and mothers against idealised images of domesticity and femininity. Nor is Jimmy's recantation unique.

Since the publicity given to the Italian 'pentiti', the reformed terrorist has joined the defecting agent as a standard thriller device for reaffirming the acceptable limits of left idealism and the absolute illegitimacy of terrorist responses. The popular serial, *Skorpion*, (named after the hand gun favoured by the Red Brigades) was structured entirely around this device, (BBC1, 26 January to 16 February 1983). The narrative centres on Gabrielle de Faujas, the head of an international relief agency for refugees, who has used her position as a cover for terrorist activities. She now regrets her decision and is prepared to inform on her own comrades. After several attempts on her life in Paris she charters a private plane, but it crashes in Scotland and she hides out with Agatha, a former refugee worker, in her cottage in the Highlands. The security services need to locate her and get her testimony before she is found and shot by the assassin sent by the terrorists.

It has gone unnoticed that this story-line is directly derived from the factoid world of Claire Sterling and her fellow experts in disinformation. It offers a further illustration of how fiction may draw on (in this case, highly suspect) journalism. In *The Terror Network*, Sterling devotes an entire chapter to the 'strange career of Henri Curiel', a Paris-based political activist in Third World causes, who was killed in mysterious circumstances. Curiel ran a charitable agency, which according to Sterling, was just a front for organising the activities of international terrorists. In Sterling's words, 'Every major counterespionage agency in the West has a file on him, and almost anybody in the trade reading through these *would assume* he worked for the KGB.'[37]

However, Sterling's story is open to considerable doubt. When Curiel's family and associates brought lawsuits in Paris against her for slander the 'documents of the French secret police provided to the court in these and in earlier cases produced no evidence whatever of Curiel's having a KGB connection . . . Sterling lost one of the slander suits and was assessed a fine; others she slipped out of on legal technicalities and by the court's accepting her claims that she had not accused Curiel of being a KGB agent, but was merely presenting a "hypothesis".'[38]

This 'hypothesis' provided the thread for the action in *Skorpion*. The central character, Gabrielle de Faujas, regrets what she has done in helping the terror network and is now prepared to inform on her own comrades.

Although basically an action-adventure plot, the serial form allows more space to explore Gabrielle's experiences and motivations, as in this key exchange with Agatha.

Agatha: How shocked we were when we saw what we had to deal with. Do you remember that first batch arrived from Lebanon? Plonked here, plonked there, just because they had no papers. They didn't know they were supposed to have papers, no-one had told them. All they knew they were hungry and their families were sick. God they were awful, repulsive sores. It was only you could bring yourself to kiss the leper. You just don't know how much we all worshipped you.

Gabrielle: I had to do something, fight the reasons for such conditions. There seemed to be only one way. Now I think I was wrong. What did I do but create more dispossessed, more amputations, more deaths? I'm sick to my stomach.

The humanitarian impulse behind her decision to support the terrorists is further underlined by the intelligence service chief assigned to the case. As he tells a police inspector, and the audience:

'The first thing for you to understand is that the lady in question is what she claims to be. She actually does protect and sustain refugees out of human warmth and conviction. No one can or does deny that.'

But he immediately reasserts the terms of the official perspective by pointing out that she allowed her idealism to be exploited by Moscow's international terror network.

'Unfortunately, as you now know, there is more to it than that . . . She may have been recruited in Moscow. She supported Black September, Red Brigades, oh all the thuggery that you can dredge up from the sewers of politics. Predictably, she acted against the Americans, ourselves, the West Germans, the French, anyone still committed, however imperfectly, to the democratic notion. Her organisation was the ideal cover. She had every reason to be in Lybia, Somalia, Beirut . . . We learned that she had had a change of heart. The problem is that her masters don't permit one of their coven to defect. Once a terrorist always a terrorist. Hence the assassin on her track.'

Despite the intelligence service's best efforts they arrive too late. Gabrielle has been shot, not by the assassin but by her friend Agatha, who has remained loyal to the terrorist international. The message is clear; the tentacles of international terror reach everywhere, concealed behind the most respectable looking fronts. To defeat this threat, the state must take whatever measures are necessary to flush out the subversives within, and if this means curtailing civil liberties, this is regrettable but necessary.

As George Cowley tells his CI5 operatives:

'Oh, there'll be squeals, and once in a while you'll turn a law-abiding citizen into an authority-hating anarchist. There'll be squeals, and letters to MP's; but that is the price, they and we, have to pay to keep this island clean and smelling, even if ever so faintly, of roses and lavender.'[39]

By no means all popular fiction is as ideologically closed as this however. Other productions we looked at offered a rather more critical appraisal of the official arguments in favour of the tough response, and an altogether more complex view of the causes of 'terrorism'.

Law against order:
dramatising the liberal state's dilemmas

The second of these potentialities is well illustrated by *Harry's Game*, a serialisation of Gerald Seymour's 1975 thriller of the same name broadcast on three consecutive evenings (ITV, 25 to 27 October 1982) Seymour worked for ITN before turning to fiction-writing full time, and *Harry's Game*, his first novel, draws extensively on his experiences as a newsman, including 'Bloody Sunday' in January 1972 when British army paratroopers opened fire on demonstrators in Derry, killing thirteen people. At the same time, the flexibility of fiction allows him to explore the dynamics of 'terrorism' and state force from the inside, in a way not possible in news reporting.

Harry's Game opens like a standard action-adventure, with an IRA operative, Billy Downes, assassinating a British Cabinet minister, Henry Danby, outside his London house, just after he has seen his two young daughters off to school. Billy evades the police net and makes his way back to Belfast. The Prime Minister demands swift action and orders the intelligence services to bring Downes in. Without informing local army intelligence in Belfast, they dispatch an experienced agent, Harry Brown. His brief is to go into deep cover, posing as a merchant seaman returning home, to locate Billy, report back and pull out, leaving the decision on how to proceed to his 'control'.

At one level this narrative structure places *Harry's Game* firmly within the terms of the official perspective, and the subsequent action rehearses several of its key themes, notably the similarity between the IRA and organised crime. At periodic intervals Billy is taken to see the 'big man' to receive his assignments, and these scenes echo the Godfather figures familiar from Mafia movies. At the same time however, the characterisation of Billy defies the conventional labels of criminality, psychopathology and Soviet influence, and offers a more complex and political account of his actions.

Unlike the 'terrorists' in *The Professionals*, Billy is not a fanatic without a past or intelligible political motivations. He is shown as a member of a community with a long tradition of resistance sustained by continuing harrassment by the British army. This provides a political explanation for his actions. In one key scene we see Billy and his wife at a Saturday night ceilidh in a local community centre. People are drinking and dancing in a hall draped with Republican flags and the band are playing 'The Men Behind The Wire', the song dedicated to the internees of Long Kesh. Suddenly, an army unit drives up in armoured cars, crashes through the door, questions the men and takes Billy away for further questioning. After they've gone the dance starts up again. This scene reverses the normal stereotypes. It is the army which appears as an alien presence interrupting everyday life, whereas Billy appears as part of the local community, accepted and even admired by those around him.

His social integration is further underlined by the stock humanising device of showing him at home with his wife and children. Similarly, the community's support for his action is demonstrated in several scenes. On his initial return from England for example, he is sheltered by a succession of ordinary families. Later, just after he has shot a British soldier he hands the gun to a young mother with a pram who hides it under the baby's blankets. At the same time, the narrative also brings into play the official argument that popular support for the IRA is due to intimidation rather than conviction. This theme is dramatised in a scene where a teenage girl who has accidentally and indirectly provided Harry with crucial information, and is later picked up by the police, hangs herself in her cell out of fear of reprisals.

Consequently, there is a tension in the narrative between the depiction of the IRA as a ruthless Mafia-like organisation and the exploration of its social and political roots. However, unlike the world of *The Professionals*, we are not invited to forget about the political and just concentrate on the force. Billy's violence is not portrayed as indiscriminate and meaningless. His 'targets' are soldiers and policemen, or in the case of the British politician, Henry Danby, the man responsible for administering Long Kesh prison. He does not kill without reason and he does not kill civilians. This is confirmed in a key scene towards the end. He has been detailed to kill a senior policeman but at the crucial moment the man's young daughter crosses his line of fire. Billy refuses to shoot, is wounded in the arm himself and only just escapes.

This deconstruction of conventional stereotypes is also evident in the portrayal of Harry. He is not presented as a straightforward positive hero and his actions are shown to be questionable rather than admirable. He has suffered a mental breakdown as a result of his work as an undercover agent in the Aden emergency, and he sees his Belfast assignment as a chance to prove to himself and his superiors that he is still up to the job. Once in the field he disobeys his orders and sets out to kill Billy himself. The climax comes when he is approached by Billy and two associates who have orders to take him to the IRA commander. He shoots one dead and wounds another but Billy escapes in his car. Harry commandeers a car and gives chase. Billy drives his wounded comrade to a hospital, leaves the car and makes for home on foot. Harry catches up with him just as he reaches his wife in the street and shoots him, although Billy is unarmed. Harry is then shot by two British soldiers concealed in a building across the street who mistake him for an IRA man, and as he crawls past the impassive crowd gathered on the pavement he is shot again by Billy's wife with his own gun.

This is an ambiguous ending. On the one hand, Harry's unauthorised use of force against an unarmed man puts him morally and politically on a level with his 'terrorist' opponents, to the extent that he can be mistaken for one of them. At the same time, because he is acting against orders, as a freelance vigilante, his action appears as a personal lapse, due perhaps to strain and an underlying mental instability, rather than as part of a deliberate counter-terrorist strategy sanctioned by the secret state.

However, this possibility and its implications were explored more fully in another popular series, *Blood Money* (BBC, 6 September – 11 October 1981).

The narrative opens with a scene set in an exclusive private boarding school for the sons of the rich. The boys are out on a cross-country run through the sunlit landscape. One of them, Rupert Fitz-charles, is the son of the Administrator General of the United Nations and because of his father's political status he is guarded by a plain clothes policeman working undercover as a school sports master. Suddenly, figures wearing gas masks spring out from behind the hedges, spray the boys with CS gas, abduct the diplomat's son and drive him to their 'safe' house in London. They intend to release him when the authorities agree to meet their demands, but if they refuse the group intend to kill him.

As in the initial scenes of *Close Quarters*, this opening sequence calls into play two of the central themes in the official discourse: the ruthlessness of terrorists and their disregard for human life; and their characterisation as an alien incursion. And as in *The Professionals*, this opposition between terrorism and the 'British way of life' is represented by idealised images of rural and upper class England on the one hand, and by making the terrorist leader a German. As the narrative progresses, however, the framework established by this opening is rendered increasingly problematic.

On the one hand, the characterisation of the group's leader, Irene Kohl, reinforces the terms of the official perspective. She is consistently depicted as fanatical and ruthless. She shows no sympathy whatever for the kidnapped boy and the fear he feels. She sees him simply as a bargaining counter, necessary for the achievements of the group's political aims, but dispensable if things go wrong. And the fact that she is a woman is constantly used to underscore the official view that terrorism is 'unnatural' and dehumanising. On the other hand, the characterisation of the Irish member of the group, Danny Connors, leads in the opposite direction. He shows considerable sympathy for the boy's distress and eventually establishes a friendly relationship with him. He is portrayed as an essentially decent man who has been led astray by political idealism, but his choice is presented as entirely intelligible given the history of the British ruling class's treatment of the Irish people. This point is made quite early on in the narrative as Danny is handing the boy his evening meal of meat and potatoes.

Danny: That's yours. You should be grateful for it. At least it's cooked. During the famine in Ireland the people were eating potatoes raw and rotten, that's when they had any at all. The Brits, they owned all of Ireland, did you know that? And because the people couldn't pay their rents, 'cause they had nothing, no food, no clothes, nothing, they sent the troops to tear down their homes so that the landlords could have their land back to do what they liked with, Irish land. Didn't teach you that at school did they? No, I bet they didn't.

This contrast between the depiction of the terrorists as fanatical and inhuman on the one hand and as human but politically motivated on the other is never resolved and remains a permanent tension within the text. But the larger and more significant fissure opens up around the presentation of the forces of law and order.

Since the kidnap is classified as a crime the investigation is the responsibility of the relevant section of the regular police force commanded by Chief Superintendent Meadows. But because of the political status of the boy's father, Captain Percival of the Secret Intelligence Service is also assigned to the case. Meadows represents the rule of law and due process. His overriding concern is to return the boy safely to his parents and bring the kidnappers to justice. Percival on the other hand, is primarily concerned with eradicating terrorism and he is quite prepared to go behind the back of the law to achieve this. In the ensuing conflict between the two men, the normal connections between law and order are prised apart and the effective maintenance of order is presented as potentially *at odds* with adherence to legal processes. This tension is made explicit in the scene where Meadows' deputy, Inspector Clarke, hands Percival the ransom note the police have received from the terrorists.

Clarke: Sir, the actual ransom demands, they seem to me to be very moderate.

Percival: Oh indeed! Who apart from someone like myself isn't prepared to give a million pounds to Amnesty International and an awful lot of people would enjoy seeing the Prime Minister confessing on television to her crimes and those of her predecessors . . . whereas for the H-Blocks no-one really cares about them except a few Irishmen who would support the kidnap anyway. So that's clearly a bargaining counter. Expendable, but that's their strength. The terrorist can compromise. The state cannot. The State can no more compromise a little bit than a woman can get a little bit pregnant . . . As you may be aware inspector, terrorism is about propaganda. Giving the impression that the state is unable to protect the things it cares for most. It doesn't matter too much what they are or who they are, politicians, or industrialists like Aldo Moro and Hanns-Martin Schleyer, a pub or a dance hall in Belfast, the Israeli athletes at Munich, even President Kennedy.

Clarke: All the same, you'd have thought they would have made better demands than, well, those.

Percival: Not at all. They don't want to change the state, they want to destroy it, or rather, make it destroy itself.

Clarke: Well then, why not ask for more?

Percival: Because if they make demands like these, which the man on the Clapham omnibus and even you regard as reasonable, the state in responding as it has to, must either disregard public opinion or surrender. Must either appear tyrannical or impotent.

Clarke: Yes, but even a democracy has an enormous amount of power.

Percival: Yes of course, but it must not be seen to use it. Democracy has deep roots but very delicate fruit.

Clarke: So delicate, that in the end terrorism is bound to win?

Percival: Not necessarily. The terrorists may choose the game, we make the rules.

Clarke: The fact that a child's involved, the Superintendent will want the heaviest sentence that the law can hand out.

Percival: Oh I do hope it doesn't come to that. After all, they specifically say they're at war with us and in a war one doesn't have to take prisoners.

This dialogue encapsulates the essential dilemma that liberal democracies face in balancing force against consent, order against law. Either the state can play by its own rules and bring the terrorists to trial thereby giving them a platform for their views and an opportinity to mobilise public opinion. Or it can violate its principles, dispense with due process and eradicate the terrorists without a trial, thereby undermining the popular consent on which its legitimacy rests. The solution to this dilemma is to kill the terrorists clandestinely, away from the glare of publicity. To retain popular consent the law must operate in public and justice must be seen to be done, whereas force is best exercised in secret so that the repressive fist within the democratic glove remains concealed.

This tension is central to the climax of the narrative and is strongly underscored in another interchange between Percival and a police inspector, just before the final action sequence.

Inspector: You'd rather they were all killed wouldn't you?

Percival: In an ideal world yes. I'd rather there wasn't a trial. Inspector Clarke knows my views. Acts of terrorism per se are quite pointless. Terrorism is about propaganda.

Inspector: Yes I know that.

Percival: So to give a highly articulate terrorist the publicity of a trial which would be the main story in the media for weeks is rather like giving a kleptomaniac free run of Harrods.

Inspector: Under the rule of law we have no alternative.

However, as Percival has hinted earlier, there is an alternative – licenced murder by the agents of the state – and that is the solution he chooses.

The terrorists have been tricked by a fake broadcast into thinking that their demands have been met. Meadows aims to arrest them as they leave the 'safe' house. But unknown to him, Percival has surrounded the house with a crack para-military unit. As the group step into the street, he gives the order to shoot them in cold blood. The boy is unhurt, but Meadows is outraged.

Meadows: (to Percival) You bastard!

Percival: Why? The woman was armed, she was going to kill the child.

SAS operative saves boy hostage, in the BBC1 series 'Blood Money

Technically, Percival is correct, but since he has made it clear from the beginning that saving the boy's life is secondary to eliminating the terrorists, the audience is invited to read his remarks as a somewhat flimsy and inadequate justification for judicial murder and the abandonment of the rule of law. This is the last exchange of dialogue, and the narrative ends on an ambiguous note with Meadows turning his back on Percival and walking away. Although the tension between order and law is resolved, the nature of that resolution is presented as highly problematic and open to question. These same issues, of state-instigated violence and of the role and nature of the intelligence services, are also central to *A Spy at Evening*, a four part serial adapted for television from a secret service thriller using a puzzle plot in the John le Carré mould (BBC1 2–23 April 1981).

Inside the 'secret state': from force to terror

The action is set in Britain in the immediate future of the mid-1980's. The economic situation has continued to deteriorate and the country is entering a period of protracted political crisis. There has been a spate of bombings, most of them attributed to an international terrorist group calling itself Red October. (In the novel the group is called Red Banner. The change of name is significant since it gives the audience advanced notice of the Soviet connection which is central to the denouement of the plot). The government has proved totally ineffectual in dealing with the situation and people have begun to protect themselves by forming vigilante groups and private armies. The largest and best organised of these is Action England, headed by a Second World War hero, General Considine.

The central character, Tom Hart, has been recruited into the secret service straight from Cambridge but his once promising career has gone steadily downhill as the pressure of the job has taken its toll on his personal life and his personality. As the story opens we find him with a serious drink problem and suspended from active duty for having botched his last mission by nearly beating an innocent man to death in an attempt to extract information. Despite this, he still wants to work his way back into favour and get his old job back. For the moment though, he is confined to routine courier assignments. The narrative begins with him going to the Tower of London to collect a list of the Red October leadership from a contact in the Soviet secret service. (It is assumed that both sides have a vested interest in eradicating terrorism since it is a rogue factor which disturbs 'normal' relations).

Driving back in a taxi, Hart passes a pub that has just been bombed and this allows the taxi driver to express reactionary populist sentiments:

Taxi Driver: ... What about that pub eh? What sort of lunatic does that? I know what I'd do with 'em if I was this bloody government I'll tell you.

Hart: What would you do?

Taxi Driver: I'd hang the bastards for a start, or shoot 'em. Locking 'em up's no good is it? Oh, and I'd bring in that detention law like they've got abroad. We're getting just as much of it as they are.

This populist discourse is forcefully reiterated later on, in a scene where Hart is detained by an Action England road block along with a small shopkeeper, a jeweller.

Jeweller: All these mad bastards on the loose everywhere, can't go on like it can it? I think they (Action England) are doing a good job here. Reminds me of my National Service. I told them I wouldn't mind doing a bit of it myself if they're going to go on with it. I don't want to sit about waiting for the government to get their fingers out. I told them, 'you're doing a good job here. Keep it up. Anytime you want me to shoot one of these mad bombers just let me know' and I would too.

Hart however is not convinced. He is a democrat at heart and finds it hard to believe that private armies are the answer to our problems. On the contrary he sees Action England's right-wing challenge to the state's legitimate monopoly of force as a greater threat to democracy than left terrorism. However this point is put less forcefully in the television version than in the original novel where Hart is explicit that:

'as many people like myself saw it, the greatest danger in all these developments was the lurch to the Right in public attitudes. While no one imagined that Red Banner would ever achieve control in any European country, yet daily, it now seemed, we were hearing of the formation of local vigilante groups all demanding police recognition, the power to stop and search and the right to carry arms.'[40]

But Hart also has doubts about the state's own use of force and the legitimacy of defending democracy by escalating repression. As he tells Lady Considine:

Hart: You're not in uniform in the Cold War but the principle is exactly the same. It's unquestioning obedience to superior officers, to orders, to duty.

Lady Considine: And you think you were wrong?

Hart: I don't know. I think the way you fight for something is as important as why . . . I know we can't use the weapons of a tyrant and hope to preserve democracy.

While Tom Hart's characterisation as an agent with scruples allows space for the articulation of alternative views, the oppositional perspective is firmly screened out. It is articulated only once in the course of the narrative, in the form of an argument in a pub between Hart and Kevin, a young left-wing militant. But the crude presentation and Kevin's identification with the 'infantile left' immediately discredits it.

Kevin: The only thing that makes anyone sit up and take notice is a good loud bang. Who needs a vote when you've got a stick of gelignite. Look, all they're doing is demonstrating the impossibility of the capitalist structure. They've got to use the same weapons that's all. Look at the IRA. They couldn't stop them could they? It's fifteen years since it started up again over there and it's still going on. It's the same principle isn't it?

Hart: And what principle's that?

Kevin: Well it's obvious isn't it? Failure of repressive measures to defeat a determined cause, that's all.

Hart: What do you call repressive sonny?

Kevin: Oh come on. Torture, beatings, internment without trial, tanks out on the streets. It's the death throes of the Establishment isn't it? And about time too.

Hart: You've been reading too many left-wing comics.

Kevin: Yeah. What have you been reading then? *The Daily Telegraph*?

Hart: What sort of a society do you think a bunch of mindless killers like Red October's going to give you?

Kevin: Red October is about the destruction of property, vested interest. They give warnings. If the Establishment chooses to ignore these warnings and people get killed, it's so they can get a bunch of middle class grocers like you all steamed up about it and voting Tory again. Got it?

At this point Hart punches him viciously in the stomach and walks away. However, the suggestion that there may indeed be a conspiracy within the Establishment is not something he can shrug off so lightly and the rest of the narrative is taken up with his search for the source of the conspiracy. At first he suspects that the terrorism attributed to Red October has been instigated by the Right in order to mobilise popular support for the neo-fascist programme of Action England. But gradually he discovers that the conspiracy originates *within* the secret service itself and is being masterminded by his immediate superior Stevens, who is a Soviet 'mole' dedicated to the overthrow of western democracy. He has organised the acts of terrorism attributed to Red October and used Action England to undermine the legitimacy of the elected government.

This resolution provides a 'tight' ending which utilises the stock conventions of the Cold War thriller to place the narrative firmly back within the terms of the official perspective and to close off speculations that the use of terror may be a normal and *systematic* feature of the democratic state's operations, rather than the work of the occasional renegade functionary employed by a hostile power.

However, it is precisely this possibility that is explored in *Psywarriors* (BBC1, 12 May 1981).

Interrogation scenes from 'Psywarriors'.

The play is set in a high security installation whose existence is known only to selected members of military intelligence and senior Ministry of Defence personnel. The action opens with two men and a woman being brought in for questioning. They are suspected of having left a bomb in an Aldershot public house, popular with soldiers from the nearby army camp (a scenario based on an actual incident). Within the unit normal legal rights are suspended. The suspects do not have the right to call a lawyer or to inform their family or friends of their whereabouts and they can be detained without being charged or brought to trial.

The play's opening scenes display the full range disorientation techniques employed in modern interrogation. The group's leader is stripped naked and made to stand against a wall with his legs apart and a black bag over his head for hours on end. Later, he is led away blindfolded and taken up in an army helicopter and pushed out of the open door. In fact he is only a few feet from the ground but he is told he is over the Thames estuary. The second man is kept in a cage in a white-tiled room under constant glaring light and his regular patterns of sleep are interrupted by bouts of intensive interrogation. The woman's head is covered by a black bag smelling of vomit. She is forced to eat repulsive food, and when she asks to go the toilet she is forcibly marched there. These techniques of sensory deprivation and psychological warfare are all drawn from official reports of the British army's operations in Northern Ireland and elsewhere, but by displaying them in a particularly graphic way, the play forcefully raises the question of how far the state is justified in suspending basic human rights in the interests of securing confessions and information from suspected terrorists.

Thus the audience is invited to believe that they are watching a play about the way in which the state deals with possible terrorists, but the author then proceeds to overturn this assumption in order to raise less obvious questions about the legality and legitimacy of the state's operations in relation to terrorism.

After the initial interrogation scenes, the action cuts to a meeting between the directors of the unit and a visitor from the Ministry of Defence. It is revealed that the 'suspects' are not in fact terrorists at all, but army volunteers who are being tested for possible recruitment to an elite anti-terrorist unit. The training exercise the play presents, requires them to assume the identity of terrorists in order to understand their situation and motivations from the inside so that they will be able to combat them more effectively. This phase of the training programme has culminated in them leaving a live bomb in the pub. But since the exercise is top secret, the police bomb squad were not informed, a fact which once again points up the tension within the state apparatuses revealed in *Blood Money*; a tension between the *forces of law* on the one hand, represented by the regular police force whose actions are open to a certain measure of political and public scrutiny, and the *forces of order and security* on the other, who operate in secret and beyond the purview of parliament. As one of the interrogators tells the group's leader, had the bomb squad failed to defuse the bomb in time, a faked phone call would have informed the mass media that the explosion was the work of the IRA.

Group Leader (looking at a newspaper): 'Bomb Scare at Aldershot', attributed to the IRA.

Interrogator: They haven't claimed responsibility.

Group Leader: What if the bomb had gone off?

Interrogator: Then the Provisionals would have claimed responsibility. Well why not eh? We help keep the terrorist cause in the public eye and the terrorist helps us justify the need for greater security. What's called a symbiotic relationship I believe.

This scene points to several themes within the alternative perspective. Firstly, it suggests that in certain circumstances security agencies are prepared to act as an *agent provocateur* and to instigate acts of terrorism. It also draws attention to the 'secret state's' use of 'black' propaganda. But perhaps even more significantly, it suggests that ultimately, the security services may be less interested in defending democracy than in extending their reach and power, and that they may therefore have a vested interest in the continuation of terrorism; that their relation to terrorism is symbiotic rather than antithetical.

As well as raising questions about the legality of the 'secret state's' operations, the play's structure provides considerable space for the presentation of oppositional justifications for terrorism. The aim of the exercise presented in the play is to get the volunteers to understand the experience and motivations of terrorists from the inside. The narrative depicts two devices for achieving this. The first is to make them take on the persona of terrorists, act out these assumed identities, and experience the possible consequences. The other is to licence the interrogators to act as devil's advocates, putting the strongest possible oppositional case in order to deepen the recruits' insights into the terrorists' motivations and to toughen up their resistance to counter-propaganda.

The oppositional case for terrorism is particularly powerfully put in the scenes between the chief interrogator and the woman. She has begun to crack under the strain and he needs to push her to the limit ideologically in order to find out where her breaking point is. In one scene they discuss the rationality of Ulrike Meinhof's abortive attempt to send her children to be trained as guerrillas by the Palestinians.

Interrogator: A food parcel and a bag of salt are no longer the currency they used to be. For a Palestinian refugee they don't express compassion, only the privilege of the sender. We give them nothing, and we learn nothing. We know nothing of the life in the camps of the Palestinians. We choose not to know. But now, there is Black September. With Black September behind them, within them, they are no longer to be pitied but feared. They have a different identity. Not refugee. Not displaced person. The Palestinian has become a fighter. They have become the enemy. And these people, the enemy, are committed to violence, to killing. It is their last line of defence. They are forced to answer violence with violence. They use their bullets to subdue the violence of the people who exploit them. They see the harvest of this exploitation every day in their refugee camps. They kill to breathe.

Woman: Thank Christ I don't have any children. I couldn't do it. To send your children into the care of people you don't know, foreigners, terrorists, refugees, knowing full well they are to be indoctrinated into the art of maiming, killing, terrorising. It's wrong. It cannot be justified. It's fanatical.

Interrogator: Perhaps it was an act of true compassion, an act of true responsibility. If you had been humiliated for over twenty-five years

... If you were persona non grata according to international law, no identity, no passport, cannot, must not travel, no rights, not even to work, how would you act? How do you think you would act if you were regarded as though you were not really a person at all?

Woman: I don't know how I would react.

Interrogator: That in itself is an expression of privilege. Perhaps Ulrike Meinhof traded her privilege for compassion, sent her children to the Palestinians instead of a food parcel. What would you send?

Although this is the strongest and most direct justification for the Palestinian cause among the programmes we analysed, it is not entirely exceptional. As we saw earlier in the discussion of actuality presentations, the Palestinian situation fits somewhat uneasily into the standard categories of discourse, and this, together with its relative geographical distance, allows for a more 'open' treatment of the issues. Also in *Psywarriors* however, was the presentation of the situation in Northern Ireland in terms derived from the rhetoric of militant Republicanism. This depicts it as Britain's last colonial war and presents the IRA's campaign as a guerrilla offensive against an army of occupation who consistently violate human rights in the defence of an exploitative colonial power.

Chief Interrogator (addressing the woman volunteer): Mau Mau, EOKA, the NLF, the IRA. I've spent the greater part of my working life watching British troops being pulled out of places they were never going to leave. A long hard line of colonial campaigns, and on every campaign the British used internment, concentration camps, and intensive interrogation, torture-sticks up bums, bums on blocks of ice, licking the bowl clean, nudity, humiliation, running round in circles and pissing in the wind. You name it, we've inflicted it, I've inflicted it, the Empire, your heritage . . . What you see in Ulster is the rear end of the cruelty and exploitation of over thirty colonial wars. The last colonial battlefield. A dog devouring its own tail. When it reaches its arse it will be in England.

Faced with this ideological onslaught the woman has no defence and is dropped from the training programme. The second man is found to be unstable and untrustworthy and is also dropped. The group leader however comes through the ordeal with flying colours and is offered the job of heading the new anti-terrorist unit in the field. But he refuses and resigns his commission claiming that he no longer wants to be part of a service that does to people, even suspected terrorists, what has just been done to him.

From fiction to actuality: differences and continuities

In these last two chapters we have tried to show how the major programme forms employed in television journalism and fiction offer a range of different ways of presenting terrorism and the state's responses to it. These are summarised in Table 2.

Although our analysis is exploratory and limited we hope we have done enough to indicate that these differences are more important and complex than the simpler Right-wing and Left-wing critiques of television's presentation of contemporary affairs would suggest. As well as highlighting the variations in programme forms however, we hope our work also points to some interesting similarities in the way particular forms of journalism and fiction handle the issues. The standard devices of the action-adventure series for example, combine to produce the same stress on dramatic events and

Table 2: Actuality and fiction forms compared

audience reach	extended		restricted
Journalism	news stories	current affairs	'authored' documentaries
Fiction	action-adventure series	serials and serialisations	single plays
Programme space	relatively closed		relatively open

the same privileging of official perspectives as in news coverage. On the other hand,the space allowed for extended interviews and investigative reporting in current affairs programmes parallels the greater openness provided by the narrative structure of serials. And the ethos of authorship which underpins the playwright's licence to dissent and provoke extends the same privileges to personal documentaries.

Looking across the whole spectrum of programme forms employed in British television, we can see a range of spaces and openings for alternative and oppositional perspectives. How often and how extensively they are actually used however, depends on the complex network of external pressures and institutional controls that govern programme making. Consequently, the next chapter is devoted to an analysis of these constraints and the way they work.

Chapter 4

The British way of censorship

The official line on political violence may set the terms of reference in most types of television programme, but it does not usually hold exclusive sway. The more we move away from the most popular forms of television, the more complex the interplay of views becomes. However, although television has the potential for representing alternative views, and very occasionally, even oppositional ones, how this space is used needs to be seen in the wider context of state propaganda warfare strategies, and the various forms of news management and censorship currently in play.

British broadcasting has been severely limited in its coverage of political violence, as the record on Northern Ireland shows, but it has been more than a simple conduit for official views. There are real divergences of interest between broadcasting and the state. While the state wishes to secure predominance and complete credibility for official views on television, it is hampered by some genuine barriers. Broadcasting, while politically and financially dependent upon the state, does nevertheless occupy the public sphere, in which it is legitimised by an ideology of 'independence' and of public service. It simply cannot afford to be seen as a subordinate apparatus of the state as its identity, especially in the case of BBC, is underpinned by its claim to be a national forum for competing views, some of which inevitably conflict with those of the government in power.

In certain respects therefore, the way in which broadcasting has been constituted historically offers some scope for certain kinds of dissent, much hedged about with restrictions and conditions, it is true.

When any given government attempts to mobilise broadcasting, therefore, it needs to face the fact of television and radio's relative institutional autonomy from the state. Naturally, these conditions are not immutable, and shifts towards a stronger state and increased privatisation are likely to erode further the public sphere within which broadcasting currently operates. Nevertheless, any explanation of the degree of openness – however limited – which presently exists in covering contentious questions such as political violence, needs to begin by taking account of the considerations just outlined.

Varieties of war, degrees of censorship

The extent to which the state can effectively censor broadcasting and other media during an armed conflict varies considerably. It is important to distinguish what has happened during a total war (World War II), limited engagements (the Suez Crisis, the Falklands adventure), and a counter-insurgency campaign within the national territory (Northern Ireland). Each of these has occupied a distinct position on the sliding scale of state control.

At the present time, one of the state's great problems in its efforts to win the propaganda advantage in the 'war against terrorism' in Northern Ireland, derives precisely from the fact that it is not waging a war as such. There is no general mobilisation, nor is there a large enemy power to be defeated. Rather, in Robert Taber's felicitous phrase, Britain has to contend with the war of the flea.

Total war simplifies matters. It allows the liberal-democratic state to exercise control over the production of news, without thereby risking the legitimacy of the system because in national emergencies security prevails over free expression. Moreover, if, as has been the case in Britain, such centralised control is exercised in a way which permits an 'apparently unimpeded and unguided flow of information'[1] then so much the better for the state's credibility in the propaganda war.

During World War II, after a rather inept start, a centralised system of censorship and propaganda was developed within the Ministry of Information. Control of news in all its forms was seen as central to the war effort. John Reith, the BBC's first Director-General, and briefly Minister of Information, described news as 'the shocktroops of propaganda'. The government operated a system of pre-censorship and guidance for the press, labelled 'voluntary censorship', a neat touch of newspeak which survives, slightly modified, today. It is noteworthy, given the emphasis attached to the impact of broadcasting, especially television, in contemporary discussion, that even forty years ago the BBC and the newsreel companies were the objects of special controls.

The newsreels, precursors of today's TV news, were thought to have a unique effect because of their visual quality. Throughout the war the BBC was controlled by exceptional powers. Although the corporation remained formally independent, this was a matter of form rather than of substance. Placed under the guidance of the Ministry of Information and with government advisors in key positions inside broadcasting itself, the BBC was in fact linked to the government machine. And it is hardly surprising that the corporation saw itself as having a central role as the Voice of Britain fighting the war of words.

Nevertheless,the BBC was not simply the government's mouthpiece, and was given considerable leeway by the Ministry of Information in making its own decisions, some of which resulted in parliamentary rows. The fact that government control was uneven and inconsistent reinforced the BBC's claim to independence and was a potent propaganda weapon, providing legitimacy for the BBC's domestic and overseas broadcasts which were seen as more reliable, accurate and objective than those of Germany.[2]

But limited engagements do not permit the exercise of such far-reaching government powers. During the Suez affair in 1956, the Prime Minister, Sir Anthony Eden, defined the situation as a war-time one, and therefore objected deeply when the BBC insisted on broadcasting newspaper criticisms and the views of the Labour opposition over the invasion of Egypt. There is some dispute over whether Eden planned to 'take over' the BBC. He could have invoked already existing powers under the Corporation's charter to veto specified items. However, given that national security was not threatened and given the existence of deep public and political divisions over the Suez adventure, the Corporation was able to resist government pressures.[3]

During the recent Falklands adventure in 1982, the BBC was once again the principal target of government attacks because of its exposed nature as the major producer of news and current affairs programmes and its peculiar status as a 'British' institution. The media in general were subject to Ministry of Defence security regulations. But the management of censorship as a whole, as the evidence to the Commons' Defence Committee inquiry has revealed, was rather haphazard and ill organised. Technical problems for correspondents in the field were compounded by sheer obstructionism on the part of the Ministry of Defence and the armed forces. All the techniques of news management were employed in addition to a system of double censorship both in the task force and in London, which, together with disinformation, meant that the government had a tight grip on how the war was reported. The journalist Robert Harris has remarked that 'the Government had unique control over how the war appeared on television. Because there were no satellite facilities, the MoD could regulate the flow of pictures and deodorize the war . . . '.[4] When *HMS Sheffield* was sunk – the first British loss – the extent of government control was evident in the television coverage. Harris describes it thus: 'the terse official statement in London, the restrictions on filming and reporting imposed by the Navy, the use of non-televised question-and-answer sessions to minimize the impact of bad news, the painfully slow progress home of pictures, so that they were of little more than historical interest by the time they arrived.'[5]

The BBC came under heavy attack when *Newsnight* was seen as 'unacceptably even-handed' and unpatriotic for using Argentine film and questioning the extent of British losses. Tory critics of the BBC, including the Prime Minister herself, harked back to World War II standards of 'loyal' reporting when they attacked the BBC's scepticism. The Corporation's chairman, George Howard, while noting that the BBC was not 'neutral between our country and the aggressor', nevertheless argued that the Corporation's duty was to supply 'as much information as possible'.

Further Conservative ire was aroused when, in the most controversial programme of the conflict, *Panorama* had the temerity to air the views of some of those opposed to the war. The BBC was this time accused of outright treachery and its Chairman and Director-General designate, Alasdair Milne, were given a mauling at the Commons by the Conservative Party's backbench media committee. Milne's defence of the Corporation was particularly alive to the distinction between different kinds of conflict:

'The notion that we are traitors is outrageous. There is no-one in the BBC who does not agree that the Argentines committed aggression. But this is not total war. One day we will be negotiating with the enemy so we must try to understand them.'[6]

Significantly, it was indicative of the room for manoeuvre which exists in such limited engagements that the BBC was defended by the Labour and Liberal leaders, an SDP spokesman, the Prince of Wales, Tory moderates, and more centrist quality press.

Controls over the media reporting of political violence in peacetime are considerably weaker than those enforced during a full-scale war; they are also a notch down from those applied during limited engagements. However, it is in the interest of the state to suggest that the 'war against terrorism' is *like* a real war, and that therefore, extra 'responsibility', self-restraint and understanding are needed from the media to assist in the state's struggles to preserve order.

From the 1970s onwards, we can discern the gradual piecing together of techniques of control, news management and 'voluntary' agreements between the media and the state. Cumulatively these have come to have an important bearing on the reporting of political violence both on the British mainland and in Northern Ireland.

Gentlemen and their agreements

Perhaps the most striking feature of the state's current approach to controlling media coverage of terrorism is the way in which wartime 'voluntary censorship' has once more resurfaced in quite different conditions. Nowadays, the euphemisms are a little different: 'voluntary self-restraint', 'voluntary self-denial' – formulae which hint at a stern Victorian struggle against one's more bestial tendencies. If we live in peacetime, it is a troubled peace, one in which the state must strengthen its defences against subversion and call upon the understanding and responsibility of the press in the interests of national security. Given the historic tradition of establishment chats in the club, what better way of settling matters than a gentleman's agreement? No need, then, for the state to spell things out in legislation, nor for a public code of practice.

The most significant initiative came from the then Commissioner of the Metropolitan Police, Sir Robert Mark, in 1975. In September that year, Mark held a conference for the media at Scotland Yard with the aim of working out agreed procedures for 'mutual aid' during sieges, kidnappings and hostage takings. It was stressed that the lives of victims should be the paramount concern, and that 'any self-denying measures adopted by the press should apply to all'. A distinction was made between 'commercial' and 'political' offences, political ones being excluded from the agreement. However, as things transpired, this distinction was very quickly revealed to be quite irrelevant in practice.[7]

The policy was rapidly tested at the Spaghetti House and Balcombe Street sieges, and in the case of Aloi Kaloghirou, a girl kidnapped for ransom. All of these incidents occurred in 1975. During the Spaghetti House siege, when black gunmen who claimed political motives held restaurant managers hostage, the media agreed to suppress news of the capture of one of the gunmen's accomplices, as this was helpful to the police.

The media also proved helpful during the Balcombe Street siege, which since it involved the IRA, was of major political importance. ITN's foreign editor, John Mahoney observed that 'all branches of the media gave the story massive coverage, but only within the strictly defined limits of cooperation with the police in their aim of securing the release of the hostages and the capture of the gunmen.'[8] An IRA active service unit was cornered in a flat belonging to an elderly couple whom they had taken hostage. The police knew that the gunmen were watching television news and made sure that BBC and ITN cameras were positioned to show police activity and the lack of an escape route, without at the same time giving too many details of deployment away. When, after four days, power was cut off, the gunmen made use of the radio and the police used this to their advantage. They leaked news of the presence of a squad of SAS marksmen at the scene, as the area was being screened off, evidently prior to an attack, and this was broadcast on BBC radio. According to Sir Robert Mark, the fear of being killed in a fatal shoot-out led the IRA-men to give up.[9]

In the kidnapping case, the police succeeded in achieving a total news freeze for nine days in return for daily press briefings and the story was published only when the girl was finally released unharmed. Such extensive media cooperation was unprecedented. Following the Metropolitan Police's successes, the Home Secretary, then Roy Jenkins, held further informal discussions with the provincial police and media. The Home Office extended the London model to the provincial press in order to 'establish a groundwork of mutual understanding', as Sir Robert Armstrong, Permanent Undersecretary, phrased it. Its guidance circular, issued in 1976, now made no distinction between 'political' and 'commercial' offences, and has been interpreted by some chief constables to mean that they can ask for a news blackout whenever publicity might conceivably endanger life.[10]

Following the Balcombe Street siege, ITN's John Mahoney, referred to the positive achievements of the 'partnership' between media and police. However, his worries about 'the voluntary aspect of the unwritten agreement'[11] being lost were echoed by other editors. The 'Sir Robert Mark Arrangement' was rapidly endorsed by his successor at the Metropolitan Police, Sir David McNee, who also called a conference with a wide range of editors and senior executives in May 1977 which 'examined the aftermath of the Kaloghirou case and explored the possibilities of extending this understanding.' As it turned out, the Yard was 'gratified to find that the understanding was endorsed without exception.'[12] The establishment of such common procedures lay in the background to media-state cooperation during the celebrated Iranian embassy siege.

Television's 'finest hour'?

For some media professionals, such as Alan Protheroe, the BBC's Assistant Director-General, the coverage of the Iranian embassy siege was one of television's 'finest hours'.[13] True enough, millions of viewers watched the denouement of the siege broadcast 'live'.

The moment when the SAS actually attacked, however, was in fact videotaped, and evidently the decision to hold back on live coverage for some minutes on both channels was the result of an 'understanding' with the authorities. The siege bust actuality coverage was pure spectacle without explanation as the commentators at the scene were woefully ignorant of what was happening. This might be thought surprising as, certainly at senior levels in broadcasting, close consultations with the authorities took place, and some top editors, such as Protheroe, had special briefings.[14] Seemingly, the government's intention to use the SAS was not known by reporters at the scene, which is odd, as the likelihood of an SAS intervention on such occasions, where ordinary methods of civil policing had failed, had been publicly known since Balcombe Street. In case editors had been left in any doubt, Lord Harris, Minister of State at the Home Office, had informed them during a private seminar in 1978 that 'the attack on terrorists taking hostages was likely to be made by the SAS.'[15]

Unlike Balcombe Street, despite the dramatic pictures at the close of the siege, television did not, on this occasion, play a major role in keeping the gunmen informed. This time, radio, especially the BBC's news service, was of crucial importance. This was because one of the express objectives of the gunmen was to achieve publicity through broadcasting for their demand for autonomy for the Khuzistan area of Iran. The authorities had an equally clear strategy of preventing them from communicating their demands. One way in which this was achieved was by cutting off all telex and telephone links between the embassy and the outside world: these had been used at first by the media to make contact with the gunmen.

The media as a whole were subject to guidelines issued by Sir David McNee. These requested restrictions on publicising the deployment of personnel and the use of specialist equipment. So far as the authorities were concerned, the broadcasters behaved themselves well during the siege. Home Secretary William Whitelaw said afterwards that there had been no need to ask for 'restraint'. Alan Protheroe, at the time Editor of BBC Television News thought that the authorities ought to have trusted the media more and that there might in future be 'some kind of system where much more information can be given to editors'.[16]

Broadcasting, especially the BBC, was closely involved in the government's management of the siege. Though no-one this time openly spoke of a 'partnership', Alan Protheroe did offer a guarded recognition of the exceptional terms under which broadcasting might work directly with the state:

'I think that any journalistic organisation should resist being used by the state *except in terms of national security*; and except in very, very precise circumstances, and even at the time of the siege we sat back and considered very carefully the requests which came in from the police *and other organisations* asking us either not to do something or to do something.'[17]

As the gunmen had radio receivers, the process of attrition was assisted by delaying the achievement of their publicity objectives. The security forces knew what these were, because, as in the other sieges, they had the building bugged. One of the extraordinary twists in the tale lay in the fact that two BBC television newsmen were among the captured hostages. It was they who transmitted the gunmen's initial demands to their newsroom.

One of these – a demand for mediation by the ambassadors of several Arab countries – was suppressed by the BBC at the request of the British government, which was unwilling to yield its control over the bargaining process. This decision was part of the government's pursuit of a 'no surrender to terrorists' policy which had been developing during the 1970s. It was also part of this policy to develop the SAS's 'counter-revolutionary warfare' role, not just in Northern Ireland, but also on the British mainland itself.[18]

The BBC was more than usually involved because of the presence of its personnel as hostages. It became even more deeply concerned when one of its senior executives was brought into the bargaining process and was instrumental in ensuring that publicity was traded for the release of some hostages. The close cooperation of the BBC and ITN with the security forces could be seen as a further step in the absorption of the broadcast media into the crisis management apparatus of the state on exceptional occasions. Of course, suspicions and mistrust persist, as the Falklands episode has shown, and the process is one of continual negotiation rather than the mythical frictionless conspiracy some believe in. It cannot seriously be doubted, however, that the measure of cooperation achieved during the Iranian embassy siege built upon the earlier agreement initiated by Sir Robert Mark and now being continued by his successors at Scotland Yard and chief constables elsewhere in the country.

An effort has also been made to extend the gentleman's agreement over the coverage of political violence to Britain's D-notice system, though quite with what effect still remains unclear. The D-notices are guidelines on defence matters issued by the Defence, Press and Broadcasting Committee, a body which draws on senior officials from the Ministry of Defence, Home Office and Foreign and Commonwealth Office together with senior representatives of the various press and broadcasting organisations. The *Observer* journalist David Leigh has described the D-notice committee as 'a front-line of censorship for the press on so-called national security matters' which 'involves secret collusion between the press and government officials to keep news from the public'.[19] Others such as

Mr Richard Francis, former Director of News and Current Affairs at the BBC, have seen the committee more positively: 'it is unique in the sense that it represents two separate estates, and in that respect it does require the build-up of confidence, particularly across the table.'[20]

As Mr Francis's remarks indicate, the D-notice committee works on the basis of 'voluntary' censorship. The notices themselves have no legal force and the committee is a long-established peacetime vehicle for censorship, which, during both of the World Wars, was replaced by fully-fledged controls.

In operation since 1912, the committee has fallen into disrepute, being attacked by investigative journalists, civil libertarians and also from within the mainstream media for the way in which it perpetuates cosy establishment links between the media and Whitehall, and for its general ineffectiveness.[21] Despite its own professed dissatisfaction, in August 1980 the Commons Defence Committee recommended keeping the existing system, though with some reforms. In April 1982, the Defence Secretary, John Nott, finally announced the new guidelines. A noteworthy departure was the addition of a reference to terrorism in the 'General Introduction to the D Notice System' under a section labelled 'The need to protect information':

'Hostile intelligence services draw on information from a variety of sources both overt and covert, and by piecing it together can build up a composite picture of a subject. The dissemination of sensitive information can make their task easier and put national security at risk. It can also be of value to terrorist groups who lack the resources to obtain it through their own efforts . . . '[22]

This explicit incorporation of terrorism into the guidelines' general rubric for the first time is not without significance. On one previous occasion the D-notice committee had warned that publishing the names of the heads of MI5 and MI6 could be dangerous should such information fall into the hands of 'the IRA and its various maverick offshoots'.[23] During the presentation of evidence to the Defence Committee, the Permanent Undersecretary, Ministry of Defence, Sir Frank Cooper, also chairman of the D-notice committee, observed that it had been considered too difficult to develop guidelines for the coverage of Northern Ireland and that it was preferable 'to get good journalists and deal with them on a people-to-people basis'.[24]

In 1976, in fact, the Northern Ireland Secretary, Roy Mason, had suggested that a news blackout on 'terrorist activities' in the North would help win the war. He had considered using a regional

D-notice, an idea that was dropped only after his civil servants had convinced him of its impracticality, most notably, that such restrictions could not be used to muzzle the Dublin newspapers. Rear-Admiral W.N. Ash, D-notice committee secretary, however, drew attention at the hearings to the 'upsurge of various different forms of terrorism' and distinguished what could be done in relation to 'Northern Ireland in particular' and 'terrorism in general'.[25] The fact that 'terrorism in general' has now been incorporated into the guidelines suggests that the defence establishment sees some value in placing it on the agenda of a forum in which the media and the state have routine contacts, presumably because chats around the table can always be useful.

'Seminar and discussion country'

Giving evidence at the D-notice hearings, Sir Frank Cooper made the following observation:

'On the whole what you might call the terrorist field in general is one which seems to me very much in seminar and discussion country rather than any clear view emerging as to how best to deal with it in relation to the media generally . . . '[26]

In some respects the various talking shops may be seen as yet a further extension of how the gentlemen reach their agreements, or, at least, disagree within acceptable boundaries.

'Seminar and discussion country' is characterised by the fences which surround it and the 'No Admittance' sign at the gate. The meetings which have taken place have been of a semi-private nature, and have proved sufficiently attractive to draw in some very influential and busy participants: ministers, senior civil servants, police chiefs, academic specialists, counter-insurgency theorists, editors of major newspapers, senior broadcasting executives, prominent journalists. It is in these circles that virtually all of the debate has been conducted and as such it can hardly have been said to have involved the wider public. While it should not be thought that the representatives of these different institutions take a uniform view of the problem of 'terrorism and the media', there is, nevertheless, a common underlying assumption: such encounters are seen as a constructive way of keeping lines open, and despite real differences of view, regular consultation on neutral ground is thought to help resolve emergencies when they arise, because the people concerned will know one another. It is quite consistent, therefore, that the convening and organisation of the continuing discussion should have been in the hands of private establishments rather than state bodies.

The London-based International Press Institute (IPI) has been especially active in promoting contacts, and other bodies have dabbled in the field, notably the Institute for the Study of Conflict, the Royal United Services Institute for Defence Studies and latterly the Centre for Contemporary Studies. For the most part the content of the discussions has hardly been easily available. Two of the IPI's conference reports are labelled 'Not for Publication', one of them also bearing the legend 'Strictly Confidential'. Other publications are expensive, obscure or require access to a well-stocked library. Entry to the conferences themselves is either strictly by invitation or beyond the pocket of most individuals.[27]

IPI's conferences in the late 1980s seem to have been the most influential in building up contacts both at national and European levels, and the Institute's initiatives took place when the 'Europeanisation' of the anti-terrorism campaign was first gathering steam. In November 1977 it organised a one-day conference in London on 'Terrorism and the Media', attended by editors, government officials and senior police officers. Sir Denis Hamilton, chairman of IPI's British Executive, disclosed that the initiative for the conference had actually come from Sir Robert Armstrong, Permanent Undersecretary of State at the Home Office, 'who had said it was the kind of dialogue he would like'.[28] The main address came from Lord Harris, who said that the government could not defeat terrorism without the cooperation of the media and indicated the kind of help he had in mind:

'I would not for a moment advocate a policy of total silence. That would be absurd. I have heard the theoretical case that since the object of terrorism is publicity, and that if the media ignored terrorism altogether, it would stop. But in the real world this kind of approach is not remotely practicable. Nevertheless, I hope that we can ask you for your discretion, and sometimes your silence, on particular matters.'[29]

The main examples she had in mind involved keeping quiet about tactical moves which would reveal to terrorists that they were about to be attacked and not publicising the tactics used after the event.

The IPI subsequently organised two further major meetings in 1978, one in London, the other in Florence, both of which were again addressed by Lord Harris. The London conference, on 'European Terrorism and the Media', was attended by over one hundred delegates from 15 countries, and drew upon the same circles as before. The conference chairman, Sir Edward Pickering, observed that the conference had made it possible to envisage an extension of contacts 'on a European and international scale'. He was backed up by the Home Office's Sir Robert Armstrong who pointed out that 'in

the European Community there were exchanges between the authorities, governments, the media and the police' as well as by the IPI's
Director, Mr Peter Galliner, who urged that 'all those concerned
with combating terrorism should have a close relationship and
understanding with the media'.[30] Subsequently, discussion of the
media's role in 'the defence of democracy against terrorism' has
taken place at the Council of Europe.[31]

Taking sides

The gentlemen's agreements over 'terrorism in general' have
evidently worked rather well, and look likely to hold. But an event
such as the Iranian embassy siege, however dramatic, is merely a
critical and fairly self-contained episode. The Northern Ireland conflict is on another plane altogether: it calls into question the very
integrity of the state. Since 1969, Britain has been engaged in a con-
tinuous counter-insurgency campaign. Propaganda has been central
to this, and in the pursuit of its goals the state, as in previous colonial
campaigns, has frequently had recourse to dirty tricks, fabricated
scare stories, cover-ups of excesses by the security forces, and the use
of smears against opponents.[32]

The media have been of key importance in fighting the propaganda war, and television, as the medium with the largest news
audiences and the highest credibility, has been regarded by all sides
as of particular importance. Without doubt, in the debate about
censorship, broadcasting has figured far more centrally than the
press. This is because broadcasting, particularly the BBC, is legitimised by an ideology of public service under which it is seen as owing
obligations to the community as a whole. As during other conflicts
this wider view of its role implies a tense relationship with the state if
governments conceive of broadcasting's primary duty as an instrument in the battle against the internal enemy. At issue, therefore, is
the extent to which broadcasting has been permitted to engage in a
serious investigation into the roots of the Northern Irish crisis,
expose the shortcomings of state policies and provide an intelligible
account of oppositional views.

The televising of 'terrorism' in Northern Ireland is subject to the
limitations imposed by the double mechanism of continual political
pressure and routine internal self-censorship. The basic rules of the
game were first laid down during the course of 1971, and, with the
passing years, have tended on the whole to become tighter and more
all-encompassing.

In 1971, the broadcasting authorities' formal adherence to the
impartial reporting of matters of controversy was explicitly

abandoned over Northern Ireland. In August that year, Lord Carrington, the Defence Secretary, wrote to the BBC's Chairman, Lord Hill, demanding that he should prevent the repetition of reports 'which are unfairly loaded to suggest improper behaviour by British troops'.[33] Shortly thereafter, in November, Christopher Chataway, the minister accountable to Parliament for broadcasting, turned the demand into a prescription. He said that broadcasters were not required to strike an even balance between the IRA and the Unionist government at Stormont, or between the British army and the 'terrorists'. He reminded them that they should exercise editorial judgement within the context of 'the values and the objectives of the society that they are there to serve'.[34] The speech was a warning to the broadcasting authorities to choose sides.

The BBC's Chairman assured the Home Secretary that the Corporation and its staff 'abhor the terrorism of the IRA and report their campaign of murder with revulsion'. He went on to say that 'as between the British Army and the gunmen the BBC is not and cannot be impartial'.[35] Lord Aylestone, his counterpart at the ITA (predecessor of the IBA) was even more forthright: 'As far as I'm concerned, Britain is at war with the IRA in Ulster and the IRA will get no more coverage than the Nazis would have done in the last war.'[36]

These declarations came at a time when the British army had become increasingly involved in direct conflict with the IRA. Broadcasting was expected to align itself formally with the state in combating its principal enemy. However, although the acceptance of the Chataway prescription has proved a decisive limitation, it is important to recognise that it has not totally closed off all the options available to the broadcasters. Since 1971 there have been sporadic rows, and successive governments have denounced broadcasting's irresponsibility and its reprehensible (and utterly fictive) tendency to peddle 'terrorist propaganda'.

'Reference upwards', or internal self-censorship?

As state pressure for 'responsible' broadcasting mounted, the BBC and the ITA began to develop detailed internal guidelines and supervisory practices which amounted to self-censorship.[37] This approach was rationalised early on by the BBC's Chairman and Director-General as a means of averting outside interference.

Central to the mechanism of self-censorship has been the installation of a process of 'reference upwards', according to which all editors, producers and reporters wishing to produce programmes or items about Northern Ireland have had to take their requests to the highest editorial levels of their organisations. The same applies to proposed interviews with members of illegal organisations. The web of restrictions, moreover, has been woven not just around news and current affairs reporting. From the very beginning, there has been intense sensitivity at the top of broadcasting about the dangers presented by all forms of output, particularly plays and historical documentaries. Far from diminishing with time, the rules have become tighter.

Currently, inside the BBC, programme ideas concerning Northern Ireland, and the Republic of Ireland too, are scrutinised at every level of the editorial hierarchy. First, the proposal has to be cleared with the programme editor, next the head of the department in question. If the topic is at all controversial it will be referred to the most senior news and current affairs executives, and ultimately to the Director-General himself. From the start, the Controller, Northern Ireland has been routinely referred to with highly restrictive implications for coverage; that role was further strengthened in 1979 following the Carrickmore affair, which is discussed below. Any proposal for interviewing a 'terrorist' (essentially the Provisional IRA and the INLA) has to go to the Director-General, a restriction which works as a virtual, but not total, ban.[38]

Whereas the BBC is a unitary organisation, with a single integrated hierarchy, the ITV network has a federal structure. Consequently, reference upwards is different. All programme ideas on Northern Ireland are first scrutinised within the individual television companies, where they are generally referred to the managing director. Advice is sought as a matter of course from the Managing Director of Ulster Television, whose notions of acceptability are much more restricted than his British counterparts. The IBA's Northern Ireland Regional Officer is also involved in the process of consultation. The IBA exercises its right under the Broadcasting Act to view all programmes before transmission, and has the final say on interviews with members of banned organisations. It has made increasing interventions since the early 1970s.[39] On a number of occasions, it has banned, censored or delayed programmes which it felt overstepped the boundaries of the consensus acceptable to Westminster politicians. So has the BBC, but because its exercise of self-censorship is in-house it has not been so glaringly obvious.[40]

As numerous disaffected broadcasters have noted, the general effect of the reference upwards system is inhibiting. David Elstein, formerly producer of Thames Television's *This Week* has written: 'A producer instinctively avoids conflict with his superiors. Sensitive subjects (like Northern Ireland) are avoided. A safe line is pursued.'[41] In similar vein, the BBC television reporter, Jeremy Paxman has observed that 'if you have a referral procedure about stories about Northern Ireland you are asking people to decide beforehand what exactly the story is about and what kind of conclusions you are going to come to.'[42]

The tighter controls have meant that certain topics are virtually off-limits and that reporters and producers have had to make immense efforts to persuade the broadcasting authorities of the need to pursue them. Torture and severe brutality during interrogation have been the prime examples. In the words of television reporter Peter Taylor, 'If Northern Ireland is the most sensitive issue in British broadcasting, interrogation techniques are its most sensitive spot.'[43]

In 1977, for instance, Peter Taylor, and his producer on *This Week*, David Elstein, had a series of clashes with the government, the RUC and the IBA over their revelations of conditions in Long Kesh prison, ill-treatment at the Castlereagh interrogation centre, and a film which reflected upon the divisive impact of the Queen's visit to Northern Ireland. The following year, in June, after increasing hostility towards the programme, the IBA in an act of what Taylor calls 'political censorship pure and simple' banned a programme altogether. This had dealt with Amnesty International's report on RUC brutality towards suspects.

The BBC also encountered similar problems in March 1977, when a *Tonight* report about the ill-treatment of an alleged IRA suspect at Castlereagh was broadcast. The report, by Keith Kyle, a highly experienced current affairs reporter, had involved painstaking investigation into a story which the BBC was not at all keen to air. It received detailed scrutiny by the BBC's highest echelons, including the Governors, before it was broadcast.[44] The report was condemned by the Northern Ireland Secretary, Roy Mason, and by Airey Neave, Opposition Northern Ireland spokesman, as helping enemy propaganda.

To take a rather different example, it has also proved difficult to provide a serious historical treatment of Irish partition as part of the essential background to current events. In 1980–81, two major historical series were broadcast: the BBC's *Ireland: A Television History* and Thames TV's *The Troubles*. Both of these dealt with events after 1968 as well as a considerable span of Irish history. It had taken more than a decade to put this kind of material on the air, and the series were fortunate in being transmitted at a time when political relations between Britain and the Irish Republic were cordial and the 'Irish dimension' was being acknowledged in London. As the times were auspicious, there were no serious rows.

But behind this success lay a long series of acts of censorship. The most stark were those against the historical programmes made by film-maker Kenneth Griffith. In 1973, *Hang out your Brightest Colours*, his biography of Michael Collins, which also examined the circumstances of Irish partition, was banned by the IBA.[45] A subsequent film, *Curious Journey*, which contained interviews with Irish men and women who had fought the British in 1916 and 1918, was dropped in 1980 by Harlech TV after Griffith had refused to remove quotations considered objectionable.

The boundaries of the permissible

Despite the strictness with which the internal rules are applied, there have been significant moments when the broadcasting institutions have been prepared to beard the wrath of the political establishment. Most controversy has surrounded the broadcasting of interviews with members of the IRA and the INLA. On each occasion that this has occurred there has been an entirely predictable response, with the broadcasters being accused by ministers, MPs and the right-wing press of transmitting enemy propaganda, endangering lives by carrying inflammatory statements, and even of treachery. There is a classic *post hoc* style to the orchestration of political outrage, so no-one can be accused of censorship. But, unquestionably, each time such a storm occurs it has an intimidating effect. So far as 'terrorist interviews' are concerned, it would appear that no formal ban is needed because the cumulative protests over ten years have effectively brought them to an end.

Decisions to permit interviews with members of illegal organisations are taken either at the top of the BBC or by the IBA as the concluding point of the reference upward procedure. In a careful analysis of such decisions, Liz Curtis has been able to trace only four occasions on which BBC television has transmitted interviews with current professing members of the IRA or INLA, and four such occasions featuring only the IRA on ITV.[46]

The BBC interviewed David O'Connell, a leading figure in the Provisional IRA once in 1972 and once again in 1974, and has interviewed no IRA man or woman since. Only two other interviews with republican paramilitaries have been transmitted by the BBC, both of which were with the INLA. One of these was on the Northern Ireland current affairs programme *Spotlight* in 1977, and the other was the infamous INLA interview on *Tonight* in July 1979.

ITV's record is much the same. London Weekend Television's *Weekend World* carried two interviews with David O'Connell, one in 1973, and once again in 1974. A unique Thames Television *This Week* documentary in 1974 interviewed three acting or former IRA chiefs of staff, in the wider context of a programme about five years of conflict which also included politicians, British generals and loyalist paramilitaries. Since them, the only IRA appearance has been in a Channel Four documentary on the censorship of Northern Ireland coverage in 1983, but the interviews in question were extracts from foreign television programmes.

It is undoubtedly significant that the Provisional IRA have not been interviewed since 1974. The last such interview, on *Weekend World*, came four days before the Birmingham pub bombings, which were part of a wider IRA bombing campaign that precipitated the passage of the Prevention of Terrorism Act (PTA). During the debate on the PTA, the role of television was of especial concern, some speakers, both in the Commons and the Lords, holding the interview with O'Connell responsible for the Birmingham outrage itself.[47] At the time, the Home Secretary, Roy Jenkins, observed that as the enactment of the anti-terrorist legislation would make the IRA an illegal organisation, he would regard any such future broadcast as inappropriate.

There can be little doubt that, immediately following its passage, the PTA was instantly seen inside television as constituting an effective ban. Michael Tracey's study of *Weekend World* shows how LWT's top management took a very restrictive line right away. Although the IBA was careful to point out that it was not going to introduce any blanket ban it certainly made it clear that it wished be consulted.[48] When, finally, some four years later, *Weekend World* and LWT management went to the IBA to request permission for a further interview with O'Connell (now a leading figure in Provisional Sinn Fein), the IBA's position had become more restrictive and it refused. This was a particularly instructive instance because the interview was part of a programme intended to assess the Provisionals' political and military strength and its implications for Britain's security policy. The IBA questioned LWT's journalistic judgment and its Director of Television, Colin Shaw, noted that 'it is very important that we should avoid any possibility of handing a propaganda advantage to those who would seek to use violence for political ends'.[49] According to David Cox, the programme's editor, it was banned twice before it was allowed on air, three weeks behind schedule.[50]

However, the full inhibiting effects of the Prevention of Terrorism Act only became fully apparent some years, and some rows, later. The INLA interview on *Tonight* in July 1979 would seem to have marked a turning-point. It was the first such networked interview in four and a half years and to date, the last. In Chapter 2, we noted the exceedingly careful way in which it was handled. One can see why. The broadcast resulted in representations to the BBC from the Northern Ireland Secretary, Humphrey Atkins, questions in the House of Commons, a reaction of shock from Airey Neave's widow (heavily emphasised by the *Daily Telegraph*, criticism from the Opposition Northern Ireland spokesman, Merlyn Rees, and Mrs Thatcher's comment that she was 'appalled it was ever transmitted'. Mrs Thatcher asked the Attorney-General to consider taking legal action, and it became clear that he was considering prosecuting the BBC under Section 11 of the PTA, a completely new departure in the relationship between broadcasting and the state. Under Section 11, it is a criminal act not to disclose information to the police about suspected terrorism, with the attendant possibility of five years' imprisonment, or an unlimited fine, or both.[51]

The BBC rapidly found itself in trouble again, this time by merely filming an IRA roadblock in the Northern Irish village of Carrickmore. Again, this led to frenzied declamations in Parliament against the BBC, which had not even transmitted the film, and which invariably gives painstaking attention to any decision to screen manifestations of IRA strength under the reference upwards rules. The row deflected attention from the failings of the state's security policy to the ostensible misdeeds of the broadcasters. Again, this had been part of a proposed programme on Provisional IRA strength, a virtually taboo area, which included interviews with leading Sinn Fein members and ex-IRA men. In Parliament, Mrs Thatcher called on the BBC to 'put its house in order', and was backed up by the Labour Opposition. The police – for the first time – used the PTA to seize an untransmitted copy of a television film. The BBC took disciplinary measures against *Panorama*'s editor and the Head of Television Current Affairs, and only action by the National Union of Journalists averted dismissal of the editor. The BBC further tightened up the reference upwards procedures to cover the filming of 'terrorists'. Most crucially, the wider investigation into the Provisionals was abandoned.[52]

The government's views on the PTA finally became clear in August 1980, when, in a letter to BBC Chairman, Sir Michael Swann, the Attorney-General, Sir Michael Havers, said that he thought that both the INLA interview and the Carrickmore filming constituted offences under Section 11. While denying any intent to censor, Havers accused the BBC of aiding terrorist propaganda, and decried the fact that BBC personnel had not attempted to 'contact the appropriate authorities to pass on the information required' to apprehend or prosecute terrorists.[53] As the government has not chosen to test its opinion in the courts, the legal force of Havers' view remains unclear. What is apparent, however, is the way in which the intimidatory use of the PTA has moved out of the shadows of 1974 into the harsh light of day in the 1980s. Its use has been an ideal object lesson in how outside political pressure has reinforced the processes of internal self-censorship.

Taking an Irish lesson?

Inasmuch as IRA and INLA spokesmen have virtually disappeared from the television screen, the state has largely succeeded in eliminating the voice of armed republicanism from public debate. However, one problem has been replaced by another. As we pointed out in Chapter 2, the election of Provisional Sinn Fein representatives to the institutions of the state has raised new difficulties. Where no proof exists of membership of an illegal organisation, such individuals can hardly be treated as 'terrorists'. The BBC anticipated this problem when it made it the business of senior executives to determine which individuals might be 'closely associated with a terrorist organisation', for here too, interviews 'may not be sought or transmitted – two separate stages – without the prior permission of the Director-General'.[54]

Precisely who officially is to be regarded as a terrorist depends on the law. The main loyalist paramilitary organisation, the Ulster Defence Association (UDA) is not illegal, despite the fact that its leaders acknowledge sectarian killings. Interviews with UDA figures have been more frequent than those with Republicans, but have generated no protests.[55]

The attempt to draw lines around those who are 'terrorists' and those who are not does not resolve the problem of how to deal with those who are ambiguous figures. In practice, with the election of Sinn Fein members to representative bodies in Northern Ireland and to Parliament, the problem has been resolved by using the hostile interview technique. Whereas the broadcasters can hardly refuse to give airtime to elected representatives, they can give it in an exceptional framework, and thereby signal the questionable status of the interviewee, thus warding off political criticism. For its part, the government can hardly insist that these are purely 'terrorist voices' to be kept off the air. The situation could only once again become quite unambiguous if it moved in an even more restrictive direction.

A model periodically advocated, mainly by politicians on the Right, and, for instance, by the *Daily Telegraph* following the INLA interview, is the one currently in force in the Irish Republic. There, legal provisions under Section 31 of the Broadcasting Act have been used to introduce a complete ban on the broadcasting of interviews with the IRA and Sinn Fein. Until 1972, the rules had allowed some leeway, and the Irish broadcasting service, RTE, transmitted an interview with the Provisionals' chief of staff, in November that year. As a result, the entire RTE authority was sacked and the reporter who had conducted the interview was jailed.[56]

The new authority introduced a set of unambiguously restrictive guidelines which completely banned the broadcasting of interviews with the Provisional and Official IRA. They also imposed tight reference upwards procedures for proposed interviews with Provisional and Official Sinn Fein.[57] A further step was taken in October 1976, when Dr Conor Cruise O'Brien, the Irish Minister for Posts and Telegraphs, banned interviews with members of Provisional Sinn Fein altogether. Liz Curtis notes that the 'directive also explicitly banned not only interviews, and reports of interviews, with both IRAs, but also with all organisations banned in the North'.

The contrast with British practice is striking. In Britain, the crudity of such direct government intervention has been avoided, and those who call for RTE rules have seriously missed the point of the present arrangements — although they have contributed to keeping alive a cautious atmosphere. The British way of censorship relies upon a mediated intervention which sustains the legitimacy and the credibility both of the state and of the broadcasting institutions. Naturally, this has a price for the state, which has managed to secure only indirect and partial control of broadcasting's output. But it has nevertheless significantly defined the terms of reference under which the broadcasters operate, and in this respect the project of excluding its republican enemies from the air as much as possible has in practice been very successful.

A liberalism for hard times

The most articulate official statement of broadcasting's role in relation to contemporary political violence has come — not unexpectedly — from Dr Conor Cruise O'Brien. Dr O'Brien begins from the argument that 'a liberalism, relevant to the dangers of the day should be concerned to support and strengthen the principle of authority under the law.'[58] Underlying this view is the assumption that the liberal democracies are presently highly vulnerable, especially when confronted by publicity-seeking terrorists. The consequence is that such regimes need to resort to exceptional measures, censorship being one such justifiable means of self-defence. This argument, in turn, has been justified not just pragmatically but also in terms of the principle that since terrorists are essentially irrational it is pointless to try and argue rationally with them, and positively damaging to expose the public to their arguments.

Dr O'Brien has waged something of a crusade against what he sees as the lapses of British broadcasting. It has been pointed out that in Ireland 'O'Brien never saw himself just as the Minister for Posts and Telegraphs. Conscious always of himself as an intellectual and an international intellectual into the bargain, he let it be known that he was not just playing a role in government but a role in history. The role he had selected for himself was the man of intellect, of reason, confronting the forces of irrationalism that beset the country'.[59]

In keeping with this role, O'Brien has consistently intervened in the British debate, such as it is. One of his prime targets has been Richard Francis, former Director of News and Current Affairs at the BBC, and former Controller, Northern Ireland. Until recently, Francis has himself been the main exponent inside broadcasting's senior circles of a kind of 'realistic' liberalism that clashes directly with O'Brien's variant.

Rather than seeing broadcasting as an instrument of the state, Francis has argued that it is part of the 'fourth estate' of the press generally. There has been an undoubted rhetorical overstatement in this since in practice he has supported the general BBC policy of caution and of infrequent forays into issues which are likely to threaten its institutional position. He has also quite expressly endorsed Lord Hill's waiver of the impartiality principle.[60] Nevertheless, whatever might be thought about the limitations of this stance, it has been important in representing the argument that the public interest as defined, respectively, by the state and by broadcasting, necessarily differs.

Francis has repeatedly defended the principle that the views of those fighting the state should be examined as part of a democratic information policy. For instance, following the row over the INLA interview, he said:

'I start from the presumption that the media have a very real contribution to make, in particular, a contribution to the maintenance of the democracy which is under threat, both by providing a forum where the harshest differences of opinion can be aired, and by reporting and courageously investigating the unpalatable truths which underlie the problems of the province.'[61]

This notion of broadcasting as a forum, however, is coupled with a clear recognition of the infrequency with which the principle is put into operation:

'...the simple fact is that the amount of publicity given to the effects of terrorist action is far and away in excess of the highly selective exercise involved in the occasional programme which seeks to illuminate the underlying reasons for these acts.'[62]

O'Brien has found these arguments rather unimpressive. In early 1981 there was an illustrative interchange between him and Francis over the question of journalistic ethics. The nub of O'Brien's argument was this:

'Even if only for the defence of his functional integrity, the journalist should see himself as on the side of the democratic society against its armed enemies. Many journalists do not see it that way. They take a stance that looks very much like neutrality between cops and robbers, police and terrorists, the law and those whom Mr Richard Francis politely calls 'persons beyond the law'. In my view, that amounts to a *trahison des clercs*: betrayal of the very system that enables the clerk to discharge his functions.'[63]

In reply Francis observed that few objections were raised when the press printed statements by terrorists. However,

'when television chooses to use its unique ability to put such people in the spotlight for the public to make its judgment, the moralist is more than likely to say the game has gone too far . . . that television is too potent a medium for such dangerous people to be given access to its platform. But is it a platform or a scaffold?'[64]

He was in no doubt himself that 'the public knows a bad 'un when it sees one'. In evidence he cited a BBC audience survey conducted in 1979 following the clamour over the INLA interview, which showed that four-fifths of those asked thought it right to broadcast the item, and that it had increased hostility to the IRA and INLA and made respondents more sympathetic towards the security forces. The survey also indicated that most of those questioned felt the need for such information.

Aside from this kind of exchange, the debate on the nature of coverage has not been lively. Most has been generated during the periodic rows, and has involved very stylised position-taking. Most contributions have come from reporters, producers, and film-makers who have protested about interference with their work. It is only a handful who have gone on record to reflect on their experiences, most prominent amongst them being Jonathan Dimbleby, David Elstein, Kenneth Griffith, Mary Holland, Jeremy Paxman, Anthony Smith, Peter Taylor, Colin Thomas. To Dimbleby must go the credit for being amongst the first to speak out at an early stage, when the self-censorship process was first being instituted. He also, uniquely, succeeded in reviving the debate for a while in 1976 by speaking out during a David Frost show looking back on twenty-five years of television:

'I do not want to go into detail about Northern Ireland, but the fact is that there has not been on British television since 1968 a serious, detailed account of the history of Northern Ireland. And that is because it is very delicate, politically sensitive issue which is very difficult to do adequately on television, and therefore the job has been baulked. It should not be baulked, and the reason why it is baulked is because of the political institutions, BBC, IBA, British Government, British Opposition, who don't wish us to know too much too well about Northern Ireland.'[65]

As against the bureaucratic realism of the broadcasting institutions' practice, the critique from below has really been for greater autonomy and a dismantling of the rigid supervisory structures. As we have seen, such arguments have had no perceptible effect, and if anything, the drift is towards greater control.

What is most striking, viewed in the round, is the limited character of the debate. When the broadcasting authorities have been under most pressure they have generally been supported by newspapers such as *The Guardian*, *The Observer* and *The Sunday Times*, as well as by liberal-minded television critics and organisations such as the National Union of Journalists and the various broadcasting unions. But there has been little in the way of wider popular support or interest.[66] Although the unions have defended their members, and have sometimes criticised the inadequacies of coverage, they have also, on occasion, been seriously divided themselves, especially over their stances on Irish republicanism and the British presence in Northern Ireland.[67] In such circumstances, it has been the establishment-oriented and 'responsible' liberalism espoused by Francis which has been the front line of defence, and that position is likely to come under ever-increasing pressure.

Censoring fictions

It is not just actuality coverage which has been judged dangerous. Drama production has also been affected by the net of restrictions, and as Richard Hoggart has pointed out 'anything on the troubles is very sensitive and involves reference upwards, discussion, sometimes stalling; and so a number of plays have been delayed, denied repeats or relegated to late-night slots.'

Most significant, though, is that very few have been commissioned, and that some, once commissioned, have been dropped.

Writing in 1980, Hoggart found that there had been some 19 plays in 12 years on the 'current troubles, whether about Ulster itself or about the effect of those troubles here in England'. Most drama on the subject, he considered, used 'stock characters and stock attitudes' and 'imaginative insights into the complexity of the situation are largely denied us'. 'Terrorists' with rare exceptions were absent from the television play, the result being 'that we are largely denied the help of drama in enabling us to see the fullness of this situation'. He concluded that there was not 'very much evidence of overt censorship' but that writers and television drama heads were definitely engaged in practising self-censorship on the grounds that Ireland was a 'switch-off subject' or 'dangerous' because drama, being subjective, could be 'inaccurate'.[68]

In terms of our argument, the plays which are most vulnerable are those at the more 'open' end of the range of programming, because it is there that drama has the greatest potential for exploring the tensions of political violence. The ideology of authorship, especially within the context of a wider public service broadcasting ethos which formally encourages that form of creativity, provides a certain licence and space for individual statements. However, in the case of plays about Northern Ireland there is a marked bureaucratic caution which takes the road of censorship if a given drama looks likely to rock the boat.

What is noteworthy about *Harry's Game* and *Psywarriors*, is that they were broadcast, although they dealt with themes which have run into censorship problems on other occasions, particularly the vexed question of brutal interrogation techniques and sensory deprivation.

One play which did not successfully clear the hurdles was *Article 5* (1975), commissioned by the BBC from Brian Phelan. They play's title came from the Universal Declaration of Human Rights, which, in one section states 'No-one shall be subjected to torture, or cruel inhuman treatment, or punishment'. It was written with the assistance of Amnesty International. Recorded in January 1975, it was viewed by Aubrey Singer, Controller BBC2, several months later: he refused to screen it. The play was against the use of torture and referred only once to Northern Ireland in passing, as an illustration. According to Singer in 1976 'The play would have caused such offence to viewers that its impact would have been dulled and its message negated'. A year later, the BBC's head of Drama, Shaun Sutton, publicly dismissed the work as a 'bad play'. It is relevant to point out that the BBC's decision was taken at a time when British interrogation techniques were still under investigation by the European Commission for Human Rights, which, the following year, found that they did indeed constitute torture.[69]

Another case which illustrates particularly well a more limited degree of censorship concerns *The Legion Hall Bombing* (1978), like *Psywarriors* a BBC 'Play for Today'. Once again, the play dealt with a very sensitive aspect of the state's activities in Northern Ireland: the Diplock non-jury court system, in which confessions are allowed as evidence, even if extracted by brutal interrogation methods.

The play was based on the trial transcripts of Willie Gallagher, who was sentenced to twelve years' imprisonment for bombing the British Legion Hall in Strabane in 1976, on the basis of his own confession. The director, Roland Joffé has discussed the play's intentions: 'We felt one thing it should ask is what's a terrorist war, what's a terrorist and how does the law make these distinctions.'[70] He also wanted to make clear to a British audience 'how a Diplock Court functions, ergo what the role of the courts is in terms of the state apparatus'.

Not surprisingly, given the contentious subject-matter, the BBC's Head of Plays referred it upwards, and had discussions with the BBC's Director of News and Current Affairs Richard Francis, and with the Controller, Northern Ireland. At one stage, Francis suggested that the play might be put out as a current affairs programme, a suggestion which Joffé resisted as he felt that a play stood a better chance of surviving censorship than journalism, given the conventions surrounding authorship. The director and the writer, Caryl Churchill, quite properly, had to take immense care over the use of the court transcripts, and the entire development of the production was closely scrutinised by the Controller, Northern Ireland.[71]

In the event, despite the precautions, the play's transmission was repeatedly postponed, and the BBC insisted that the original commentary be changed because it 'editorialised'. In the judgment of the BBC's Head of Programmes, Northern Ireland, 'The prologue and epilogue were pure, naked political propaganda. I got the script and I tore [them] off and I said: "Forget it, that's for the birds ... You want to make that kind of statement, go to Hyde Park!"'[72] The prologue was altered and the epilogue completely cut. It ran as follows:

'The Diplock Courts were set up to make it easier to get convictions, and they have been successful. Recent research at Queen's University, Belfast, shows that the rate of acquittals in these courts has dropped steadily in each year. If courts can accept signed statements put forward by the police with no corroborative evidence and reject the evidence of a defence witness without explanation it is reasonable to ask whether it is worth while for the defence to put a case at all.

The courts have a tradition of independence but at the same time they carry out the will of Parliament. In peaceful times the role of the courts is generally accepted. In times of stress their role may change.'[73]

Because of these acts of censorship, the writer and the director made unsuccessful legal efforts to prevent the screening, and, given their failure in this, they insisted on having their names removed from the credits. The play was put out at a later time than normal for the 'Play for Today', its screening was delayed for six months in all, and the original intention of having it coincide with a discussion of the Diplock Courts on the *Tonight* programme was dropped. Once again, it is important to recognise the general political climate at the time: the play was produced at a moment when unpalatable truths about RUC interrogation methods had surfaced, and, as we have seen, had already caused serious problems for *Panorama* and *This Week*.

Bearing these instances of censorship in mind, it is instructive to look once more at *Harry's Game* and *Psywarriors*. The considerations surrounding their commissioning, transmission and reception may be gleaned, if only somewhat obliquely, from remarks made by senior television decision-makers. Paul Fox, Managing Director of Yorkshire Television, has described his worries about whether or not to go ahead with *Harry's Game*, and the circumstances under which it might not be shown:

'I have a play on my desk at the moment about Northern Ireland, and it is a very, very difficult decision to make, whether that play should be made, and when it's made, whether it should be shown. It's an extremely difficult decision, and very delicate . . . I'm concerned that when that play is made, and a transmission date happens, and the transmission date coincides with an attack or a bombing attack in London, what do you do? Do you show that play? Or do you pull the play out? . . . It's written by a newspaperman, it's an exceptionally good script, it's been read by people in Northern Ireland who approve it, and yet I have enormous doubts about it.'[74] This is as clear a demonstration as one could want of how even a popular drama goes through the hurdles of reference upwards.

As it transpired, Fox's fears were groundless, and the three-parter was repeated in June 1983, on a Saturday night, spliced together as a full-length telefilm.

Psywarriors was the subject of a retrospective discussion by the BBC's top management. The observations made give some insights into the difficult negotiations that probably preceded its transmission, and even its commissioning:

'Shaun Sutton (H.D.G.Tel.) thought it necessary for the Service to put on once every two years a play of quality that was also tough. This had been tough, but it had been very carefully edited and well done. C.BBC-1 argued that it had been well performed. He and others considered the later starting time of 10.15pm had not been a second too early. C.BBC-1 said his remaining doubts really concerned the commissioning of such a play. Mr Sutton did not think the element of violence nearly as great as that in the Peckinpah film of the previous week, which had not been universally condemned. Mike Fentiman (Editor, Community Programmes) said all the violence in the play had been totally integrated into the story.

Keith Williams (H.P.D.Tel.) thanked C.BBC-1 for going ahead with the play. All the things portrayed in the film did go on. It had been very carefully researched. Even he himself could recall some of the training involved, in case of enemy capture when he had been a volunteer for the R.A.F. The play was an illustration of man's inhumanity to man; he did, however, accept that the writer did present a viewpoint that was radical rather than conservative . . .'[75]

One noteworthy point is that such plays should be performed only 'once every two years', which one may assume represents an accurate index of how often the BBC's drama bosses think that they can take risks in this area. The Controller BBC-1's doubts about whether such plays should even be commissioned at all suggests an even more pessimistic and restrictive strand in executive thinking, and the passing remark about 'radicalism' hints at another dimension of the complexities. Given the lack of enthusiasm in some quarters it seems reasonable to conclude that the play was helped by the fact that interrogation methods were not a current bone of contention. This again points up an important implication: that the way the television system as a whole is organised does create spaces for trenchant statements running counter to official thinking, but it may be possible to fill them only 'once every two years', under the right political circumstances.

Conclusion

The representation of 'terrorism' on television is constrained not only by the different kinds of programme form available but also by the complex modes of control and pressure which the state and the wider political establishment can bring to bear on broadcasting. This exercise of power is usually discreet, but when it is judged worth having a row, it may take a highly public form.

As we have shown, some areas of potential dispute have been accomodated by recourse to the gentleman's agreement, rather than to a formalised and visible system of intervention in decision-making inside the institutions themselves. It is noteworthy that, even during total war, the legitimising fiction of broadcasting's formal independence from the state was sustained. At a time of lesser conflict, the autonomy of broadcasting is greater, and where the state is waging an undeclared internal war, the unacceptability of overt intervention in broadcasting's practices increases further. Nevertheless, developments throughout the 1970s, whether in relation to a containable single crisis such as the Iranian embassy siege, or whether in relation to the long-running Northern Irish question, suggest that the state has largely succeeded in imposing its terms of reference. To achieve such sway, however, does require continual work, and as some of the rows we have examined indicate, the system is subject to a certain amount of slippage.

We have also sought to demonstrate that broadcasting is not a push-over for the state. The BBC and the IBA have their own long-term institutional needs. Rightly enough, they recognise that their public credibility and acceptance is a crucial resource, and that to sustain these they must at times be seen to diverge from the immediate national security goals of the state. For instance, briefly or not, it became necessary to lift the lid on brutality and ill-treatment in Northern Ireland.

As presently constituted, broadcasting offers several sources of resistance to the blanket imposition of an official perspective. Notwithstanding the limitations of the present system, the fact that it is based in notions of public service is crucial. In the vexed area of political violence it has justified divergences from *raison d'état* on quite distinctive grounds. For instance, the interviews with members of illegal organisations were presented by senior spokesmen as an essential part of broadcasting's social obligation to inform in a democracy. Of course, this was coupled with a ritual denunciation of the enemies of the state. But however hedged about, the commitment to the idea that the electorate is *entitled* to such information is one to build upon.

It is at this point that more radical forms of resistance have come in. The demand for an honest and untrammelled investigative journalism, and for film-making and dramatic authorship which can address issues without continually engaging in self-censorship, have gone beyond the 'responsible' accommodations made by the official spokesmen of broadcasting. Faced with the impossibility of working properly under self-censorship, criticisms from within have periodically surfaced, and are bound to do so again. While, at one level such arguments necessarily criticise the cautious practice of the BBC and the IBA, they are also sources of internal pressure which may add to the institutions' willingness to push further at the boundaries of the permissible.

Outside broadcasting itself, the world has hardly been set alight by these questions. Sympathetic journalists, some trade-unionists in the media industries, a scattering of campaigners and odd intellectuals have spoken out now and again. There are few signs of large-scale popular support in the fight to develop discussion of a highly contentious area which, by raising the question of state repression, inevitably brings to light the contradictions of liberal-democratic politics. Much more effort is needed to ensure that further openings for rational debate and criticism are created in the future.

Meanwhile the arguments for censorship and increased control continue. They rest upon unfounded assumptions about the impact of television, and about the irrationality of the ordinary viewer, as we argue in the next chapter.

Chapter 5

Television: the insurgent's friend?

Roads to reaction

Official thinking on the media coverage of 'terrorism' in western capitalist democracies draws on two main sources: counter-insurgency arguments about the state's need for psychological warfare strategies, and more general assertions about the causal links between popular imagery and social violence. While the counter-insurgency theorists have set the framework for debate, their arguments borrow extensively from a powerful tradition of conservative commentary on popular entertainment dating back to the beginning of the last century. Although this ancestry is seldom acknowledged, its key concepts of imitation and contagion still underpin official views. So, before we dissect the contemporary debate in more detail it is worth pausing briefly to examine the origin of and backing for these ideas.

Popular imagery and contagious ideas

Early conservative fears centred on the popular theatres and 'penny gaffs' which catered for the new urban proletariat with plays that showed state agencies as unjust or corrupt and made selected law-breakers into popular heroes. Commentators were quick to connect the popularity of these shows with the rising levels of crime and political protest since most shared Gabriel Tarde's view that 'one kills or does not kill, because of imitation . . . one steals or does not steal, one assassinates or does not assassinate, because of imitation.'[1] However, critics were careful to exempt themselves from these influences, on the grounds that their superior knowledge and training effectively insulated them from imitation effects. Conversely, they felt that the popular audience's lack of education and judgement made them permanently vulnerable, more easily swayed by dramatic images and emotional appeals, and more likely to act out what they had seen. 'Nothing', proclaimed Le Bon, 'has a greater effect on the imagination of crowds than theatrical representations' and 'sometimes the sentiments suggested by the images are so strong that they tend to transform themselves into acts'.[2] These early critics are seldom quoted now, but their views remain firmly embedded in the conventional wisdom. The idea of terrorism as a form of theatre provoking imitation is still very much part of official thinking. Present-day commentators also continue to apply the double standards of yesteryear. They still exclude themselves from the processes they describe and call for greater controls on media representations in the name of the 'others' who cannot resist.

Imitation effects were not the only dangers early critics detected in popular culture. They felt that glamourised images of law-breaking were seriously eroding popular support for state authority, and from this perspective even public executions presented a problem. It was widely felt that the official rationale of providing a salutary reminder of the state's power was persistently subverted by the performance of the condemned and the positive response of the crowd.

The last public execution in England took place outside Newgate prison in May 1868. The condemned man was Michael Barrett, who had killed 12 people and injured 120 more while trying to blow a hole in the wall of Clerkenwell gaol to release the Fenians held inside. The fact that his crime had been committed in the cause of Irish liberation made his execution a political occasion and gave the Fenians a propaganda opportunity which Barrett was quick to exploit, apparently with some success. As *The Daily News* complained the day after, the crowd's 'bastard pride in his animal courage and the brutal delight that he died game made the law and its ministers seem to them to be the real murderers, and Barrett to be a martyred man'.[3] This assumption, that given the chance popular audiences will identify with 'terrorists' as underdogs and be more than willing to believe the worst about the authorities, also remains a standard part of official thinking.

By the 1870s the popular theatres had been 'cleaned up' and executions moved behind closed doors, though these reforms did little to dispel the fears of conservatives. They now simply shifted their focus to the *Illustrated Police News* and the other commercial papers aimed at the bottom end of the mass market. This new popular press continued where the 'penny gaffs' had left off and provided 'much the same kind of entertainment as public hangings'.[4] Not only did it make reports of crime and social disorder a major feature of its coverage, it presented them with the same stress on dramatic imagery and lurid detail. Moreover, thanks to the new telegraph system, sensational stories could be rapidly disseminated throughout the country and abroad. And, as many observers saw it, this meant that imitation effects could also spread more rapidly and widely than ever before. The process was frequently compared to the spread of contagious diseases, an idea neatly encapsulated in Corre's dictum that 'infectious epidemics spread with the air or the wind; epidemics of crime follow the line of the telegraph'.[5]

The supporting evidence for contagion effects was somewhat thin however. Corre, for example, claimed that the massive publicity given to the details of the Jack the Ripper murders was responsible for a spate of copy-cat killings around the world, including the disembowelling of four negroes in Birmingham, Alabama. This is a classic case of mistaking correlation for causality. The fact that events occur closely together in time does not mean that one is caused or even influenced by the other. They may both be the product of other factors that are common to both situations or they may be totally unrelated. In Corre's case it certainly was not necessary to evoke contagion effects to explain a racial murder in Alabama at a time when the mutilation, lynching and burning of negroes was a standard vigilante activity. But it is characteristic of this argument and of the way it is mobilised in official thinking, that it constantly detaches events from their specific historical and political contexts and regroups them as part of the same general phenomenon because they look the same, employ the same techniques, or occur together in time. By doing so it glosses over crucial differences between them and the situations from which they spring.

The idea of media contagion is still central to current debates and official thinking on 'terrorism' continues to rely heavily on impressionistic evidence and selective examples. Consider this contemporary example from the work of Professor Yonah Alexander of New York State University, a leading figure in 'terrorism studies':

'Several weeks after Argentina's Montoneros removed the body of ex-President Pedro Aramburu to secure the return of Eva Peron's body from Spain, Burmese terrorists stole the body of U Thant for the purpose of using it in negotiations with the Burmese government.'[6]

This is Jack the Ripper all over again. It surely needs pointing out that a particular technique, body-snatching, cannot be considered in isolation from the social relations in which it occurs. We need to specify the mediating conditions which explain *why* such acts occur. It is not enough to assert loose correspondences between actions in Latin America and in Asia with the supposed explanation that the 'theatrical attraction' of the act in one place causes people to do it in another. Why do they do it? Under what conditions? Do they have alternatives? Such questions are simply not asked.

It is true that Len Berkowitz and other interested researchers have tried to provide more systematic support for the contagion

thesis. Their efforts are certainly an advance over the standard assertions but they are not conclusive. The problems are illustrated well
by the study of aircraft hi-jacks conducted by Albert Bandura,
another leading figure in the field. Using government records he
shows that there was a marked increase in hi-jacks in both the USA
and elsewhere after 1967. This leads Berkowitz to conclude that the
publicity given to American incidents 'seemed to influence the hijackings elsewhere' and that 'the contagion spread with the television camera and newspaper headline'.[7] This seems plausible but it
ignores relevant factors. How reliable are the records of hi-jacks for
example? Is what counts as a hi-jack defined consistently at all times
and in all countries? To what extent was the sudden rise in hi-jacks a
function of the rapid growth of airline traffic in the second half of
the sixties? Were the other nations where hi-jacks took place also
countries where US incidents got extensive publicity? The evidence is
not quite as solid as it looks at first.

Despite the technical sophistication of recent research, the argument still depends on detaching incidents from their contexts and
making unwarranted leaps from correlation to causality. Elsewhere,
Berkowitz comes close to admitting this. He concedes that news
reports are not the only factor and that 'contagious influences
operate on top of (other) determinants and probably in conjunction
with them'.[8] But he does not draw the obvious conclusion; that if
media 'contagion' is only one factor among others and not necessarily the most important one, the whole argument for direct and
powerful effects collapses.

These difficulties with the argument have not stopped the
counter-insurgency theorists from taking the contagion thesis as
read. Nor has it stopped them from mobilising it to support calls for
greater controls over reporting, and here too there are strong continuities with the past. On 9 December 1893 for example, August
Vaillant, a badly-paid sugar refinery worker, threw a nail bomb on
to the floor of the French Chamber of Deputies from the public
gallery. No-one was killed but the incident followed an anarchist
bombing the previous year which had left five policemen dead and
created widespread panic in the city. The morning after Vaillant's
bomb one of Paris's leading papers, *Le Journal*, quoted a well-
known celebrity as saying 'What do the victims matter if it's a fine
gesture?' This was widely seen as open encouragement to further
outrages, and the next day the Chamber rushed through a new law
making it an offence to print any direct or 'indirect' provocation to
terrorist acts.[9]

Present-day concerns are now focused on the power of television
but the essential arguments remain the same. Demands for more res-

trictions on the coverage of 'terrorism' are still made, backed by the same appeals to notions of imitation and contagion. Indeed, because television combines the visual impact of popular theatre and film with the mass audience of the daily press, it has attracted and reinforced all the arguments that grew up around these older media. Its privileged place in the debate on 'terrorism' has been further secured by the rise of counter-insurgency theories which see the state fighting a continuing battle for hearts and minds, in which television, as the dominant mass medium, plays a strategic role.

Counter-insurgency and the Cold War crusade

The debate about media reporting of 'terrorism' in Western capitalist democracies has primarily developed in the context of the psychological warfare aims of the state. During the past decade or so, and especially since the mid-1970s, an international conventional wisdom has been elaborated within official and semi-official circles in which the media are conceived as tools which can contribute to, or impede, final victory in the 'war against terrorism'. Although mere expediency might seem to dictate direct censorship in order to deny violent opponents of the state the supposedly clear-cut advantages of publicity, matters are not so simple. Overt censorship threatens the legitimacy of the liberal-democratic order. Therefore it is advantageous for the state to adopt an information policy which integrates the media into a national-security design, while, at the same time, keeping up the appearance of the media's complete independence.

National security doctrines, which define the media as tools to be used by the state, rather than free institutions of a democratic society, are usually thought of as characteristic of dictatorial systems of rule. Indeed, such doctrines have been fully developed in Latin America since the mid-1960s when a military dictatorship was established in Brazil. National security doctrine is founded on a Cold War conception of the world in which Christian, civilised values are under threat from godless communism. Thus, it is argued, the state needs to mobilise for a 'total war' under the leadership of the military, which is best equipped to counter internal 'subversion'.[10]

However, there are other sources of national security doctrine which issue from the heartland of the 'Free World', the United States. In its post-war confrontation with the Soviet Union, the US has made national security and the search for internal enemies a centrepiece of state policy. As part of its 'hemispheric defence' this ideology and its associated repressive practices have been exported to Latin America, not least through the extensive military contacts which exist. A further input into national security doctrine has been the counter-revolutionary ideas developed by the *guerre révolutionnaire* school of French military writers, drawing upon their Vietnamese and Algerian experiences. Of particular note is the emphasis which the French counter-insurgents (in time followed by the Americans, and therefore the Latin Americans) laid upon the role of 'psychological warfare', for which they used the term *action psychologique*. The use of propaganda is a crucial part of winning the 'hearts and minds' of the civil population in any battle between the state and its enemies.[11]

Naturally enough, given its long experience of fighting colonial wars, there is also a British variant of counter-insurgency theory which has much in common with the French school. The most celebrated exponent of British counter-insurgency writing has been General Sir Frank Kitson, whose *Low-intensity Operations*, published in 1971 caused some concern that ideas potentially threatening to democracy were circulating among the British military. Kitson, who drew upon his experiences in Kenya, Malaya and Cyprus, as well as synthesising British, French and American material, subsequently commanded a Brigade in Northern Ireland in the early 1970s.[12]

Subversives everywhere

Kitson offers a generous definition of subversion as 'all measures short of the use of armed force taken by one section of the people of a country to overthrow those governing the country at the time, or to force them to do things which they do not want to do'.[13] 'Insurgency' is when these purposes are pursued by the use of armed force. However, 'non-violent subversion' includes all those activities which others might see as the legitimate exercise of democratic rights: political and economic pressure, strikes, protest marches, propaganda. The very functioning of political life is therefore seen as subversive. Governments, needing to anticipate the worst, are urged to prepare themselves for joint civil, military and police administrations, to shift to exceptional forms of rule as insurgencies become more threatening. Within this broad strategic conception lies the use of propaganda:

'The government must promote its own cause and undermine that of the enemy by disseminating its view of the situation, and this involves a carefully planned and coordinated campaign of what for want of a better word must regrettably be called psychological operations.'[14]

But while Kitson has not developed a critique of how the British media work from a counter-insurgency point of view, there has been no shortage of contributors. Dr Richard Clutterbuck may be singled out amongst the counter-insurgents for having devoted an entire book to this theme *The Media and Political Violence*, published in 1981, with a foreword by Sir Robin Day, doyen of British current affairs broadcasters.[15] Although Day disagreed with Clutterbuck's substantive recommendations, he nonetheless endorsed the book as one to be taken seriously and widely debated. 'Let us make sure', he wrote, 'as Dr Clutterbuck argues, that the heavy armour of television is on the side of reason and the democratic process'.[16] Others have been less flattering. Christopher Wain, the BBC's Defence Correspondent has remarked 'This book lacks substance both in the quantity and quality of evidence offered. Its analysis is unsatisfactory, its conclusions are questionable and its recommendations neither practical nor desirable'.[17]

Clutterbuck's study illustrates particularly well the general shortcomings of counter-insurgency writing. No less than 'terrorism', 'political violence' is a notoriously diffuse term. It could refer to the practices of terroristic regimes, to insurgent terrorism from below, even to a Clausewitzian view of acts of war between states.[18] Clutterbuck, fully in keeping with the canons of counter-insurgency characterises 'political violence' as that which comes from below. Not only is the definition of violence loose, so is the scope of what is taken to be politics.

Clutterbuck lumps together 'violence in industrial disputes; violence in political demonstrations; and terrorism' as instances of the 'political use of violence and disruption'. These, he claims, have been 'used to destabilise parliamentary democracy and to poison the reasonable society'.[19] Clutterbuck groups legitimate forms of political protest together with the use of illegal armed force. This kind of slippery thinking is consistent with the counter-insurgency approach: it is tantamount to arguing for guilt by association, a tactic which he has used elsewhere, when, for instance, similarly associating 'protest and the urban guerrilla'.[20]

The heavy armour of television

Counter-insurgents all agree that the media, and particularly television, are crucial in the battle for 'hearts and minds'. Not surprisingly, given the simple instrumental goals which they pursue, arguments about contagion and imitation are adapted uncritically to their purposes. In a typical formulation a conference report published by the Institute for the Study of Conflict in 1978 opined that the 'mass audience tends ... to lack independent criteria for judgment'. On the other hand, 'by definition, the leaders of society – whether in politics, industry, business or administration ... are the people who have the means of critical judgment'.[21] If an easily-persuaded, irrational mass audience, highly susceptible to televised propaganda, is assumed, it becomes logical to suppose that 'a television programme may be an act of war', and one with seriously negative consequences if the wrong people are in charge. Richard Clutterbuck, fond of the pithy military metaphor, has put it this way:

'In the battle for survival of the reasonable society the television camera is the super tank – the Queen of the Battlefield. Ordinary mortals are wise to learn her ways and treat her with respect, but those who serve in her entourage have an awful responsibility.'[22]

Whether they are talking about its programmes or its technology, therefore, counter-insurgents attribute an immense power to television. The classic example offered to support the power-of-television thesis is that of the Vietnam War. The ISC report's tone is set by quoting an axiom of Sir Robert Thompson's, a celebrated British counter-insurgent with experience of fighting 'communist insurgency' in Malaya and Vietnam. According to Thompson, the Vietnam War 'was lost on the television screens of the United States'.

As journalist Phillip Knightley has noted, 'Television's power seems to have impressed British observers even more than American.'[23] Both in military circles and in some journalistic ones, Sir Robert Thompson's nostrum has become an accepted truth, and this has profoundly conditioned counter-insurgency thinking. Moreover, as Robert Harris has pointed out, it also deeply influenced the media management of the Falklands campaign.[24]

Maurice Tugwell, a former paratroop colonel who was head of the 'Information Policy' department which conducted 'psychological warfare' in Northern Ireland, has also singled out what he calls the 'Vietnam Syndrome'. Tugwell is careful to point up the full subversive potential of the media, taken *en bloc*:

'the United States news media turned what had in fact been a considerable military success for the South into a massive political and psychological victory for the North, one was that was ultimately to contaminate the whole campaign. The power of the media to influence public perceptions of conflict situations and to undermine political will was established, to the satisfaction of radicals and many liberals, and to the chagrin of established power and those responsible for countering violence. The revolutionary basked in the warmth of public admiration, while the police and the military leaders tended to be portrayed as misguided or wilful oppressors.'[25]

In the battle for public opinion, therefore, the authorities have to learn the lessons of Vietnam if they are not to be the losers.

But, how correct is the assumption that there was a 'Vietnam Syndrome'? In a careful assessment of the available evidence on Vietnam, Robert Entman and David Paletz cast some doubt:

'Television news is widely credited with bringing the war in all its cruelty and futility into Americans' living rooms. It is said to have spurred antiwar sentiment, forcing leaders to end the war sooner than they might otherwise have done. *Our analysis indicates television's contribution to undermining official policy was limited mainly to the first half of 1968. Generally before and after that, it legitimized presidential actions.* Television helped generate public support for ever deeper entrapment in the quagmire, then served to mute opposition to the pace of Nixon's four-year policy of extrication. At the end, it went along with the concerted efforts of American leaders to stifle consideration of the guiding policy assumptions that had led the country into Vietnam in the first place.'[26]

Obviously, the issue is complex, and we cannot go into details here. However, the crux of Entman and Paletz's argument is that when US television coverage seemed to be undermining the war effort, it was at that time largely echoing views of the Johnson administration's establishment critics. In essence, it was only the divisions within the foreign policy elite which gave television the impetus to reflect respectable opposition as credible. And that phase, they argue, lasted only a short while.[27]

One need not accept this argument in its entirety to acknowledge that the so-called 'Vietnam Syndrome' is at least open to serious challenge.

The unacceptable face of television

According to Clutterbuck, 'while news and current affairs reporting has generally reflected the public support for the police and for the rule of law, this has not always been the same for television documentaries and drama'.[28] Underlying this assertion is an implicit distinction between programmes which are politically 'acceptable' and those which are not. The acid test for him is whether or not such programmes ultimately sustain the rule of law. However, he offers no criteria as to how we are to judge this.

Hardly surprisingly, the programmes which he finds most acceptable are those which under our definitions are relatively

'closed', whereas those which present the greatest danger of supposed misrepresentation are those which are most 'open'. Documentaries and dramas which Clutterbuck sees as rooted in the realities of
British life are *Dixon of Dock Green, Z Cars, Softly Softly, Task
Force*. These represent the acceptable face of British policing, while
the series of plays *Law and Order* produced by Tony Garnett in 1978
are singled out as decidedly harmful, as 'a calculated attempt to
discredit the police and the law' because they suggest that corruption
and bending the rules are general features of the legal system. The
effect of this, thinks Clutterbuck, is to encourage the 'criminal
fraternity' and 'sow doubts in the minds of potential jurors as to the
fairness and integrity of both the police and lawyers involved in
presenting the case before them'. Clutterbuck suggests that those
writers, directors and producers of television drama who set out to
promulgate 'political propaganda at the expense of dramatic truth'
should not be given access to broadcasting.[29]

He goes on to say that while most reporters in broadcast news
and current affairs are not 'unduly influenced by any personal
motivation to discredit the police . . . a few programmes like
Jonathan Dimbleby's *A Force to Reckon With* must raise doubts'.
On the basis of such doubts we are asked to be 'vigilant' that the
media should not be abused. Such abuse is best tested by inquiring
into the 'motives' (i.e. the political beliefs) of reporters and
producers as these 'may be easier to detect than distortions or
inaccuracies'. But if such distortions are invisible even to the naked
eye of Dr Clutterbuck then what do the motives matter? To advocate
investigating the attitudes of broadcasters towards the rule of law
and the democratic order pushes the argument perilously close to
suggesting that 'loyalty' tests be applied as a condition of access to
broadcasting.

The Institute for the Study of Conflict concurs with
Clutterbuck's diagnosis. It too singles out the 'documentary drama'
as a television 'black spot' one in which 'people of admitted and
indeed proclaimed Marxist views have been allowed to present
slanted accounts of past events as fact. The BBC's *Days of Hope*
series is one example among others'. The 'Personal View' type of
programme is also seen as dangerous.[30] A majority of those
participating in the ISC conference found fault with 'the content of
the main ITV current affairs programmes *This Week, World in
Action* and *Week-end World*, and pointed questions were asked
about the political affiliations of those connected with the presentation of the programmes'.[31] The broadcasting authorities were urged
to be much more careful in the 'appointment and supervision of
broadcasting staff'.[32] If the television companies are indeed stuffed

full with subversives, it is hardly surprising that the ISC's Brian Crozier should opine that 'Over the years there has been a constant thread of anti-Establishment, anti-institutional, anti-free enterprise, anti-parliamentary and anti-American attitudes.[33]

But our analysis, and that of others, does not support Crozier's contention.

When the counter-insurgents move on to discuss specific cases rather than general impressions they still fail to supply convincing arguments based on sound evidence. Wilkinson has singled out television as especially prone to exploitation by terrorists. Taking a well-known example, he alleged that the INLA interview was one in which 'the programme makers concerned actually became accessories to terrorism . . . providing a propaganda coup for the Irish National Liberation Army, trivialising the enormity of their crime, and according them a spurious legitimacy if only by implying that such atrocities are within the tolerance of a civilized society'. Wilkinson offers the INLA interview as an example of how television will seek 'spectacular and dramatic visual imagery', pursued by 'ruthless' television producers. The interview may well have been *sought* on sensationalist grounds, but it was in a hostile framework. There is no basis for asserting that the interview legitimised the INLA: the BBC's audience research, referred to in the last chapter, suggests quite the contrary.

Wilkinson has further inveighed against the *Panorama* team at Carrickmore, asserting that they 'decided to cooperate with the Provisional IRA in filming a PIRA roadblock'.[34] However, he produces no evidence of collusion between the programme makers and the Provisionals. Wilkinson has deplored the failure to prosecute the BBC and has called for a strengthening of the law.

Clutterbuck makes a more serious attempt to offer a number of case studies, the most important of which for our purposes concern the role of broadcasting in Northern Ireland. In his foreword to Clutterbuck's book, Sir Robin Day asks 'is he right in suggesting that the BBC television interview with one of Airey Neave's INLA assassins may well have goaded the IRA to assassinate Lord Mountbatten?'[35] Since this is, seemingly, a clear-cut instance of postulating an imitation effect for a television programme, it is worth illustrating the kind of evidence which is presented in support of the claim. Clutterbuck's suggestion is based upon the following passage:

'Merlyn Rees . . . ex-Northern Ireland and Home Secretary . . . warned that the Provisional IRA would have regarded the broadcast as giving extra status to the INLA in their competition for ''who are the greatest guys on the terrorist scene'' and asked ''are they going to outdo each other?''. *His anxiety proved to be justified* by the murder of Earl Mountbatten by the Provisional IRA on 27 August 1979, which though it probably rebounded against them both in the Republic of Ireland and in the USA, certainly brought them a matching publicity splash. *This likelihood of cause and effect cannot be overlooked.*'[36]

This is an evasive argument. On the one hand Rees' anxiety allegedly 'proved' justified: that is, it supported the view that television played a role in causing a competitive act of killing. On the other, Clutterbuck hedges his bets by asserting that the causal link is only 'likely'. It is true that the INLA interview generated 'enormous publicity', but virtually all was in reaction to the screening of the interview, was heavily critical of the BBC, and offered no elaboration whatsoever concerning the aims of the INLA.

Indeed, Clutterbuck understates things when he talks of a 'matching publicity splash': the Mountbatten killing was far more extensively and elaborately covered. There can be no doubt at all that the Provisionals were well satisfied by the propaganda effects of both the Mountbatten and Warrenpoint killings. In fact, Warrenpoint was the more important to them militarily, and recognised as such by the British army. It is one thing to acknowledge the competition between the INLA and the IRA and quite another to allege a *direct link* between the killings and the appearance on television of a heavily disguised interviewee.

The IRA would seem to have decided against this kind of exposure. Richard Francis, then BBC Director of News and Current Affairs, has said that 'an approach was made to the INLA after the IRA had rejected the opportunity'.[37] Liz Curtis has provided further details of this refusal: 'According to Sinn Fein spokesman Richard McAuley, the IRA refused to do a back-to-camera interview because of the negative impression that would be given. Instead, the Republican Press Centre offered to provide a spokesperson who would answer any questions *Tonight* wanted to ask about the IRA, on condition that it was made clear at the start of the programme that the interviewee was not a member of the IRA.'[38]

It is difficult to conclude from this that the IRA were piqued by the INLA gaining a form of public exposure which they had rejected. Although an IRA spokesman somewhat disparagingly referred to the INLA as a 'small republican organisation' by comparison with the Provisional's claim to be the 'spearhead of resistance', the Neave killing was, nevertheless, commended as a successful breach of security at Westminster.[39] It would be perfectly possible both to hypothesise a competitive killing and at the same time accept that the role of the INLA interview was completely irrelevant in causal terms.

For, after all, Neave's death had already caused considerable publicity in its own right. Clutterbuck's case for greater restrictions on journalists is based on this kind of defective reasoning. Before turning to his proposals let us consider a further instance.

The siege of the Iranian embassy in London in 1980 was noteworthy for the crucial role played by broadcasting. Clutterbuck praises the way in which the Mark strategy of media control was applied, and notes that the police were successful in allocating 'specific and controlled vantage points' to the TV cameras at the scene.[40] Cameras were not stationed at the rear because the police were concerned about disclosing their surveillance equipment to the gunmen and did not want to risk losing the advantage of a surprise attack by the SAS, thereby putting hostages' lives at risk.

ITN, however, smuggled a camera to the rear of the building and was able to record the preparations for the SAS assault. From this, Clutterbuck raises the spectre of a potential disaster. First, he wonders, what if the SAS had attacked during an ITN bulletin:

'there would have been at least *a possibility* of the editor or studio director, unaware of the shots on the back camera videotape, switching them on to the transmitter before the SAS had actually gone through the windows, with *potentially disastrous results*.'[41]

Then he speculates about the dangers of 'live' reporting from the scene:

'There could, however, have been a terrible risk if the pictures from the illicit ITN camera at the back had been broadcasting (*sic*) live, so that the SAS were seen on the roof before anyone realized what they were doing – *anyone, that is, except the terrorists watching their screen in the Embassy*.'[42]

But the terrorists were *not* watching their screen then, nor indeed at any other time, as was presumably known by virtue of the surveillance equipment installed at the beginning of the siege. Clutterbuck's worries were not shared either by the Home Office or by the police; or, if they were, they have not been made public.

While irresponsibility in such a situation is to be deplored if it puts lives at risk, all the evidence suggests extremely close consultation between the broadcasting authorities and the state, a context in which Clutterbuck's disaster scenario, although conceivable, is unlikely in the extreme. Upon such tenuous bases Clutterbuck demands greater restrictions.

Major Alan Hooper of the Royal Marines has further elaborated Clutterbuck's arguments, though in a book which is generally noteworthy for its clear-sighted recognition of how news values work and how they frequently conflict with the needs of the military. After accepting Clutterbuck's rather incomplete account of the role of the media during the siege, Hooper also focusses on the placement of ITN's camera. Hooper accepts the denial by ITN's editor, David Nicholas, that ITN smuggled its camera 'in defiance of the police request'. He acknowledges that the likelihood of accidental transmission was negligible. His main argument, therefore, is not that ITN potentially jeopardised the operation. Rather, he maintains, by disclosing the SAS's abseil technique ITN's report closed 'an option for the future'.[44]

This argument is implausible. The siege was such a major story, and interest in it so intense, that the media, British and foreign, would have been bound to try to reconstruct the way the siege bust was carried out, as at Entebbe and Mogadishu. Moreover, abseiling is hardly a secret technique and is known to be part of the repertoire of counter-terrorist forces. ITN's pictures were hardly revealing state secrets. Hooper's argument is a standard one, and echoes Paul Wilkinson's more general point that 'the unrestrained revelation of police tactics and resources' has been of value to terrorists.[45] Not surprisingly, the counter-insurgents have turned their thoughts to what controls may realistically be exerted.

What is to be done?

The solutions canvassed by the counter-insurgents are aimed at securing greater control by the state over the operations of the media. Within this broad goal, however, there are some differences of emphasis over how the end is to be achieved. The options range from invoking legal sanctions to securing a gentleman's agreement on a voluntary basis.

As noted in the previous chapter, during the Carrickmore Affair, the British government made use of the Prevention of Terrorism Act, although the full legal implications of this remain to be tested. Well before the Attorney-General took this step, the Institute for the Study of Conflict had pointed out that although interviews with 'terrorists' were subject to the provisions of the 1976 Act, nevertheless, *the relevant section in the Prevention of Terrorism Act is inadequately drafted if there is to be an obligation to hand information over to the police.* The phrase "with lawful excuse" enables newsmen to argue that it is part of their journalistic duties to maintain their sources of information, so they do not need to hand it over'.[46] Consequently, said the ISC report, 'what was required was some enforcement of the present law, particularly in the production of visible filmed evidence of membership of the IRA, which would enable the police to proceed'.[47] The subsequent seizure of non-broadcast BBC film in November 1979 following the Carrickmore incident was a definite step in that direction, and it remains to be seen whether the PTA will, at some future time, be redrafted to make it 'both clear and obeyed', in the ISC's phrase.

This example demonstrates the way in which small, quite influential bodies may contribute to shaping the political climate. One need not suppose that the Attorney-General's decision was a direct outcome of such pressure, merely that such allies tip the balance a little in decision-making and help create the right ideological climate for moving in a restrictive direction.

Paul Wilkinson has also seized on the INLA and Carrickmore incidents as just cause for a tightening of the law: 'Wilfully aiding and abetting terrorist propaganda in their (*sic*) campaigns of murder and destruction is surely a crime in the legal code of most member states in the Council of Europe. If it is not then it certainly ought to be. And the free media, because of the power for harm that they possess, must not be placed above such laws.'[48]

Along with calls for legislative intervention has gone the demand for more effective regulation. Richard Clutterbuck, in common with other counter-insurgents, has advocated 'voluntary self-control' as a decent British solution to the problems of excess. However, besides suggesting that much tougher codes of practice be applied by the media unions and professional bodies, he has also distinguished himself by arguing for a corporative body, an 'Institute for the Mass Media', on the lines of existing medical and legal professional bodies. The so-called 'IMM' would have the power to strike offending members off its register for disobeying police instructions by putting lives at risk or assisting criminals to escape justice. This body bears more than a passing resemblance to the Central General Council of the mass media proposed by South Africa's Steyn Commission. Which is not surprising, since they were also looking for a way to instil greater 'responsibility' into the coverage of 'terrorism'. And like Clutterbuck, they wanted to ensure that journalism was 'not infiltrated and damaged by undesirable elements' whilst maintaining the outward appearance of a free and open news system. As they candidly put it; 'so unruly a horse as that of the media needs a strong bridle, even with retention of the "adversary relationship" between State and media profession'.[49]

It is not clear how charges against individuals falling foul of Clutterbuck's IMM would actually be adjudicated. Those guilty of offences would, in effect, be condemned to lose their livelihood since registered members would be required 'to cease to employ or to publish in the defined mass media the work of any journalist or contributor who had broken the code'.[50] Of course, concedes Clutterbuck, such miscreants could try and find work with the non-mass media, where they would be doing less damage. Failing the success of such corporatist regulation of the media, Clutterbuck accepts that tightening up the law would be the only resort. Here, then, is a significant step left out by the ISC and Wilkinson. Corporatist control, if ever adopted, would be much tighter than the *ad hoc* 'gentleman's agreement', but it would also have the advantage of not involving anything that could justly be called overt state censorship.

Alongside these various forms of legal or regulative constraint, calls have also come for 'closer consultation between the broadcasting authorities and people with political, military and security experience'.[51] As we showed in the last chapter, such contacts have become increasingly common, and represent a significant informal link between key media personnel and the state apparatus. It is hardly surprising, therefore, that in addition to calling for tougher controls, the counter-insurgents, have also advocated this classically British clubland approach.

Alan Hooper, at the more sophisticated and liberal end of the spectrum, has praised Sir Robert Mark's strategy for gaining the confidence of the media and observed that his

'approach would appear to be readily adaptable to the military-media relationship. An early rapport should be established between the editors and the appropriate personalities in the media. Once the principle has been established the rapport should be passed on to the subsequent military officers in the relevant appointments . . . The fundamental issues to be resolved at such meetings are the media's requirement to publish and the military's desire for non-disclosure of certain information on the grounds of security.'[52]

This last position recognises the need to co-opt the media by means of persuasion rather than *force majeure* at a time when 'low-level conflict', in Major Hooper's phrase, is a permanent part of the country's political life. It also advocates a longer-term strategy of forging permanent institutional links between the media and the state, positively supported, of course, by 'goodwill' and 'mutual understanding'.

Whether this traditional approach will remain in the ascendant is open to question, for the drift of recent counter-insurgency thinking, and of actual political developments, begins to suggest otherwise. Paul Wilkinson's writings give some indication of the shifting climate. Whereas his most recent pronouncements have been hard line, only a few years ago, in 1978, he was arguing strongly for 'informal understanding', 'goodwill' and 'voluntary self-restraint on the part of the media'.[53] Furthermore, the present rethinking of censorship strategies by the government in the wake of the Falklands adventure may well have implications for the way in which the internal war at home will be fought via the media.

Chapter 6

Television: instrument of the state?

Is violence communication?

The arguments of the counter-insurgents have dominated the debate reinforcing the official perspective.

Fully worked-out statements from the alternative point of view are rare, and have anyway gone largely unnoticed. The most significant intervention from this quarter has come from two Dutch peace researchers at Leiden University, Dr Alex P. Schmid and Janny de Graaf. In their book, *Violence as Communication*, published in 1982, they provide a comprehensive review of the literature on the relationships between Western news media and what they term 'insurgent terrorism'. While there is much in their book with which we would agree, there are also some points about which we have strong reservations.

Schmid and de Graaf's guiding thesis is that we should not treat 'acts of terrorism as "senseless violence"' but rather 'as a kind of violent language'. So, bombings, hijackings, kneecappings, murders which lay claim to a political character are to be understood as a form of communicative action, directed at an audience. Thus, they argue,

'In our view *terrorism can best be understood as a violent communication strategy*. There is a sender, the terrorist, a message generator, the victim, and a receiver, the enemy and/or the public. The nature of the terrorist act, its atrocity, its location and the identity of its victim serve as generators for the power of the message. Violence, to become terroristic, requires witnesses.'[1]

While, at first glance, this might seem plausible, there are serious difficulties. Political violence is not reducible to communicative behaviour alone, even though certain acts have made prime-time viewing of late. The thesis assumes that violent acts take place only, or primarily, because they will achieve media coverage. But the evidence which the authors themselves provide runs counter to this. Two instances which they examine in some detail, the kidnappings and assassinations of Hanns-Martin Schleyer by the Red Army Fraction, and of Aldo Moro by the Red Brigades, reveal the internal contradictions of their argument particularly clearly.

Schleyer was kidnapped in order to secure the release of members of the Baader-Meinhof group, and the quest for publicity during his kidnap was subordinate to this goal. His killing was obviously going to generate publicity, but was also a retaliation for the failed hijack at Mogadishu. Similarly, the purpose of Aldo Moro's abduction was to disrupt the accord between the Italian Communist party and the Christian Democrats, which he had been instrumental in forging. The Red Brigades succeeded in demonstrating the Italian state's vulnerability to attack. But in both these cases, it is important to distinguish between the symbolic demonstration and the wider political strategy to which it was subject. As the deaths themselves testify, acts of political violence are not *just* linguistic statements using a particularly brutal form of expression: they have real, material consequences too.

There are further difficulties in the way in which Schmid and de Graaf define the problem. The key for them lies in 'the interaction between insurgent terrorism and the mass media', where 'insurgent terrorism' is defined as directed against the power holders in a state. The authors, however, rightly recognise that 'political terrorism' can also include 'state or repressive terrorism, directed against less powerful segments of society' and they also note the existence of 'vigilante terrorism' practised by 'non-state groups'.[2] Although Schmid and de Graaf periodically make reference to these other forms of political violence, it is 'insurgent terrorism' which dominates their entire analysis.

They offer two main grounds for this. First, its interaction with the media is 'much denser' than the others, state terrorists being media shy. And second, most of the data available bears on 'insurgent terrorism', and, especially, 'the relationship between government and media'.[3] On the first count, as Chomsky and Herman have shown, the role of the media in misreporting state terrorism is, despite the difficulties, open to quite a revealing analysis. Secondly, by defining the main focus of their study in line with the preoccupations of the official perspective, the authors end up by devoting an entire book to looking at a relationship between the media and a strand of terrorism which they go on to describe as unimportant in global terms:

'informed only by the mass media, the average news consumer gets the impression of a unilateral upsurge in mainly left-wing insurgent terrorism. *Yet state terrorism is a much more serious problem.* In terms of victims the state terrorism in Guatemala, for instance, has cost many more lives in one year than all the international insurgent terrorist incidents of the last ten years together.'[4]

Schmid and de Graaf do not let the oficial perspective overwhelm their argument completely. They recognise very clearly that the media are subject to news management in liberal-democratic states such as Britain, Italy and West Germany, and produce evidence to demonstrate this. Indeed, they are plainly aware of the central theme which we have been developing in this book – that the representation of 'terrorism' is closely bound up with the exercise of definitional power. From this recognition they then go on to build a specific kind of anti-censorship case:

'In a democratic society no-one's definition should prevail. The same act perpetuated with the same motives, should be labelled with the same word independently of whether it is committed by those in power or by those less powerful.'[5]

Underlying this comment is the presumption of a society without any form of domination whatsoever, be it of class, ethnicity or gender. The implicit yardstick is some form of ideal and unconstrained communication in a non-contradictory universe.

This is a vision which we do not share, as we can see no immediate end to definitional struggles which are themselves part of wider struggles for the hegemonic domination of given societies. The abolition of fundamental social differences does not seem to be on the agenda of either today's or tomorrow's politics, and is hardly a realistic assumption from which to proceed to the fair exchange of equals on the level of ideas. It is this unconvincing foundation, however, on which Schmid and de Graaf build the libertarian recommendation with which they end their own book:

'Where people have gained control over the law the terror of the law has ceased. When public control over the mass media is gained, the media might also cease to serve as instruments of terror. *A right to communicate for aggrieved minorities, in turn, is likely to stop many of them from having recourse to terrorist violence.*'[6]

This implies that blockages of communication rather than economic and political factors are a major cause of political violence. Schmid and de Graaf's position raises more problems than it resolves. How large is an 'aggrieved minority'? Are all minorities, larger and smaller, to be treated equally? Who decides how they are to be treated? Under what institutional arrangements could we envisage access to the media being accorded? Why should we assume that those with a message to send will necessarily command the audience they seek, or is that unimportant? Why should we believe that 'communicating' will *alone* somehow dissolve objective differences of interest and domesticate those who espouse armed struggles?

By stressing the overwhelming publicity effect of anti-state political violence Schmid and de Graaf fit in neatly with official conventional wisdom. Furthermore their espousal of 'contagion' and 'imitation' arguments, on what they themselves judge to be inconclusive evidence, further undermines their case.[7] But there is enough in their argument to provoke Paul Wilkinson to judge them guilty of 'dangerous naivety'.[8] The dangers seem to us to be far from immediately obvious, for alternative critiques are more usually ignored or denigrated than taken seriously. As for naiveté, one can hardly assume that Schmid and de Graaf seriously expect Western states to open their airwaves to their enemies in the manner suggested. One must suppose that they have overstated the argument for effect.

Their advocacy of opening up existing global structures of communication does not carry much conviction, nor are they likely to generate debate at national level – which is where it counts – about how to ensure that opportunities for rational public discussion are kept open. In our view, it is much more pertinent and realistic to recognise the specific ways in which the media are contested sites, and to begin from a sober appraisal of just how much space does exist for genuine debate. An abstract standard of equality for all is not attainable, nor does such a goal pay adequate attention to the particular contexts in which political and ideological conflicts are being waged.

Schmid and de Graaf do have some useful things to say at a more practical level. For instance:

'If restrictions are imposed on the news people get, the least the public should demand is that the nature of these restrictions is known. The present guidelines are often secret and if manipulation of news for higher purposes such as saving hostages has to be introduced, the public should have a right to know this.'[9]

This is a proposition which can be debated in a serious manner, and in which the outcome is bound to be decisively influenced by local experience. A related constructive suggestion is: 'The proper body to formulate guidelines in matters of media coverage of terrorism should . . . be a public body'[10] – that is, a *non*-governmental one. Such points have the virtue of focussing attention on the secrecy which characterises current state practices, and begin to raise the question of developing mechanisms for accountability.

Cultivating compliance

George Gerbner and his colleagues at the University of Pennsylvania have also contributed to the debate from within a broadly alternative perspective. For over a decade they have analysed the contents of prime-time programming on the American networks and explored the ways in which it 'cultivates' certain ways of looking at the world among the audience. Although they do not deal specifically with terrorism, their analysis of images of violence and their impact extends the discussion in this area. Unlike most previous studies Gerbner's focus on fiction rather than news. Moreover, the critique of the official orthodoxy is backed by a massive research effort.

Gerbner and his colleagues begin by contesting official thinking's fixation with imitation and contagion:

'Conventional wisdom . . . might stress the one or two in a thousand who imitate violence and threaten society. But it is just as important to look at the large majority of people who become more fearful, insecure, and dependant on authority, and who may grow up demanding protection and even welcoming repression in the name of security.'[11]

This definition of the 'problem' highlights television's contribution to securing popular consent for tough measures to counter 'violence' as well as the medium's role in mobilising sympathy and support for terrorist causes or encouraging imitation effects. It also suggests a different way of looking at the costs of crime and violence, though it has been left to others to develop this point. While acknowledging the real and obvious human costs to victims and their relatives, sociologists such as Stinchcombe point to the hidden social costs of support for the strong state. Civil liberties are reduced and public services run down as expenditure is transferred from welfare to warfare against both internal and external enemies.[12] These arguments are important and provocative, with mounting empirical evidence in their favour, although they still rest on somewhat shaky conceptual foundations. Gerbner's own analysis raises three particular problems. In the first place, he works with a crude instrumental and functionalist view of the relationship between the media and the wider power structure, arguing that 'throughout history, once a ruling class has established its rule, the primary function of its cultural media has been legitimization and maintenance of its authority'.[13] By way of illustration he frequently compares contemporary television with the medieval church. 'Television' he maintains 'relates to the State as only the Church did in former times . . . People attend to television as they used to attend to church except that they do it more often and more religiously.'[14] As a consequence, they are 'held in thrall by the myths and legends of the new electronic priesthood' which make them 'perceive as real and normal and right that which fits the established social order.'[15] At first sight this metaphor seems convincing enough. Television's command of mass communications and symbolisation approaches the centrality if not the near monopoly of the church, and like the church its influence pervades and structures everyday life. But this is a relatively superficial reading of ecclesiastical history.

The church did not legitimate state power without problems. There were continual tensions between the sacred and secular authorities as the church fought to retain its autonomy and historic privileges, and the rulers of emergent nation states battled to consolidate their authority. Nor did the church present a united ideological front. Even before the Reformation it was shot through with schisms and heresies. Dissident sections of the clergy and laity constantly contested official orthodoxies and pointed up the gaps between ideals and institutional practices.

Television has indeed replaced the church at the centre of national cultural life, but it has also inherited the historic difficulties of that position. It too has an uneasy, often abrasive, relationship with the state marked by struggles over the balance between autonomy and control. It also has internal disputes over the implementation of key principles such as the public's right to know and the author's right to provoke. We have argued that these conflicts produce a symbolic field which is a good deal more open and contested than Gerbner's one-sided stress on television's legitimating role allows for.

This narrow view of the way television works as a cultural and ideological system also restricts the analysis of fictional output. Gerbner concentrates on the central features of prime-time programming because they are the core of most people's television experience. He aims to show that prime-time television is quite uniform in content across all the major formats and very resilient to change. He admits that the networks occasionally carry productions which break the rules but dismisses these as too rare to significantly counter the ideological thrust of mainstream programming. He is on reasonably firm ground here. Unlike Britain where the public service ethos still ensures a space for dissent and experiment in the prime-time schedules (albeit a restricted and contested one) 'authored' productions have all but disappeared from the US networks.

However, Gerbner's dismissal of contradiction also extends to his view of popular fiction. He tends to treat action-adventure series as though they were paradigmatic and to assume that the commercial pressures which shape them operate equally on other forms. Hence, according to Gerbner, the 'economics of the assembly line and the requirements of wide acceptability assure general adherence to common notions of justice and fair play, clearcut characterisations, tested plot lines and proven formulas for resolving all issues'.[16] This leads him to see popular television fiction as overwhelmingly closed and tight, without complex personalities, unclear motives or ambiguous outcomes.[17] This supposition is amply confirmed by his content analyses, since by focussing on the continuities and communalities across forms, he effectively neglects the variations and breaks.

Our analysis strongly suggests that the ideological field of popular fiction is rather more complex than it looks at first sight. Once again, national differences may well be at work here, producing less consistent closure and convergence in British television fiction, though other researchers who have recently looked at crime fiction on American television have pointed to some of the same tensions and ambiguities as we found in our British sample.[18] Gerbner's 'message system analysis' takes no account of the way that notions about power and violence are differently inflected by differences in genre, plot format and narrative style. For him, variations in form and style are irrelevant to the central task of mapping 'the repetitive pattern of television's mass-produced messages and images'.[19]

This too simple approach to television as a system of representations is matched by an equally simple view of its impact on the audience. Gerbner's main concern is to show how viewers' overall conceptions of reality are 'cultivated' and reinforced by repeated exposure to the recurrent features of mainstream programming. He tries to demonstrate a strong relationship between heavy television viewing and certain ways of looking at the world, including support for tougher law and order policies.

However, the way in which the audience is conceived of is unsatisfactory. In the early 'cultivation' studies, Gerbner treated the audience as relatively undifferentiated and played down the significance of inequalities in social situation and experience. Although now he has acknowledged that the audience is complexly stratified, his approach is still inadequate. Because he mostly relies on standardised interview schedules, Gerbner is unable to catch the nuances and contradictions in peoples' attitudes to law and order, or the subtle ways in which their outlooks are formed by social experience and draw upon popular memory.

Gerbner's somewhat one-dimensional approach to media organisation and effects is by no means unique among researchers arguing from a broadly alternative position. It is also shared by Professors Noam Chomsky and Edward Herman, whose books, in our view, provide the most cogent and morally engaged alternative account of the 'problem' of terrorism currently on offer.

Brainwashing and the free press

Unlike Alex Schmid and Janny de Graaf, Chomsky and Herman decisively reject the importance attached to 'insurgent', or in their terms 'retail' terrorism. Their counter-texts, while systematically criticising the official orthodoxies, are much more concerned to provide detailed instances of state terrorism sponsored or maintained by the United States. A central thesis of their work is that routine coverage by the US media lends support to a Cold War version of reality emphasising 'Communist terror' which is 'positively and urgently needed as a diversion and to show that while we may be awful they are worse'.[20] Establishment scholarship, and the pronouncements of many leading intellectuals and commentators also tend in this direction, they argue.

The general method adopted by Chomsky and Herman in building their case is to expose the logical and evidential flaws in many mainstream accounts. Alongside this detailed level of analysis they offer a more general framework of explanation which is held to account for why the press and television operate in the way that they do. Here, we wish to consider this level of their analysis because we have some reservations about it.

Like Gerbner their basic model is both functionalist and instrumentalist. Fundamentally, they argue, the mass media are governed by an economic and political logic:

'Mass media selectivity, suppressions, exaggerations, and sometimes plain lying are . . . subject to an entirely rational explanation in terms of primary systemic interests, whatever may be the precise mechanics whereby the system's "line" is implemented.'[21]

Where US economic and political interests are involved, the press works just like a 'state agency'. The factors which make this so are various: concentrated capitalist ownership and control, sponsors' control over news content via threats to refuse advertising, the preeminence of government and big business sources, close ties between the business, administrative and mass media elites.[22] This is a very deterministic model, and Chomsky and Herman frequently suggest that the media as a whole work as a conscious instrument of state propaganda. They are careful, however, to point out that they do not believe a conspiracy exists to produce a particular Cold War version of the world, rather this flows 'from basic structural facts, relationships, and resultant values, the internalisation of these values on the part of media personnel, the importance of government and business as information sources and sponsors, and the interplay of all these forces in generating systematic bias via self-censorship'.[23]

While it is by no means the primary purpose of Chomsky and Herman's work to offer a fully theorised analysis of class, power and the media, their sketches of these interrelations suggest that they have not adequately thought through a number of complex questions. For instance, while they argue that the US media in practice are as monolithic as those of a totalitarian state, they need, at the same time, to account for the existence of a measure of diversity. They acknowledge the range of variation in three specific ways.

First, they accept that 'alternative views and analyses' exist in 'fringe media', but that these reach a 'minuscule sector of the population'. Second, they note that 'facts contrary to the line are available in the mass media in small, isolated doses, and may be culled out by the assiduous reader aware of the overwhelming bias'. Finally, they point out that 'where powerful domestic interests are at odds over an issue (Nixon and Watergate, or to a lesser extent, Vietnam) there may be no uniform line, or the line may be subject to a fair amount of undercutting in the mass media'.[24] Such spaces are 'important and valuable' and consequently the 'Free Press' is better than a state-censored press.

Given their focus, it is not surprising that Chomsky and Herman should stress the uniformity rather than the diversity (however limited). What they do say about diversity is acceptable enough: fringe journals are sustained by dissenting movements; 'reading' a newspaper critically is a definite skill; and divergent accounts do emanate as a result of squabbles within elites.

In our terms, however, this is not an adequate account. Perhaps our divergence can be partly traced to differences in the media systems in Britain and the United States. Certainly, the existence of a public service broadcasting system and the complex relationships it has to the state are of great importance. However, there is something more fundamental too.

Our approach has set out to enumerate distinct television forms and to see them as contested spaces. Chomsky and Herman do not begin from that assumption. For them the television system is much more closed. The output of US television is sufficiently well explained for them by citing commercial and political pressure, just as in the case of the press. They do make the point that account should be taken of the ideological impact of 'action-drama-spy series'. This, however, is assumed to simply reinforce dominant views.[25] We believe that an analysis such as ours on US television would be potentially fruitful for the discoveries it could make. But Chomsky and Herman's approach closes off this possibility. They adhere to a mass manipulative model of the media which allows no space for negotiation either within the production process or by those consuming media products:

'The 99% of the population unreachable by US dissidents are subject to the selective processes of the mass media that do not allow serious criticism of patriotic myths and untruths, with a brain-washing effect comparable to that of systems with explicit government censorship.'[26]

This is a pessimistic account, which suggests that all but one per cent are likely to live in ignorance of the truth most of the time. Behind this is a notion of the media every bit as simplistic as that of the counter-insurgents.

Chapter 7

Conclusion

This book has taken issue with the prevailing orthodoxies of Right and Left. We reject the counter-insurgents' claim that television gives extensive publicity to 'terrorist' views and mobilises sympathy and support for their causes. We also reject the commonplace radical characterisation of broadcasting as a largely uncritical conduit for official views. In opposition to these one-dimensional accounts we have drawn attention to the diverse ways in which television handles 'terrorism' and the problems this question poses for liberal democracies. We have shown that some programmes are relatively 'closed' and work wholly or mainly within the terms set by the official perspective. Others, though, are more 'open' and provide space for alternative and oppositional views. However, the extent of this diversity should not be overstated. Although television is the site of continual struggle between contending perspectives on 'terrorism', the contest is not an equal one. 'Open' programmes appear far less frequently than 'closed' ones and they reach smaller audiences.

Table 3: Average audience size of selected programmes

Fiction programmes	audience in millions	Actuality * Programmes	audience millions
The Professionals (Nov 82-Feb 83)	13.0	ITN *News at Ten*	7.6
Harry's Game (25-27 Oct 1982)	9.5	BBC *Nine O'Clock News*	6.8
Blood Money (8-23 Apr 1983 repeat)	4.1	*Nationwide*	6.8
Psywarriors †	1.7	*Panorama*	3.7
		Tonight †	1.9
		Newsnight	0.9

Source: BARB (Broadcasters' Audience Research Board).
* All figures refer to the last quarter of 1982, except the figure for *Tonight* which refers to the last quarter of 1978.
† These figures were gathered before the present BARB system came into operation are therefore not directly comparable with the other figures in the table.

As Table 3 shows, there is a strong relationship between 'openness' and audience size. *Psywarriors*, the most 'open' fiction programme in our sample, had an audience of only 1.7 million, low even for a single play. In its latest series in Spring 1983 for example, *Play For Today* averaged 4.9 million viewers, with the most popular single production reaching 7.1 million and the least popular, 2.1 million. *Psywarriors* however, had the disadvantage of being moved to a later time than usual because of its sensitive nature. Similarly, around the time of the highly controversial INLA interview, *Tonight* was attracting only 1.9 million viewers a night.

Table 4: Proportion of the population reached by selected programmes

Programme	Number of programmes	Average % of the population watching each programme	% of the population seeing at least 1 programme
BBC *Nine O'Clock News* (July 1982)	20	15	75
ITN *News at Ten* (July 1982)	20	16.5	73
The Professionals	11	24.2	67
Harry's Game	3	16.7	29
Blood Money	3	7.7	17

Source: BARB (Broadcasters' Audience Research Board).

Of course, these figures only tell us how many people watched a given programme. They say nothing about what they thought of it, how it affected their views on 'terrorism', or whether they took any action as a result. These are important questions which deserve more detailed investigation than they have so far received. On the basis of other work on audiences we can be reasonably sure that the viewers will have responded in a variety of ways, depending on their prior knowledge of the situation, their involvement with the issues, their political commitments, and a range of other factors. Certainly their reactions are likely to be more varied and complex than any simplistic assertion of direct effects allows for. Given the relative scarcity of 'open' programmes, the restricted nature of their audiences and the uncertainty about their impact, the counter-insurgents are quite unjustified in using them to support calls for tighter controls in general over television's treatment of 'terrorism'. Indeed, in our view, the official perspective is already over-represented in peak-time viewing.

The Professionals, one of the most 'closed' programmes looked at, averaged 13 million viewers per episode during its latest series, easily the largest audience for any of the fictions in our sample. Similarly, the major news bulletins had the largest audiences of the actuality programmes studied, with ITN's *News at Ten* attracting 7.6 million people a night on average, and 6.8 million watching the *Nine O'Clock News* on BBC1. Moreover, as Table 4 shows, over time these regular productions reach a much wider audience than the mean figures suggest. In an average month, around three-quarters of the population see at least one edition of each of the major news bulletins, while just over two-thirds caught at least one episode of *The Professionals* during its most recent series. Conversely, only 17 per cent saw any of the repeat episodes of *Blood Money*.

Still, the figures also show that relatively 'open' programmes can command quite sizeable audiences. *Harry's Game*, for example, averaged 9.5 million viewers per episode, and over a quarter of the population (29 per cent) saw at least one. Similarly, although the average audience for *Panorama* is only around half that for *News at Ten*, it is still seen by almost four million people. The spaces such programmes may provide for alternative and oppositional perspectives are an essential precondition for an informed public, capable of making considered choices between competing policies towards political violence. They must be defended and extended. We must preserve the current affairs producers' right in principle to examine all sides of an issue and to cast a sceptical eye over the policies of governments and state agencies. We must also defend the right of documentary makers and playwrights to ask awkward questions about officialdom and to challenge off-the-shelf story-lines and stock characterisations. Furthermore we should explore how popular fiction might engage with crucial issues in more varied and complex ways, without sacrificing the commitment to entertainment that keeps people watching. The right to dissent and the opportunity to innovate are supported by the ethos of public service which has regulated television until now. The practice has not always lived up fully to the ideals, but the ideals themselves are well worth defending.

Public service provision rests on three cardinal principles; 'independence', 'authorship', and universal availability. 'Independence' implies the broadcasters' right to make programmes with relative freedom from interference by government or state agencies. Ideally an 'independent' service to the public should provide information and arguments that people need to exercise their political judgement to the full, including material critical of current policy and official practice. The principle of 'authorship' insists on the programme makers' right to challenge prevailing attitudes and pre-conceptions, to provoke and annoy sections of the audience, and to experiment with new formats and forms. Where the commercial logic of the marketplace makes popularity the major arbiter of production, the public service principle defends the producers' right to be unpopular and to offer the widest possible range of viewpoints and perspectives. Lastly, the principle of universal availability maintains that the whole output should be offered equally to all those who have paid the licence fee. These principles, and the spaces and opportunities they keep open, are now under sustained attack from the combination of free enterprise and strong state and the sheer logic of technical change which together define Britain's emerging social market economy. There has been considerable drift towards greater political control over programme making in recent years. If this continues it will further restrict the range of views and voices allowed access to the public communications system, and make access to strategic information on official policies and actions even more difficult to obtain. These threats are well known and have been widely discussed. Less publicised, but no less important, are threats posed by the aggressive commercialism of the 'new' television industries.

Until now television has existed in a mixed broadcasting economy where the pure logic of the market place has been held in check, to a greater or lesser extent by the requirements of public service. But this is now changing. The 'new' television industries of video, cable and direct broadcasting satellite are conceived by many simply as profit-making ventures in which serving the public is equated with giving people what they want (as measured by sales or ratings) or what advertisers and sponsors are willing to subsidise. This development is likely to have a profound effect on public service broadcasting if it proceeds unchecked. In the long term it could lead to its eventual disappearance.

If competition from the 'new' television industries were to reduce the BBC's share of the total audience beyond a certain point the case for the compulsory licence fee would become untenable. There would then be mounting calls for the Corporation to be dismantled and for the more profitable sectors to be sold off to private enter-prise. Competition for audience attention and advertising revenue will also undoubtedly erode the economic viability of the ITV com-panies, producing increased pressure to relax present public service requirements. The future of the Fourth Channel in its present form will also be put seriously at risk. More immediately, both BBC and ITV will be tempted to respond to increased competition by using peak-time programming formats with proven audience appeal to keep up their share of total viewing. This will mean less diversity of views and styles, less risk taking and more 'closed' presentations. 'Open' programmes will continue to be made but may be made with fewer resources and transmitted less often in peak viewing slots. Moreover, as competition intensifies so the price of the creative labour and strategic information required to make these programmes will rise, leaving the relatively impoverished public service organisations unable to match the bids of the transnationals at the heart of the 'new' television industries, thereby further reducing diversity.

Nor can viewers simply transfer their custom to the new commercial operators. Under the system now developing, choice is not free, it has to be paid for. As well as renting or buying the necessary equipment, customers have to pay for the goods and services they consume, either singly (as in pay-as-you-view systems) or in packages (as with basic cable and satellite services). Consequently, access to televised information and entertainment will be tied more and more securely to ability to pay, creating a sizeable and permanent information gap between rich and poor.

Against this we want to argue for a resolute defence of public service broadcasting as the best way of defending and extending the present range of information and debate on 'terrorism' and political violence. Indeed, the argument applies to the whole range of broadcasting output.

This does not imply uncritical support for existing institutions but any criticism must recognise that although public service broadcasting may not be the best way to maximise broadcasting freedom and popular access, it is the best we have, and more importantly, the best we are likely to get for the forseeable future. In the present political climate, support for public service principles will have to be actively canvassed, as the arguments are tipping decisively against them. Recasting public television will require some hard thinking about finance and accountability, about the balance between authorship and access, and about the limits of pluralism. But the aim must be to strengthen the basic principles of public service television by reinforcing its relative autonomy from state and government, securing the most open and diverse expression of available views, and ensuring that the totality of this provision remains available to everyone. If these core principles are not defended against the incursions of the strong state on the one hand, and aggressive international commercialism on the other, the range of programming described in this book is quite likely to become of merely historical interest.

Notes and references

Preface
1 See *Dati per la Verifica dei Programmi Trasmessi 1981, Terrorismo e TV: Italia, Gran Bretagna, Germania Occidentale*, Introduction by Franco Ferrarotti, Turin, ERI, 1982, 2 vols. There is also an English version, 'The State and "Terrorism" on British Television', *L'Immagine dell'Uomo*, no.1, January 1982. An abridged version has been published as '"Terrorism" and the state: A Case Study of the Discourses of Television', *Media, Culture and Society*, vol.5, no.2, April 1983.

Chapter 1: Talking about 'terrorism'
1 Alex P. Schmid, *Political Terrorism: A Research Guide to Concepts, Theories, Data Bases and Literature*, Leiden, C.O.M.T., 1983 (Preliminary Version), notes that the term first entered the *New York Times* index in 1970. In Britain, its first appearance in *The Times*' index as a separate category was in 1973. Prior to that it was included under the more general heading 'guerrillas and terrorists'.
2 Christopher Dobson and Ronald Payne, *Terror! The West Fights Back*, London, MacMillan, 1982, p.1.
3 For a development of this argument see Steve Chibnall, *Law-and-order News: An Analysis of Crime Reporting in the British Press*, London, Tavistock, 1977.
4 Margaret Thatcher, speaking at the 51st Annual Conservative Women's Conference, 'Women and Employment', 20 May 1981; *Conservative Central Office News Service*, p.15.
5 B. Hayes, 'The Effects of Terrorism in Society', *Police Studies*, Fall, 1979, vol.2, p.8.
6 See Pierre Vidal-Naquet, *La Torture dans la République*, Paris, Maspéro, 1972, pp.28–29.
7 Jacques Soustelle, 'Liberty or Licence?' in 'Political Violence and the Role of the Media: Some Perspectives', *Political Communication and Persuasion*, vol.1, no.1, p.82. This was a talk delivered to the Jerusalem Conference on International Terrorism held at the Jonathan Institute, 2–5 July 1979.
8 Conor Cruise O'Brien, 'Liberty and Terror: Illusions of Violence, Delusions of Liberalism', *Encounter*, October 1977, vol.xlix, no.4, p.38.
9 Institute for the Study of Conflict (ISC), *Television and Conflict*, introduction by Brian Crozier, London, ISC, 1978, p.20.
10 Norman Podhoretz, 'The Subtle Collusion', in *Political Communication and Persuasion* as above, pp.88–89.
11 The Jonathan Institute which hosted the conference is named after Yehonathan Nethanyahu,head of one of the rescue teams in the Entebbe operation of July 1976, who was killed in action. For some details on similar institutes see Alex Schmid, *Political Terrorism*, as above, pp.264–266.
12 See AP Report, 'Close Watch on Russian Conduct', *The Guardian*, 30 January, 1981.
13 Alex Schmid, *Political Terrorism*, p.211.
14 Gerardo Jorge Schamís, *War and Terrorism in International Affairs*, Transaction Books, New Brunswick, NJ, 1980, p.75. The phrase 'new war' appears in the original title: *Las Relaciones Internacionales y la Nueva Guerra*.
15 Latin America Bureau, *Falklands/Malvinas: Whose Crisis?* London, LAB, 1982, p.67.
16 Claire Sterling, *The Terror Network: the Secret War of International Terrorism*, London, Weidenfeld and Nicolson, 1981.
17 See Alex Schmid, *Political Terrorism*, p.221; Claudia Wright, 'Terrorism: Facts and Fantasies', letter to the *New Statesman*, 21 August 1981.
18 *The Terror Network*, pp.291–2; 295.
19 The *Financial Times*, 26 February 1983.
20 See Claus Rath and Dagmar Jakobsen, 'Produzione di figure di terrorismo alla televisione tedesca occidentale', *Dati per la Verifica dei Programmi Trasmessi 1981, Terrorismo e TV*, vol.2, Turin, ERI, 1982, p.147.
21 *Terror!* as above, p.196.
22 Paul Wilkinson, 'Fascism has never believed in waiting for a democratic

mandate', pp.4–5. Paper presented to the Conference on 'Defence of Democracy against Terrorism in Europe: Tasks and Problems', Parliamentary Assembly, Council of Europe, Strasbourg, 12–14 November 1980.

23 Bruce Hoffman, 'Right-wing Terrorism in Europe', *Contemporary Affairs Briefing*, vol.2, no.5, November 1982, London, Centre for Contemporary Studies.

24 The entire report is reproduced in facsimile in Roger Faligot, *Britain's Military Strategy in Ireland: The Kitson Experiment*, London, Zed Press, 1983, pp.223–242. The book was originally published in French as *Guerre Spéciale en Europe: le laboratoire Irlandais*, Paris, Flammarion, 1980.

25 *Terrorist Trends*, para.64 in Roger Faligot, *Britain's Military Strategy*, as above, p.241.

26 *Terrorist Trends*, para.3; emphasis added, in Faligot, p.224.

27 *Terrorist Trends*, paras. 65 and 67, in Faligot, p.241.

28 51st Annual Conservative Women's Conference, as above, p.16.

29 Quoted in Simon Hoggart, 'Neave broadcast episode dropped', *The Guardian*, 17 July 1979.

30 Brian M. Jenkins, 'Responsibilities of the News Media', in *Terrorism and the Media*, London, International Press Institute (IPI), 1980, unpaged. This was a paper delivered to the international conference organised by the IPI and the semi-official foreign affairs journal *Affari Esteri* (Rome), in Florence, June 1978.

31 Walter Laqueur, *Terrorism*, London, Weidenfeld and Nicolson, 1977, p.223, emphasis added.

32 José M. Desantes Guanter, 'Relationship between Freedom of Press and Information and Publicity given by the Mass Media', p.2, Council of Europe, Strasbourg, as above.

33 Lord Chalfont, 'The Climate of Opinion', in *Political Communication and Persuasion*, as above, p.80.

34 Daniel E. Georges-Abeyie, 'Terrorism and the Liberal State: A Reasonable Response', *Police Studies*, vol.4, no.3, Fall 1981, p.37.

35 For an authoritative account of these developments concerning industrial relations see Keith Jeffery and Peter Hennessy, *States of Emergency: British Governments and Strikebreaking since 1919*, London, Routledge and Kegan Paul, 1983. Their account suggests that there has been no conclusive shift towards a fully-fledged strike-breaking apparatus, although the idea has at various times been canvassed.

36 There is by now quite a substantial literature dealing with these questions. Amongst the most informative texts are Carol Ackroyd *et al.*, *The Technology of Political Control*, 2nd edition, London, Pluto Press, 1980; Tony Bunyan, *The History and Practice of the Political Police in Britain*, London, Julian Friedmann, 1976; Duncan Campbell, *Big Brother is Listening: Phonetappers and the Security State*, London, New Statesman Report No.2; Peter Hain (ed.), *Policing the Police*, London, John Calder, vols I and II, 1979 and 1980. The *State Research Bulletin*, now sadly defunct, is an indispensable source.

37 For such a criticism see Catherine Scorer and Patricia Hewitt, *The Prevention of Terrorism Act: The Case for Repeal*, London, National Council for Civil Liberties, 1981. For an excellent analysis of pro- and anti- positions in the Parliamentary debates over the anti-terrorism legislation see Matthew Lippmann, 'The Abrogation of Domestic Human Rights', in Yonah Alexander and Kenneth A. Myers (eds.), *Terrorism in Europe*, London and Canberra, Croom Helm, 1982.

38 On *Channel Four News*, 7 March, 1983.

39 *Hansard* (House of Commons), 7 March 1983, columns 569–570.

40 See, for instance, Juliet Lodge, 'The European Community and Terrorism: Establishing the Principle of "Extradite or Try"', and David Freestone, 'Legal Responses to Terrorism: Towards European Cooperation?' in Juliet Lodge (ed.), *Terrorism: A Challenge to the State*, Oxford, Martin Robertson, 1981.

41 Paul Wilkinson, 'Proposals for Government and International Responses to Terrorism', in Paul Wilkinson (ed.), *British Perspectives on Terrorism*, London, George Allen and Unwin, 1981, p.191.

42 'Liberty and Terror', as above, p.38.

43 *Political Terrorism*, as above, p.285.

44 Noam Chomsky and Edward S. Herman, *The Washington Connection and Third World Fascism*, Nottingham, Spokesman Books, 1979, p.85.

45 *The Washington Connection*, as above, p.6.
46 Edward S. Herman, *The Real Terror Network: Terrorism in Fact and Propaganda*, Boston, South End Press, 1982, p.8. Alex Schmid, *Political Terrorism*, pp.259–260, discusses how the CIA figures were massaged to produce *twice* as many incidents.
47 *The Washington Connection*, p.87.
48 *The Real Terror Network*, pp.212–214.
49 On this, see Noam Chomsky, 'Introduction', *Towards A New Cold War: Essays on the Current Crisis and How We Got There*, London, Sinclair Browne, 1982, pp.47–57.
50 Quoted in James P. Terry, 'State Terrorism: A Juridical Examination in Terms of Existing International Law', *Journal of Palestine Studies*, vol.x, no.1, Autumn, 1980 p.100.
51 Luigi Bonanate, 'Some Unanticipated Consequences of Terrorism', *Journal of Peace Research*, vol.xvi, no.3, 1979, p.205.
52 Alessandro Silj, 'Case Study II: Italy', in David Carlton and Carlo Schaerf (eds.), *Contemporary Terror: Studies in Sub-State Violence*, London, MacMillan, 1981, p.151.
53 Sebastian Cobler, 'The Determined Assertion of Normalcy', *Telos*, no.43, Spring 1980, pp.48.
54 'The Year of the Terrorist', *The Guardian*, 3 January 1983.
55 'Terrorism and the Liberal Fallacy', *The Observer*, 9 January 1983.
56 For a detailed analysis of this whole process in relation to 'Red Ken' Livingstone see Liz Curtis, *Ireland: the Propaganda War*, ch.9, to be published by Pluto Press, London. All references to this text are to particular chapters in the typescript version and may well diverge from the final published version.
57 Sebastian Cobler, *Law, Order and Politics in West Germany*, Harmondsworth, Penguin, 1978, p.92.
58 See the 'Introduction' to Bommi Bauman, *Terror or Love? The Personal Account of a West German Urban Guerrilla*, London, John Calder, 1979.
59 See Alfio Bernabei, 'The Italian Inquisition' in Red Notes, *Italy 1980–81: After Marx, Jail!*, London, Red Notes, 1981.
60 Catherine Scorer and Patricia Hewitt, *The Prevention of Terrorism Act*, as above, p.5.
61 Reginald Freeson, MP, *Hansard* (House of Commons), 7 March 1983, column 587.
62 Interview on *Channel Four News*, 7 March 1983.
63 Willem Nagel, 'A Socio-legal View on the Suppression of Terrorism', pp.2, 4. Council of Europe, Strasbourg, as above.
64 *La Torture dans la République*, as above, p.61. All translations from French or Italian originals by Philip Schlesinger.
65 A searching account is to be found in Peter Taylor, *Beating the Terrorists? Interrogation in Omagh, Gough and Castlereagh*, Harmondsworth, Penguin, 1980. Also see John McGuffin, *The Guinea Pigs*, Harmondsworth, Penguin, 1974. An example of the relevant official literature is *Allegations against the Security Forces of Physical Brutality in Northern Ireland* (The Compton Report), Cmnd 4823, London, HMSO, 1971. The interrogation techniques portrayed in *Psywarriors* (see Chapter 3 below) are based on those whose use was confirmed by Compton.
66 John le Carré, 'Introduction' to *The Observer, Siege: Six Days at the Iranian Embassy*, London, MacMillan, 1980, p.6.
67 See Stuart Hall, 'The Great Moving Right Show', *Marxism Today*, vol.23, no.1, January 1979.
68 Hugh Davies and Colin Brady, 'UDA leaders call for power to the people', *The Daily Telegraph*, 17 November 1981.
69 On *Panorama*, BBC1, 22 November 1982.
70 Quoted in Michael Farrell, *Northern Ireland: The Orange State*, 2nd revised edition, London, Pluto Press, 1980, p.296.
71 Quoted in 'Prior denounces threats from both sides', *The Guardian*, 19 November 1981.
72 Quoted in Hugh Herbert, 'Why the weary major believes in selective assassination', *The Guardian*, 19 February 1980.

73   Quoted in Jim Cusack, 'Hume criticises security policy', *The Irish Times*, 31 December 1982.
74   See Bob Lumley and Philip Schlesinger, 'The Press, The State and its Enemies: The Italian Case', *The Sociological Review*, vol.30, no.4, November 1982 for a general survey. Specifically on the Moro affair, see Alessandro Silj, *Brigate-Rosse-Stato: Lo scontro spettacolo nella regia della stampa quotidiana*, 2nd edition, Florence, Vallechi, 1978, esp. ch.4.
75   From communiqué no.3, 29 March 1978. Quoted from Bruno Di Biase (ed.), *Terrorism Today in Italy and Western Europe*, Sydney, Circolo 'G. Di Vittorio', 1978, p.85.
76   See, for instance, Carlo Marletti, 'Immagini pubbliche e ideologia del terrorismo', in Luigi Bonanate (ed.), *Dimensioni del Terrorismo Politico*, Milan, 1979, pp.249–251.
77   *The Daily Mirror*, 28 August 1979.
78   Quoted from Roger Faligot, *Nous avons tué Mountbatten: L'IRA parle*, Paris, Editions Jean Picollec, 1981, pp.17–18.
79   *Nous avons tué Mountbatten*, as above, pp.30–31.
80   As above, pp.117, 118, 120.

Chapter 2: Reporting 'terrorism'

1   Stuart Hall, Ian Connell and Lidia Curti, 'The "unity" of current affairs television', *Working Papers in Cultural Studies*, no.9, Spring 1976.
2   Howard Davis and Paul Walton, 'Death of a Premier: Consensus and Closure in International News', in Howard Davis and Paul Walton (eds.), *Language, Image, Media*, Oxford, Basil Blackwell, 1983.
3   There are far too many studies to list here. Some of the better-known which deal particularly with television include: Edward J. Epstein, *News From Nowhere: Television and the News*, New York, Random House 1973; Herbert J. Gans, *Deciding What's News: A Study of CBS Evening News, NBC Nightly News, Newsweek and Time*, New York, Pantheon Books; Todd Gitlin, *The Whole World is Watching: Mass Media in the Making and Unmaking of the New Left*, Berkeley and Los Angeles, University of California Press, 1980; Glasgow University Media Group, *Bad News* and *More Bad News*, London, Routledge and Kegan Paul, 1976 and 1980. Gaye Tuchman, *Making News: A Study in the Construction of Reality*, New York, Free Press, 1978. The present authors' main contributions are: James D. Halloran, Philip Elliott and Graham Murdock, *Demonstrations and Communication: A Case Study*, Harmondsworth, Penguin, 1970; Philip Schlesinger, *Putting 'Reality' Together: BBC News*, London, Constable, 1978; Peter Golding and Philip Elliott, *Making the News*, London, Longman 1979.
4   Stuart Hall, Chas Critcher, Tony Jefferson, John Clarke, Brian Roberts, *Policing the Crisis: Mugging, the State, and Law and Order*, London, MacMillan, 1978.
5   See Philip Elliott, 'Press performance as political ritual', in Harry Christian (ed.), *The Sociology of Journalism and the Press*, Sociological Review Monograph no.20, Keele, University of Keele, 1980; Yves Lavoinne, 'Presse et cohésion sociale: le cas des prises d'otages', *Revue Française de Communication*, Winter, 1979, no.2.
6   Philip Elliott, 'Reporting Northern Ireland', in *Ethnicity and the Media*, Paris, UNESCO, 1977.
7   David L. Paletz, Peter A. Fozzard, John Z. Ayanian, 'Terrorism on TV News', in William C. Adams (ed.), *Television Coverage of International Affairs*, Norwood NJ, Ablex, 1982, p.149.
8   'Terrorism on TV News', as above, p.150.
9   'Terrorism on TV News', p.162.
10   See, for instance, the extensive discussion in Philip Schlesinger, *Putting 'reality' together*, as above, ch.8; and see below 'Taking sides' in Chapter 4.
11   See, for instance, Philip Elliott, 'Press Performance' as above and Philip Schlesinger, '"Terrorism", the Media, and the Liberal-democratic State: a Critique of the Orthodoxy', *Social Research*, vol.48, no.1, Spring 1981.
12   Davis and Walton, 'Death of a Premier', as above, p.48; emphasis added.
13   Examples of such coverage were shown on the Channel Four documentary, *Ireland: The Silent Voices*, 7 March 1983. For an analysis of how the IRA have

been presented on Italian television, see Luciano Li Causi, 'Il terrorismo degli altri: movimenti politici illegali in contesti stranieri', in *Terrorismo e TV*, vol.2, as above. Li Causi notes that the existence in Northern Ireland of groups such as the IRA and the UDA 'is explained in terms of the troubled history of that country, by the centuries-old subjection of Ulster to British rule, and so far as Republican irredentism is concerned, by the economic and cultural oppression of the Catholics by the Protestants, and finally by the presence of the British army' (p.226).

14 For an analysis of this programme's populism see Charlotte Brunsdon and David Morley, *Everyday Television: 'Nationwide'*, Television Monograph No.10, London, British Film Institute, 1978.

15 See Cary Bazalgette and Richard Paterson, 'Real Entertainment: The Iranian Embassy Siege', *Screen Education*, no. 37, Winter 1980-81; Philip Elliott, 'Press Performance', as above, pp.148 onwards.

16 The opening sentence was false when it said that 'civilians die too', although it was, of course, true that civilians had been very badly injured. According to the documentary *Sefton* (see below), the final death-toll was eleven, all of them soldiers.

17 For a detailed account of both the Rats and Sefton cases, see Liz Curtis, *Ireland: the Propaganda War*, as above, ch.6. Sefton's biography is J.N.P. Watson's *Sefton: Story of a Cavalry Horse*, Souvenir Press, 1983. A further collection, proceeds to the Army Benevolent Fund, has been published: Brigadier-General Landy (ed.), *Sefton: 'The horse for any year'*, London, Quiller Press, 1983.

18 Max Halstock, *Rats: The Story of a Dog Soldier*, London, Corgi Books, 1982, p.8.

19 Donatella Ronci, 'Terrorismo e sistema politica nel rotocalco televisivo', *Terrorismo e TV*, vol.1, as above, pp.174–176.

20 Luciano Li Causi, 'Il terrorismo degli altri', as above, p.231.

21 *Report of the Tribunal appointed to Enquire into the Events on Sunday 30th January 1972 which led to loss of life in connection with the Procession in Londonderry on that day*, (The Widgery Report) HL 101/HC 220, London, HMSO, 1972; The Compton Report, as above.

22 Brian Lapping (ed.), *The Bounds of Freedom*, London, Constable/Granada Television, 1980, p.211. 'Hypothetical' no.6 is titled 'Terrorism', and offers some revealing insights into the relationships between journalism, the broadcasting authorities and the state.

Chapter3: Dramatising 'terrorism'

1 Quoted in Edward Jay Epstein, *News From Nowhere: Television and the News*, New York, Vintage Books, 1974, p.241.

2 Quoted in Edward Epstein, as above, p.241.

3 See Cary Bazalgette and Richard Paterson, 'Real Entertainment: The Iranian Embassy Siege', as above.

4 For further discussion of the siege and the decisions surrounding its coverage, see below 'Television's finest hour?' in Chapter 4.

5 John Hartley, *Understanding News*, London, Methuen, 1982, p.145. The narrative qualities of the *whole* embassy siege story were brought out in *Siege*, a compilation video-tape made for the 1980 Edinburgh International Television Festival by Mairéde Thomas, Richard Paterson and Philip Schlesinger. This runs through the background, development, denouement and the 'return to normality'.

6 On the cult of secrecy and the use of the siege-bust imagery across the range of popular culture see Richard Paterson and Philip Schlesinger, 'State Heroes for the Eighties', *Screen*, vol.24, no.3, May/June 1983.

7 Quoted in Christopher Wicking, 'Postscripts from the Termite Range', *Primetime*, vol.1, no.2, Autumn 1981, p.7.

8 Quoted in *Screen International*, 17 May 1980.

9 Publicity brochure for the film released by Rank Film Distributors.

10 James Follett, *The Tiptoe Boys*, London, Corgi Books, 1982, p.85.

11 Publicity brochure, as above.

12 Quoted in *Film Review*, vol.32, no.10, October 1982, p.13.

13 From a discussion on 'Did You See?' BBC2, 13 May 1981.

14   See 'The Single Play', *Television and Radio* 1980, London, The Independent Broadcasting Authority, 1980, pp.24–5.

15   The notion of 'authorship' and its role in television fiction production is discussed in greater detail in Graham Murdock, 'Authorship and Organisation', *Screen Education*, no.35, Summer 1980, pp.19–34.

16   Mairéde Thomas 'A Play for Today: An Interview with Roland Joffé', *The British Media and Ireland*, London, Information on Ireland, 1979, p.12.

17   The origins of the secret service thriller are interestingly discussed in David Stafford 'Spies and Gentlemen: The Birth of the British Spy Novel, 1893–1914', *Victorian Studies*, vol.24, no.4, Summer 1981.

18   Tony Bennett, 'James Bond in the 1980s', *Marxism Today*, vol.27, no.6, June 1983, p.38.

19   Ken Blake, *'The Professionals: Where the Jungle Ends'*, London, 1978, p.17.

20   John Cawelti, 'Pornography, Catastrophe, and Vengeance: Shifting Narrative Structures in a Changing American Culture' in Sam B. Girgus (ed.), *The American Self: Myth, Ideology and Popular Culture*, Alburquerque, University of New Mexico Press, 1981, pp.182–192.

21   On this see Jerry Palmer, 'Mickey Spillane: a reading' in Stan Cohen and Jock Young (eds), *The Manufacture of News*, London, Constable, 1973, pp.302–313.

22   This is the publicity slogan for the American movie *'10 to Midnight'* released in 1983, directed by J. Lee Thompson and starring Charles Bronson, who played the lead in one of the first and most successful of all the urban vigilante films, Michael Winner's *Death Wish*, released in 1974.

23   Ken Blake, as above, p.19.

24   See Graham Knight and Tony Dean, 'Myth and the Structure of News', *Journal of Communication*, Spring 1982, pp.145–161.

25   Terence Strong, *Whisper Who Dares*, London, Coronet Books, 1982.

26   Colin Dunne, 'Secrets of the SAS', *The Sun*, July 19, 1982.

27   See Steve Chibnall, *Law-and-Order News: An Analysis of Crime Reporting in the British Press*, London, Tavistock Publications, 1977, pp.112–116.

28   James Follett, as above, p.95.

29   See Ken Worpole 'The American Connection: The Masculine Style in Popular Fiction', *New Left Review*, No.139, May-June 1983, pp.79–84.

30   TV Times Extra, *Who's Who Among the TV Super Sleuths*, London, Independent Television Publications, 1979, p.11.

31   Blurb on the back cover of Ken Blake, as above.

32   Blurb on the back cover of Ken Blake, *'The Professionals 9: No Stone'*, London, Sphere Books, 1981.

33   TV Times Extra, as above.

34   Quoted in Christopher Wicking, as above, p.7.

35   ditto.

36   ditto.

37   *The Terror Network*, ch.3. Quotation from p.49, our emphasis: note the phraseology.

38   Frank Brodhead and Edward S. Herman, 'The KGB Plot to Assassinate the Pope: A Case Study in Free World Disinformation', *Covert Action Information Bulletin*, no.19, Spring-Summer 1983, p.15. For a confirmatory account see Claudia Wright, 'Terrorism: facts and fantasies', as above.

39   Ken Blake, 1978, as above, p.19.

40   Donald James, *A Spy at Evening*, London, Coronet Books, 1980, p.13.

Chapter 4: The British way of censorship

1   Nicholas Pronay, 'The News Media at War', in Nicholas Pronay and D.W. Spring (eds), *Propaganda, Politics and Film, 1918–1945*, London, Macmillan, 1982, p.182.

2   On this period see Michael Balfour, *Propaganda in War, 1939–1945: Organisations, Policies and Publics in Britain and Germany*, London, Routledge and Kegan Paul, 1979, pp.80–88; Asa Briggs, *The Golden Age of Wireless: The History of Broadcasting in the United Kingdom*, vol.2, London, Oxford University Press, 1965, *passim*; James Curran and Jean Seaton, *Power without Responsibility: the Press and Broadcasting in Britain*, Glasgow, Fontana, 1981, ch.9; Ian McLaine, *Ministry of Morale: Home Front and the Ministry of Infor-*

mation in World War II, London, George Allen and Unwin, 1979, esp. pp.230–231.

3 See Harman Grisewood, *One Thing at a Time*, London, Hutchinson, 1968; F.R. MacKenzie, 'Eden, Suez and the BBC – a reassessment', *The Listener*, 18 December 1969.

4 Robert Harris, *Gotcha! The Media, the Government and the Falklands Crisis*, London, Faber and Faber, 1983, p.61.

5 *Gotcha!*, as above, p.70.

6 *Gotcha!* p.83.

7 See Sir Robert Mark, 'The Case of Great Britain' in *Terrorism and the Media*, as above; Peter Harland, 'Terror and the Press. Politics and Greed: When lives are at stake where is the difference?', *IPI Report*, vol.26, no.10, November 1977, pp.5–7. For more details on the background to these developments see Philip Schlesinger, 'Princes' Gate, 1980: The Media Politics of Siege Management', *Screen Education*, Winter, 1980/1981, no.37.

8 John Mahoney, '22b Balcombe Street, London . . . the "television siege"', *EBU Review*, vol.xxviii, no.2, March 1976, p.17.

9 Sir Robert Mark, *In the Office of Constable*, Glasgow, Fontana/Collins, 1979, pp.193–194.

10 Peter Harland, 'Terror and the Press', as above, p.7.

11 '22b Balcombe Street', as above, p.18.

12 IPI, 'Terrorism and the Media'. Report of the IPI British Committee's one day conference held in the Council Chamber, BBC, on 10 November, 1977 p.6; marked 'Not for Publication'.

13 As he said on *The Editors*, BBC1, 16 June 1980.

14 For a discussion see 'The Media Politics of Siege Management', as above, pp.49–50.

15 IPI, 'European Terrorism and the Media'. Report on the one-day conference organised by the IPI international secretariat and the British national committee of the IPI on Thursday, 19 November, 1978, at the Royal Commonwealth Society, London WC2, p.2; marked 'Strictly Confidential. Not for Publication'.

16 As he said on *The Editors*, as above.

17 *Minutes of Evidence taken before the House of Commons Defence Committee, Report on The D-Notice System, Session 1979–80*, 6 August 1980, p.49; emphases added.

18 For accounts of these developments see 'Policing the Eighties: the Iron Fist', *State Research Bulletin* no.19, 1980, p.152; Tony Geraghty, *Who Dares Wins: The Story of the Special Air Service*, London, Arms and Armour Press, ch.6 and pp.168–169.

19 David Leigh, *The Frontiers of Secrecy: Closed Government in Britain*, London, Junction Books, 1980, pp.57–58.

20 *Minutes of Evidence*, as above, p.49.

21 For discussions, see David Leigh, *The Frontiers of Secrecy*; Bruce Page and Duncan Campbell, 'D-Notices – Mystery of British Journalism', *Index on Censorship*, vol.9, no.6, December 1980.

22 *Defence, Press and Broadcasting Committee: D Notices*, 12 January 1982, p.1. Also see Richard Norton-Taylor, 'Nott updates D Notice "censorship"', *The Guardian*, 1 April 1982.

23 Quoted in *The Frontiers of Secrecy*, as above, p.68.

24 *Minutes of Evidence*, as above, p.15.

25 *Minutes of Evidence*, p.41.

26 *Minutes of Evidence*, p.15.

27 Examples of restricted information are the two IPI reports cited above. The ISC's *Television and Conflict* cost £5 in 1978. Access to the Centre for Contemporary Studies' 1982 conference on 'Terrorism and the News Media' which brought together prominent inhabitants of seminar and discussion country such as Professors Paul Wilkinson and Yonah Alexander, Merlyn Rees and Lord Chalfont cost £85. (Information on the last point from Liz Curtis, as above, ch.7).

28 'Terrorism and the Media', as above, p.12.

29 'Terrorism and the Media', p.2.

30 'European Terrorism and the Media', pp.17, 18.

31 Council of Europe, Strasbourg, as above.

32 For material dealing with this see Campaign for Free Speech on Ireland (ed.), *The British Media and Ireland*, London 1979; Roger Faligot, *Britain's Military Strategy*, as above, ch.3; Liz Curtis, as above, *passim*.

33 Quoted in Liz Curtis, ch.1.

34 Quoted in *Putting 'Reality' Together*, as above, p.211.

35 Quoted in *Putting 'Reality' Together*, p.212.

36 Quoted in Liz Curtis, ch.1.

37 See Anthony Smith, 'Television Coverage of Northern Ireland', *Index on Censorship*, vol.1, no.2, 1972, for one of the earliest, and certainly one of the most wide-ranging accounts.

38 For more detailed discussion of the wider editorial system and 'impartiality' see *Putting 'Reality' Together*, ch's 6–8; Liz Curtis, ch.8 contains lengthy quotations from the current guidelines; Peter Lennon offers some up to date journalistic reflections in 'Broadcasting Problems in Northern Ireland', Parts I and II, *The Guardian*, 23 and 30 June, 1983.

39 See Peter Taylor, 'Reporting Northern Ireland', *Index on Censorship*, vol.7, no.6, 1978.

40 For lists of censored programmes and background information see: John Howkins, 'Censorship 1977–78: A Background Paper' and Chris Dunkley, 'Programmes on Northern Ireland, 1968–1978' in *Edinburgh International Television Festival 1978 – Official Programme*; Paul Madden 'Banned, Censored and Delayed: A Chronology of Some TV Programmes Dealing with Northern Ireland', in *The British Media and Ireland*, as above.

41 David Elstein, 'Why can't we broadcast the truth?', in *The British Media and Ireland*, as above, p.14. Originally published in *Boulevard*, no.1, 1978.

42 Speaking on *Look Here*, 5 July 1978.

43 'Reporting Northern Ireland', as above, p.5.

44 Keith Kyle, 'Bernard O'Connor's Story', *The Listener*, 10 March 1977; also see Paul Madden, 'Banned, Censored and Delayed', as above, p.19 and Liz Curtis, ch.4.

45 For the background see Liz Curtis, ch.9, which contains quotations from *Hang Out Your Brightest Colours*, still under lock and key in a safe.

46 Liz Curtis, ch.6, contains a detailed account, from which we have drawn.

47 See Michael Tracey, *In the Culture of Eye: Ten Years of Weekend World*, London, Hutchinson, 1983, pp.87–90.

48 *In the Culture of the Eye*, as above, p.102. Within Thames Television too, it was right away assumed that interviews with the IRA were illegal: see Jeremy Isaacs' memorandum of 11 December 1974, reproduced in *The British Media and Ireland*, as above, p.27.

49 Quoted in *In the Culture of the Eye*, as above, p.109.

50 He said so on *Look Here*, 5 July 1978. See Paul Madden, 'Banned, Censored, and Delayed', p.20 and John Howkins, 'Censorship, 1977–78', p.56. Oddly, despite offering the most detailed account of all, Tracey does not quote Cox's remarks about being banned, nor discuss the episode in those terms.

51 For assessments of the significance of this move see Dorothy Connell, 'Reporting Northern Ireland, 1979–1980', *Index on Censorship*, vol.9, no.3, June 1980, and Geoff Robertson, 'Panorama and Mrs Thatcher', *The Guardian*, 12 November 1979. On the general background to the legislation see Brian Rose-Smith, 'Police Powers and Terrorism Legislation', in Peter Hain (ed), *Policing the Police*, vol.1, as above.

52 See Liz Curtis, ch.7 for a fuller account, and for an analysis of the debates themselves comparing the position in Italy see Philip Schlesinger and Bob Lumley, 'Due dibattiti sulla violenza politica e i mass media', *La Critica Sociologica*, forthcoming.

53 Colin Brown, 'BBC reporters under renewed pressure over "terror" contacts', *The Guardian*, 5 August 1980.

54 *BBC News and Current Affairs Index*, 1980, p.46.

55 See See Liz Curtis, ch.5.

56 See Peter Golding and Philip Elliott, *Making the News*, as above, pp.59–64.

57 The rules are quoted in Liz Curtis, ch.8.

58 Conor Cruise O'Brien, 'Freedom and Censorship', Lecture at the IBA on 28 March 1979, p.9.

59 Anon, 'Conor Cruise O'Brien and the Media: Decline of an Irish Liberal', *Belfast Bulletin*, no.9, Spring 1981, p.4.
60 His most notable intervention has been his Chatham House speech of February 1977. An edited version is in 'Northern Ireland: Francis Answers BBC's Critics', *Broadcast*, 28 February 1977.
61 Quoted from a speech to the Broadcasting Press Guild, 12 July 1979, published in *The Listener*, 19 July 1979, p.74.
62 Richard Francis, 'Television Reporting Beyond the Pale', *The Listener*, 27 March 1980, p.390.
63 Conor Cruise O'Brien, 'A journalist doesn't stop being a citizen', *The Listener*, 22 January 1981, p.108.
64 Richard Francis, 'The journalist cannot survive as an informer except when . . .' *The Listener*, 12 February 1981, p.206.
65 Quoted in 'The Show that Broke the Silence', in *The British Media and Ireland*, as above, p.6.
66 The union-based Campaign for Press and Broadcasting Freedom has offered periodic criticisms but hardly a consistent opposition with teeth. The tiny Campaign for Free Speech on Ireland has monitored developments and has produced the widely-read *British Media and Ireland* pamphlet which has now sold 13,000 copies.
67 Liz Curtis, ch.10 discusses this.
68 Richard Hoggart, 'Ulster: a "switch-off" TV subject?', *The Listener*, 28 February 1980; quotations from pp.261–262.
69 The verdict was later modified by the European Court of Human Rights which dropped the 'torture' count. However, as Peter Taylor remarks in *Beating the Terrorists*, as above, p.14: 'the most significant finding at Strasbourg, by both Commission and Court, was that ill-treatment had constituted an "administrative practice": that is to say, the authorities knew about and condoned it.' On *Article 5* see Paul Madden, as above, p.19 and Liz Curtis, ch.4.
70 See 'A Play For Today: An Interview with Roland Joffé, Director of "The Legion Hall Bombing"', by Mairéde Thomas, in *The British Media and Ireland*, as above, p.12.
71 'A Play for Today', as above, p.13.
72 Quoted in Peter Lennon, 'Broadcasting Problems in Northern Ireland', Part II, as above, p.7.
73 Quoted in Paul Madden, as above, p.20.
74 BBC Radio 3 interview with Paul Fox, quoted in Liz Curtis, ch.8.
75 BBC Minute, 13 May 1981, p.21, para.131 continued. Thanks to Liz Curtis for drawing our attention to this.

Chapter 5: Television: the insurgent's friend?

1   Gabriel Tarde, *Penal Philisophy*, London, William Heinemann, 1912 (first edition published in 1890) p.322.
2   Gustave Le Bon, *The Crowd: A Study of the Popular Mind*, New York, The Viking Press, 1960 (first edition published in 1895), p.68.
3   Quoted in David D. Cooper, *The Lesson of the Scaffold*, London, Allen Lane, 1974, p.173.
4   Kai T. Erikson, *Wayward Puritans: A Study in the Sociology of Deviance*, New York, John Wiley and Sons Inc., 1968, p.12.
5   Quoted in Tarde, *Penal Philosophy*, as above, p.340.
6   Yonah Alexander, 'Terrorism, the media, and the police', *Police Studies*, June 1978, p.47.
7   Leonard Berkowitz, 'Studies of the Contagion of Violence' in Herbert Hirsch and David Perry (eds), *Violence as Politics*, New York, Harper Row, 1973, p.44.
8   Leonard Berkowitz and Jacqueline Macaulay, 'The Contagion of Criminal Violence', *Sociometry*, 1971, vol.34, no.2, p.260.
9   Barbara Tuchman, *The Proud Tower: A Portrait of the World Before the War, 1890–1914*, London, Hamish Hamilton, 1966, p.91.
10 On this see Noam Chomsky and Edward S. Herman, *The Washington Connection*, as above, pp.252–255; Joan R. Dassin, 'Press Censorship and the Military State in Brazil' in Jane L. Curry and Joan R. Dassin (eds), *Press Control Around the World*, New York, Praeger, 1982, pp.152–155; Armand and Michèle

Mattelart, 'L'Information et état d'exception' in *De l'usage des média en temps de crise*, Paris, Alain Moreau, 1979, pp.255–260.

11   See George A. Kelly 'The French Doctrine of *la guerre révolutionnaire*', in George A. Kelly and Clifford W. Brown, Jnr, (eds), *Struggles in the State: Sources and Patterns in World Revolution*, New York, John Wiley, 1970 and John Steward Ambler *The French Army in Politics*, Ohio State University Press, 1966.

12   For a relevant analysis, see Roger Faligot, *Britain's Military Strategy in Ireland*, as above, ch.1.

13   Frank Kitson, *Low-intensity Operations: Subversion, Insurgency, Peace-keeping*, London, Faber and Faber, 1971, p.3.

14   *Low-intensity Operations*, as above, p.71.

15   London and Basingstoke, MacMillan, 1981; 2nd edition 1983.

16   As above, p.xiii.

17   In a book review in the *RUSI Journal*, December 1981, p.69.

18   See the discussion in Alex Schmid, *Political Terrorism*, pp.20–23.

19   *The Media and Political Violence*, p.4.

20   Richard Clutterbuck, *Protest and the Urban Guerrilla*, London, Cassell, 1973. For some general criticisms of this kind of work see Philip Schlesinger, 'On the Shape and Scope of Counter-Insurgency Thought', in Gary Littlejohn *et al* (eds), *Power and the State*, London, Croom Helm, 1978.

21   *Television and Conflict*, p.4.

22   *The Media and Political Violence*, p.164.

23   Phillip Knightley, *The First Casualty: The War Correspondent as Hero, Propagandist and Myth Maker*, London, Quartet Books, 1982, p.379.

24   *Gotcha!* pp.61–62.

25   Maurice Tugwell, 'Politics and Propaganda of the Provisional IRA' in Paul Wilkinson (ed.), *British Perspectives on Terrorism*, as above, p.15. *Television and Conflict*, p.26 offers an identical view. For information on Tugwell's role and propaganda warfare in Northern Ireland more generally see Liz Curtis, ch.10.

26   Robert M. Entman and David L. Paletz, 'Tunnel Vision on Television: the War in Southeast Asia' in William C. Adams (ed.), *Television Coverage of International Affairs*, as above, p.196; emphasis added. For further evidence suggesting that the 'Vietnam Syndrome' is simplistic see Phillip Knightley, *The First Casualty*, as above, pp.379–382.

27   See, for instance, Todd Gitlin, *The Whole World is Watching*, as above, p.209.

28   *The Media and Political Violence*, p.79; the following two quotations come from the same page.

29   As above, pp.82–83; the following two quotations come from the same pages.

30   *Television and Conflict*, p.8.

31   As above, p.28.

32   As above, p.32.

33   As above, p.7.

34   Paul Wilkinson, 'Relationship between freedom of press and information and publicity given by the mass media', all quotations from p.6. Paper given at Council of Europe, Strasbourg, as above. 'PIRA', incidentally, is a typical piece of military jargon: compare Brigadier Glover's report cited in Chapter 1 above.

35   *The Media and Political Violence*, p.xiii.

36   As above, p.115.

37   Quoted in 'How interview "boosted" INLA', *Irish Times*, 17 July 1981.

38   *Ireland: The Propaganda War*, ch.7.

39   *Nous avons tué Mountbatten*, as above, p.37.

40   *The Media and Political Violence*, p.134.

41   As above, p.139, emphasis added.

42   As above, pp.140–141, emphasis added.

43   For a detailed alternative account see 'The media politics of siege management', as above.

44   Alan Hooper, *The Military and the Media*, Aldershot, Gower, 1982, p.153.

45   Paul Wilkinson, 'Terrorism and the Media', *Journalism Studies Review*, vol.3, 1978, p.3. This line strongly recalls Lord Harris's remarks at the 1977 IPI conference, referred to in Chapter 4 above.

46   *Television and Conflict*, p.17.

47 As above, p.37.
48 Council of Europe, Strasbourg, as above, p.7.
49 *Report of the Commission of Inquiry into the Mass Media* (The Steyn Commission), vol.3, 1981; quotations from pp.1344 and 1340.
50 *The Media and Political Violence*, p.162.
51 *Television and Conflict*, p.32.
52 *The Military and the Media*, pp.153–4.
53 'Terrorism and the Media', as above, p.6.

Chapter 6: Television: instrument of the state?
1 *Violence as Communication: Insurgent Terrorism and the Western News Media*, London and Beverly Hills, Sage, 1982, p.15; emphasis added.
2 As above, p.59.
3 As above, pp.2, 5.
4 As above, p.85; emphasis added.
5 As above, p.64.
6 As above, p.225; emphasis added.
7 See their own reservations in *Violence as Communication*, p.126.
8 In a review in the *RUSI Journal*, December 1982. Our thanks to Alex Schmid for drawing our attention to his own critic.
9 *Violence as Communication*, p.171.
10 As above, p.174.
11 George Gerbner, Larry Gross, *et al.*, 'The Demonstration of Power: Violence Profile No.10', *Journal of Communication*, vol.29, 1979, p.106.
12 Arthur Stinchcombe *et al.*, *Crime and Punishment – Changing Attitudes in America*, London, Jossey-Bass Publishers, 1980.
13 George Gerbner and Larry Gross, 'The Scary World of TV's Heavy Viewer', *Psychology Today*, April, 1976, p.89.
14 George Gerbner and Larry Gross, 'The Violent Face of Television and its Lesson', in Edward Palmer and Aimee Dorr (eds), *Children and the Faces of Television: Teaching, Violence, Selling*, New York, Academic Press, 1980, p.150.
15 George Gerbner and Larry Gross, 'Living with Television: The Violence Profile', *Journal of Communication*, vol.26, 1976, pp.173/176.
16 George Gerbner, Larry Gross *et al.*, 'Cultural Indicators: Violence Profile, No.9', *Journal of Communication*, vol.28, 1978, p.182.
17 George Gerbner and Larry Gross, 'The Scary World of TV's Heavy Viewer' as above, p.44.
18 Todd Gitlin, 'Television's Screens: Hegemony in Transition' in Michael Apple (ed.), *Cultural and Economic Reproduction in Education*, London, Routledge and Kegan Paul, 1982. Douglas Kellner, 'Television, Mythology and Ritual', *Praxis*, No.6, 1982.
19 Gerbner, Gross, et al. 'Cultural Indicators' as above, p.178.
20 *The Washington Connection*, p.73.
21 As above, p.74.
22 As above, pp.75–78; and compare *The Real Terror Network*, pp.145–151.
23 *The Real Terror Network*, p.15.
24 *The Washington Connection*, p.74.
25 As above, p.75.
26 As above, p.79.

Other titles from Comedia